MP3
and the Digital Music Revolution

Turn Your PC into a CD-Quality Digital Jukebox!

by
John Hedtke

MP3 and the Digital Music Revolution:
Turn Your PC into a CD-Quality Digital Jukebox!

Copyright © 1999 by John Hedtke

SAN#: 299-4550
Top Floor Publishing
P.O. Box 260072
Lakewood, CO 80226-0072 USA
http://TopFloor.com

Feedback to the author: *feedback@topfloor.com*
Sales information: *sales@topfloor.com*
The Top Floor Publishing Web Site: *http://TopFloor.com/*
The Poor Richard Web Site: *http://www.poorrichard.com/book/*
Cover Design by Doyle Communications: PHONE: 303.232.3924
Book Design by Magnolia Studio: *http://www.edithst.com/magnoliastudio*

Library of Congress Catalog Card Number: 98-96890

ISBN: 0-9661032-4-6

Information has been obtained by Top Floor Publishing from sources believed to be reliable. However, because of the possibility of human or mechanical error by our sources, Top Floor Publishing, or others, Top Floor Publishing does not guarantee the accuracy, adequacy, or completeness of any information and is not responsible for any errors or omissions or the results obtained from use of such information.

01   00   99   6 5 4 3 2 1

*This book is dedicated to Richard & Marcia Baugh, my uncle and aunt.
Thanks for everything.*

ABOUT THE AUTHOR

John Hedtke is the award-winning author of 18 books, including *Peachtree Made Easy* and *Using Computer Bulletin Boards, Third Edition*. A software expert with over 20 years of experience, John has developed and written books and manuals for many leading software products, as well as contributing frequent articles to computer magazines. John is the Past President of the Puget Sound chapter of the Society for Technical Communication. When not otherwise occupied, he plays the banjo and collects novelty tunes. He can be reached through his web site at *http://www.hedtke.com*.

CREDITS

Publisher
Peter Kent, Top Floor Publishing

Project Manager
Linda Gallagher, TechComm Plus

Developmental Editor
Kevin Murray, KJM Editorial Services

Proofreader
Fred Kloepper, PDG Editing

Cover Design
Tim Doyle, Doyle Communications

Book Design & Composition
Phyllis Beaty, Magnolia Studio

Illustrator
Linda Berry

ACKNOWLEDGMENTS

Each book is the result of a joint effort by a unique team of people. I would like to thank the members of this team for helping to create the book you are reading:

To the folks at Top Floor Publishing:

- ✦ To Peter Kent, publisher and owner of Top Floor Publishing, for doing the book.
- ✦ To Linda Gallagher for project management.
- ✦ To Kevin Murray, developmental editor on this book, who's always a pleasure to work with as well as being a model of editorial effectiveness.
- ✦ To Fred Kloepper for proofreading.
- ✦ To David Collier and Terry McCullough for their invaluable efforts in creating the CD accompanying this book.

Thanks also to Joel Diamond, without whom Peter Kent would not have learned about MP3 and I would not have had a chance to write this book nor had the pleasure of working with Peter.

- ✦ To Tim Doyle of Doyle Communications for the cover design.
- ✦ To Phyllis Beaty of Magnolia Studio for the dazzling book design and composition.
- ✦ To Linda Berry of Roxy Design & Corporate Communications for technical illustrations.
- ✦ To David Rogelberg, Neil Salkind, and Sherry Rogelberg, of Studio B, my agency. Thanks!
- ✦ To Constance, for putting up with me through yet another book.
- ✦ To Dennis Mudd, Pamela Evans, Beth Kunzie, Joeli Yaguda, Steven Cole, and Adrian Herrera of MusicMatch for permission to feature MusicMatch Jukebox in this book as well as for substantial and invaluable technical assistance and advice throughout the writing process. Thanks, everyone!

- ✦ To Paul Schatzkin (aka "The Perfesser"), President of *Songs.com*, for invaluable assistance in creating the CD.
- ✦ To Trapper for moral support, technical information, and bad jokes.
- ✦ To Jim Lane for information on speakers.
- ✦ To Michael Robertson of *mp3.com* for invaluable assistance.
- ✦ To Sandy Bradley for rounding up tracks for the CD and for being herself.
- ✦ To Angelo Sotira of Dimension Music for a wealth of background information.
- ✦ To Potential of MP3 2000, for enthusiasm and a lot of connections for MP3 hardware.
- ✦ To Jim Griffin of OneHouse for a fascinating look at the future of MP3 and digital music technology.
- ✦ To Warren Argo, generally great guy and record company executive, for support and contribution of a vast array of very cool music from Sage Arts.
- ✦ To Barney McClure for music for the CD.
- ✦ To Scott Snailham for technical information on ripping to and from cassettes and vinyl.
- ✦ To Jeff Felker for hardware support par excellence.
- ✦ To Ian K. Hagemann for invaluable computer support.
- ✦ To Richard Vanceunebrouck-Werth of Omega Organization for technical data on recording.

In addition, the following people and companies have provided valuable support and information and also deserve recognition (the list is in alphabetic order by company or product):

- ✦ To Kathryn Kelly of Adaptec for information on Adaptec's Easy CD Creator Deluxe.
- ✦ To Chris Hoffman of CDH Productions for information about CDH Media Wizard.
- ✦ To Carl Davis of CD Systems, Inc., for information on Impy3.
- ✦ To Theresa Pulido, Pilar Miranda, Hock Leow, and Carl Slater of Creative Labs and also to Gary Brotman of Golin/Harris International for invaluable technical assistance on Creative Labs speakers, sound cards, and the Nomad MP3 player.

- To Lorraine Comstock, Mary Medeiros, and many other people at Diamond Multimedia for information on the Rio portable MP3 player and on Diamond sound cards.
- To Tai Hwang and Frank Jin of Eiger Labs, Inc., for information on the MPMan portable MP3 player.
- To Steve Sanders of Empeg for information on the Empeg-car.
- To Detlef Wiese of MAYAH Communications, for information about EditPro.
- To Mixman Technologies for information on Mixman Studio and Studio Pro.
- To Rafael W. Luebbert for information about the MPecker encoder.
- To Dave Chaimson, senior product manager, for information about Sound Forge XP and Sound Forge.
- To Todd Souvignier and Arboretum Systems, for information about Ray Gun.
- To Alexandra Walsh at the RIAA for information about the RIAA.
- To Jo Gilmore at Syntrillium for information about Cool Edit 96 and Cool Edit Pro.

And finally, to the many people who contributed to the CD, my deep and abiding thanks.

CONTENTS AT A GLANCE

TABLE OF CONTENTS

INTRODUCTION

Welcome to *MP3 and the Digital Music Revolution*. This book will introduce you to the exciting world of MP3 files and digital audio.

WHY THIS BOOK IS FOR YOU

MP3 and the Digital Music Revolution is written for anyone who wants to learn about the many features of MP3 and digital music. If you haven't used MP3 files before, the book discusses each of the features in simple terms. You don't really need any prior experience with audio, the Internet, or Windows. All you need is a computer and a minimum amount of experience using it. The CD accompanying this book contains all you need to get started playing and recording MP3 files. When you're ready to move forward, you can find out about additional programs and techniques to get the best sound quality out of your computer.

ABOUT THIS BOOK

This book is meant to be a fast introduction to MP3. After learning some basics about how MP3 files work, you'll see how to install the MusicMatch Jukebox software on the CD accompanying this book and use it to play MP3 files. For the new user, there are extensive instructions on how to set up and use the MusicMatch Jukebox software.

The chapters continue by showing you how to create playlists of MP3 files, get more MP3 files online, and record MP3 files from CDs. You also see how to play MP3 files through your sound system and how to record them on cassettes and CD-ROMs using a CD-ROM burner. Throughout these chapters, you're taken through the menus and shown how to use the features and options in the MusicMatch Jukebox software.

As you progress further in the book, you see how to edit and enhance your MP3 files using other software and tools. You're introduced to a range of MP3 and audio software with which you can fine-tune your MP3 files or produce different effects and results. Next, you see how to play MP3 files away from your computer using portable MP3 players such as the Rio and the MPMan, and how to update your sound card and speakers to produce a better quality of sound. The final chapter presents quotes from luminaries in the field of digital audio about what the future will bring. There is an extensive appendix of resources for MP3 users and a brief appendix on how to use the CD accompanying this book.

HOW THIS BOOK IS ORGANIZED

This book is divided into nine chapters. Each chapter discusses one or two features of the MusicMatch Jukebox software and how to play, create, or enhance MP3 files. Chapters and concepts are organized in the order you are most likely to need them.

CHAPTER 1, "GETTING STARTED," describes the basics of MP3 files. You'll learn what you need in the way of hardware and software and how to play MP3 files using the standard Windows Media Player. You'll also see how to install MusicMatch Jukebox on your computer, play a single track with it, and learn about the basic MusicMatch Jukebox features and options. Finally, you'll also see how to use MusicMatch Jukebox with other MP3 players, such as Winamp.

CHAPTER 2, "CREATING AND USING PLAYLISTS," teaches you more about two of the features of MusicMatch Jukebox: the Play List window and the Music Library. You'll see how to use the Play List window to create and use playlists of tracks. You'll also see how to use the Music Library to create and maintain databases of tracks and how to edit track information and add your own categories.

In **CHAPTER 3, "GETTING MORE MP3 FILES,"** you'll see how to get MP3 files from the Internet by downloading them from web sites, newsgroups, and FTP sites. You'll also see how to upgrade your computer to accommodate the vast number of MP3 files you'll be getting. There is also a brief discussion of some of the issues relating to MP3 files, copyrights, and legality.

In **CHAPTER 4, "CREATING YOUR OWN MP3 FILES,"** you learn more about how digital music works. With this knowledge, you'll learn how to create your own MP3 files from CDs, cassettes, vinyl, and radio.

CHAPTER 5, "RECORDING FROM YOUR COMPUTER TO YOUR AUDIO SYSTEM," reverses the process and shows you how to play your MP3 files on your stereo and how to record MP3 files onto cassettes, DAT tapes, and CDs.

With the basics of playing and recording MP3 files covered, **CHAPTER 6, "EDITING AND ENHANCING MP3 FILES,"** shows you ways to improve the sound quality of your MP3 files by editing and filtering them using a variety of methods.

CHAPTER 7, "USING OTHER SOFTWARE," describes a wide variety of other MP3 software: players, rippers, encoders, and all-in-one programs. Macintosh users will be particularly interested in this chapter, as several Macintosh programs are discussed.

CHAPTER 8, "PLAYING MP3 FILES AWAY FROM YOUR COMPUTER," describes some of the hardware options available to you. The chapter opens with an introduction to several popular portable MP3 players, including the Rio, the MPMan, and the Nomad. The chapter also discusses hardware for your home computer that will improve the quality of the sound available to you, including better sound cards and speakers. There is also information on MP3 players for your stereo and your car.

Finally, **CHAPTER 9, "WHAT'S NEXT?"** gives a look into the future through the eyes of a number of noted luminaries and specialists in the field of digital audio.

For users who are interested in expanding their reach, **APPENDIX A, "RESOURCES,"** lists a number of web sites and newsgroups for MP3 files, software, news, and information.

APPENDIX B, "HOW TO USE THE CD," gives you basic information on how to load and use the software and MP3 files on the CD accompanying this book.

CONVENTIONS USED IN THIS BOOK

This book has several standard conventions for presenting information.

- ◆ Defined terms are in *italics*.
- ◆ The screen shots in this book show you how the software looks on a Pentium computer using an SVGA monitor with a standard 800x600 High Color (16 bit) color display in Microsoft Windows 95. What you see on your screen may be slightly different depending on your hardware and software.

There are three types of notes in the text that appear in the side margins:

There are two styles of sidebars in the text that appear at the top or bottom of the pages:

THIS IS A SIDEBAR

Sidebars are information that expand on some of the material being discussed in the text. Sidebars are larger than NOTES and may be more illustrative than NOTES or TIPS.

THIS IS A SIDEBAR

Sidebars are information that expand on some of the material being discussed in the text. Sidebars are larger than NOTES and may be more illustrative than NOTES or TIPS.

Getting Started

This chapter will introduce you to the basics of MP3 files. You'll learn what you need in the way of hardware and software and how to play MP3 files using the standard Windows Media Player. You'll also see how to install MusicMatch Jukebox on your computer, play a single track with it, and learn about the basic MusicMatch Jukebox features and options. Finally, you'll also see how to use Music-Match Jukebox with other MP3 players, such as Winamp.

WHAT IS MP3?

MPEG (pronounced "EM-peg") is an acronym for *Moving Pictures Experts Group.* MPEG is a group of standards for compressing and storing audio and video in files. MP3 is actually short for *MPEG 1, layer 3,* the portion of the MPEG standard that specifies how audio files are stored.

What makes MP3 files special is that they give CD-quality sound in a file that only requires about one megabyte for every minute of sound. (By comparison, the format used on CDs for recording requires about 11 megabytes for every minute.) This means that you can fit 10 to 11 hours of music stored in MP3 format on a single CD, compared to the 60 minutes you usually get on a CD. Furthermore, at three to five megabytes per track, MP3 files—also referred to as *tracks*—are small enough to download from web sites. This, combined with their high quality of sound reproduction, has made them enormously popular for distributing and exchanging songs and music. Many search engines list *MP3* as the second-most-popular search topic.

WHAT DO YOU NEED TO PLAY AND CREATE MP3 FILES?

There are minimum hardware requirements for playing and creating MP3 files. You also need to know a little about the variety of software available.

WHAT HARDWARE DO YOU NEED?

For Windows computers, the practical minimum for playing MP3 files is:

- Pentium 90 MHz (for playing only; for creating your own MP3 files, you'll need at least a P-133)
- 16 MB of RAM
- 256-color display card and monitor
- Windows 95 or Windows 98
- A CD-ROM drive
- A 16-bit sound card
- External speakers or headphones

For Macintosh computers, you'll need the following minimum hardware:

- A 68020 or a Power Macintosh
- System 7.5
- Apple's Sound Manager 3.1
- A CD-ROM drive
- External speakers or headphones

Regardless of the type of computer you're using, it's a good idea to have at least half a gigabyte of spare hard disk to store MP3 files. (At 3–5 megabytes per file, they can add up fast.) Both Windows and Macintosh users should also give serious thought to purchasing a CD-ROM burner, a CD-ROM drive that lets you create your own CDs. The blank CDs cost about $1 each these days. (This kind of drive is known as a *Write Once, Read Many* or WORM drive.) Rewritable CD-ROM burners and CDs will be more expensive and probably aren't the kind you'll want. You can use the burner for backing up volumes of MP3 files and for creating your own custom CDs.

WHAT SOFTWARE DO YOU NEED?

There are several different kinds of software you will need to play and record your own MP3 files.

The first and most important type of software is the *player*. Very simply, the player plays MP3 files. Many players play a variety of files in addition to MP3 files, including WAV, MIDI, AAC, and other types of sound files. Some typical Windows players include Winamp and Sonique. On the Macintosh, look for MacAMP or SoundApp.

The next type of software is a *playlist editor*. A *playlist* is a list of the MP3 files you want to play in the order you want to play them. Playlists can be set up in advance and saved, letting you create your own "albums" for a specific mood or occasion. Many players already have playlist editors built in, but you can get stand-alone playlist editors that create playlists for a range of other players. Typical playlist editors include the MP3 Explorer for Windows or Trax for the Macintosh.

To create your own MP3 files, you will need two tools: a ripper and an encoder. A *ripper* extracts the tracks from the CD and converts them into WAV files on your computer's hard disk. An *analog ripper* does the same thing but with analog signals from cassette tapes, vinyl, or radio. (MusicMatch Jukebox does both digital and analog ripping.) An *encoder* takes ripped files and turns them into MP3 files. Rippers and encoders are frequently bundled into a single product. Examples of rippers and encoders for Windows are Audiograbber and Audio-Catalyst; for the Macintosh, check out Recordit and MPecker.

If you don't want to have to pick and choose, you can get an all-in-one program that does everything you need. The best-known example of this is MusicMatch Jukebox, which is on the CD accompanying this book. The CD also includes a selection of players, rippers, encoders, and other programs. See Appendix B, "How to Use the CD" for more information about the CD and how to install it on your computer.

(MusicMatch Jukebox is not yet Mac compatible but should be by late 1999.)

While it's not to be denied that the majority of MP3 software is written for Windows and the Macintosh, there is a wide selection of MP3 software available for most other operating systems in common use, including Linux, Unix, and OS/2. There are also a number of utilities for editing and tweaking MP3 files, filtering for better sound, and adding information such as lyrics, notes, cover art, and the like. In addition, new programs and new versions of existing software are released frequently. For more information on all kinds of MP3 software, be sure to check out some of the web sites and newsgroups listed in Appendix A, "Resources."

FINDING AN MP3 FILE TO PLAY

There are thousands of MP3 files available online from Web sites and newsgroups via FTP. You'll see how to collect these later in the book in Chapter 3, "Getting More MP3 Files," but for now, you'll work with files from the CD accompanying this book.

There are a number of MP3 files on the CD. Here's how to play one of them:

1. Insert the CD in your computer's CD-ROM drive.
2. Go to the Windows Start menu. From the Program menu, start the Windows Explorer.
3. Select the CD-ROM drive and go to the \music folder.
4. Double-click one of the MP3 files. The Windows Media Player will start (as shown in Figure 1.1) and the file will start playing.

If all has gone well, you should be hearing MP3 music in all its glory... and it's pretty neat. The sound quality is good, and, looking at the files on the CD with the Windows Explorer, you can see that they're relatively small—only a few megabytes each.

This, anyway, is the way things *should* work. But this procedure might not work as described for one of a couple of reasons:

✦ You don't have the Windows multimedia options installed, in which case the MP3 file won't play. (You can find out by going to the Windows Control Panel and seeing if you have a Multimedia icon in the selections or by looking on the Windows Start menu, then going to Programs, Accessories, Multimedia, and looking for an entry for the Windows Media Player.)

FIGURE 1.1:
The standard
Windows Media
Player.

♦ You already have another MP3 player set up on your computer, in which case the other MP3 file player will play the file.

But even if everything worked perfectly, the bottom line is that Windows Media Player is only so-so as an MP3 player. Oh, it handles MP3, WAV, MIDI, and a host of other sound file formats, MPG, AVI, QuickTime, and other video formats, and the RealNetworks, RealAudio, and RealVideo formats... so many that you should always have the Windows Media Player on your system just because of the range of formats it will handle. But despite this, it's simply not the most effective or full-featured program to use for playing your MP3 files. And if you install Windows Media Player after you've installed MusicMatch Jukebox or other MP3 audio players, it will disable them without asking. To enable those players again, you have to mess around with the file associations in the View Options menu in the Windows Explorer or uninstall Media Player.

One of the most popular MP3 products these days is MusicMatch Jukebox. (A copy of MusicMatch Jukebox appears on the CD.) MusicMatch Jukebox is not just a player; it's a complete system for playing, recording, and maintaining MP3 files. You'll see how to use each of its features in this and subsequent chapters. Another popular player is Winamp (which also appears on the CD). Winamp is just a player, but it's a good one. (You'll see later how you can set up Music-

Match Jukebox to use Winamp as its default MP3 player.) Yet another very popular player is Sonique, which plays a wide range of file types.

The next section shows you how to install MusicMatch Jukebox on your system and introduces you to its basic features.

INSTALLING MUSICMATCH JUKEBOX

MusicMatch Jukebox appears on the CD accompanying this book in the MusicMatch folder. To install MusicMatch Jukebox from the CD, follow these directions:

1. Insert the CD in your computer's CD-ROM drive.
2. Go to the Windows Start menu. From the Program menu, start the Windows Explorer.
3. Select the CD-ROM drive and go to the \MusicMatch folder.
4. Double-click the MMSETUP.EXE file. The MusicMatch Jukebox setup procedure will begin. Follow the directions on the screen.

When you install MusicMatch Jukebox (or most any other MP3 player for that matter), the setup program will supplant the Windows Media Player as the default MP3 player on your computer if that option is selected during installation.

Once you've installed MusicMatch Jukebox, start it by selecting the Windows Start menu, then going to the Programs menu and selecting MusicMatch Jukebox. (If you set up MusicMatch Jukebox as an icon on the desktop, you can just double-click the icon.)

The first time you run MusicMatch Jukebox, you'll see the main screen, the Track Info window, and a welcome screen, shown in Figure 1.2. (After you've run the program the first time, you won't see the welcome screen when you run the program, although you can display it from the help files.)

The MusicMatch Jukebox main screen has many features you should take a moment to acquaint yourself with. The player window occupies the upper left half of the screen. The player controls are modeled after a cassette player. The cover art for the MP3 file (if any) appears in the cover art window. Songs in the playlist appear in the playlist window on the right side of the screen.

When you start MusicMatch Jukebox by double-clicking an MP3 file, you automatically start playing the file. The file information will appear in the player's fields (an example of this appears in Figure 1.3).

FIGURE 1.2:
The MusicMatch
Jukebox main screen,
Track Info window,
and welcome screen.

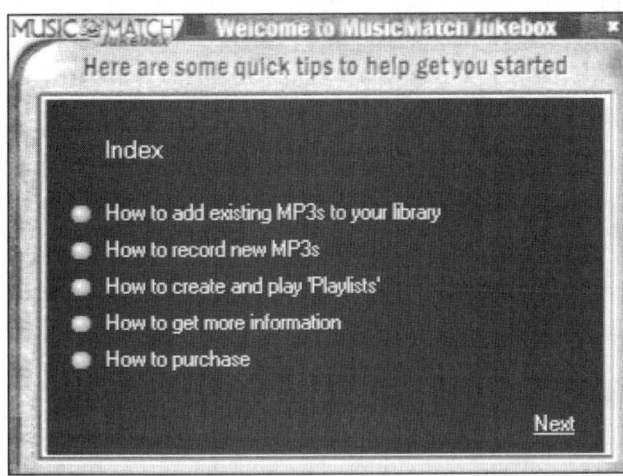

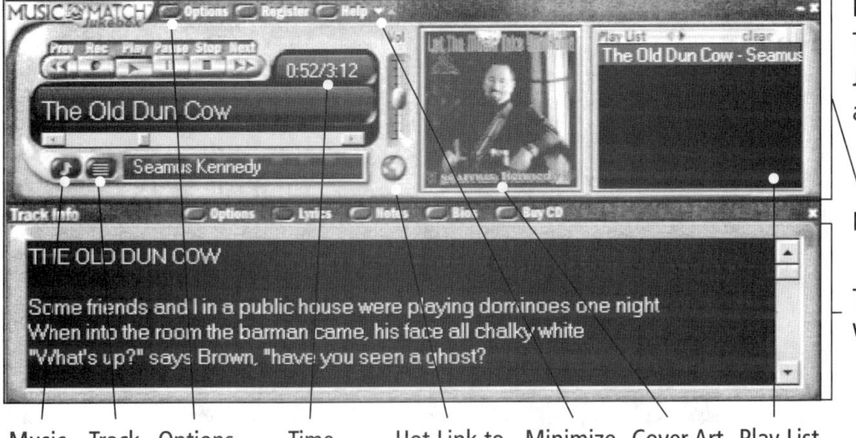

FIGURE 1.3:
The MusicMatch
Jukebox player with
a track playing.

Player

Track Info
window

Music Library button Track Info button Options menu button Time Played/Total Time of Track Hot Link to MusicMatch web site Minimize button Cover Art window Play List window

As you can see from Figure 1.3, there's often more information to
be had about the track than just the artist's name and the name of the
track. One of the versatile features of MP3 files is that they can contain a lot of text and graphics information in addition to the music

itself. The Track Info window displays information about the song you're playing. You can view the lyrics (and sing along if you like!), read notes about the song, and see biographical information about the artist by clicking the appropriate button at the top of the Track Info window. One of the really convenient features of the Track Info window is that you can also buy the CD if you like the track you're listening to. Clicking Buy CD will link you to a web page that will let you order this CD. If the Track Info window isn't visible, click Track Info ( ) at the bottom of the player.

Adding the information displayed in the Track Info window takes a little extra effort on the part of the person creating the MP3 file, though, so many MP3 files will simply contain the name of the song and the artist. You'll see later in this book how you can add lyrics, notes, cover art, and other information to an MP3 file yourself.

MusicMatch Jukebox also has a built-in database for your MP3 files, which you can open by clicking the Music Library button ( ). Figure 1.4 shows MusicMatch Jukebox with the Music Library displayed.

The Music Library contains a list of your MP3 files. When you first start MusicMatch Jukebox, there won't be any files listed. You'll see how to add MP3 files to the Music Library later in this chapter. You'll also see how to sort tracks to find all the songs by one group or of one style, such as blues or jazz.

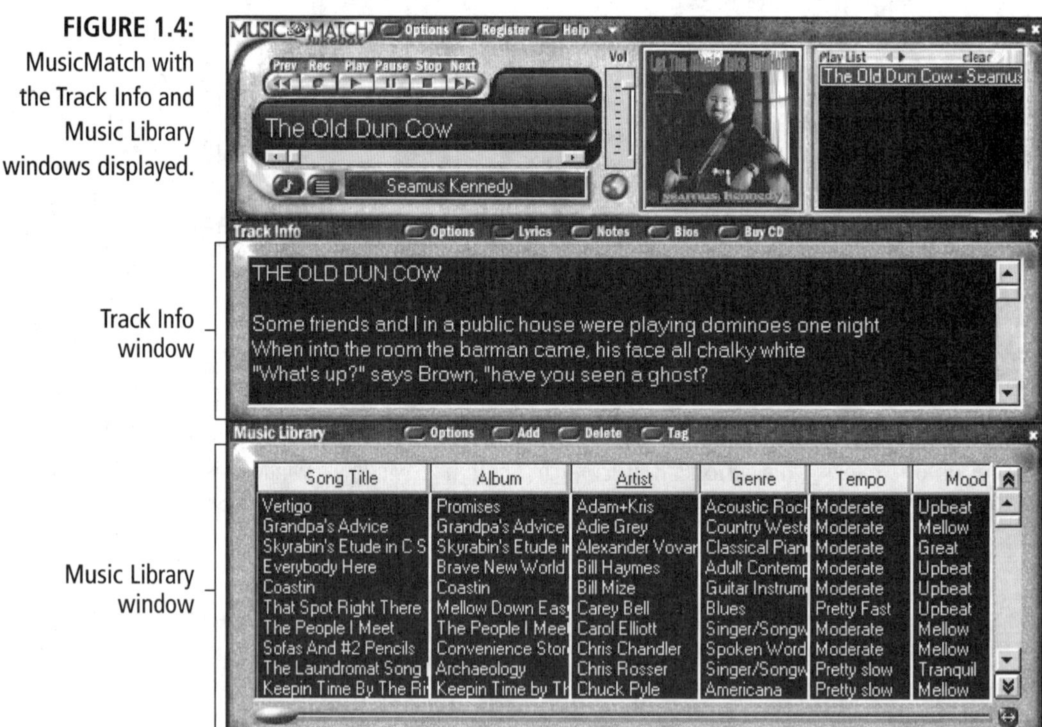

FIGURE 1.4:
MusicMatch with the Track Info and Music Library windows displayed.

Track Info window

Music Library window

Here are some tips for playing MP3s:

✦ Any time you're doing something on the computer other than playing a track, you're going to be taking the computer's attention away from the track you're playing... and you'll hear a brief dropout in the sound. This doesn't hurt the file you're playing, but it can be annoying if you're trying to listen to a symphony and then have to load programs, start software, and do other things that require a lot of computer power that should otherwise be spent on entertaining you. During recording, you don't want to run any power-hungry applications because the lack of computer power can damage the sound file. (However, I can attest that I listened to a lot of MP3 files while I was writing this book, and word processing by itself will not affect your sound output one whit.)

✦ You can play MP3 files with the built-in speaker on your computer, but who'd want to? The standard inexpensive stand-alone speakers are about 40 watts and will give you adequate sound. However, if you find you're spending a lot of time listening to MP3 files, you may want to invest in a good set of computer speakers with some bass response, or a good set of headphones if you're in an office or other setting where you can't just crank up the volume for a particularly good guitar solo. For the best sound output, you should give serious consideration to plugging your computer into your sound system as described in Chapter 5, "Recording from Your Computer to Your Audio System."

✦ Just about all the sound cards sold today will work okay for playing and recording MP3 files. If you buy a really expensive sound card, you may notice a very slight improvement, but there's no real difference in playing MP3 files on an average sound card or one of the very best.

EXPLORING MUSICMATCH JUKEBOX

The previous section showed you some of the basic features of MusicMatch Jukebox. Now you'll have a chance to explore the program in more detail. Click Options on the main screen. A drop-down list of menu options (shown in Figure 1.5) appears.

The Options menu has half a dozen different menus you can select from, as described in Table 1.1.

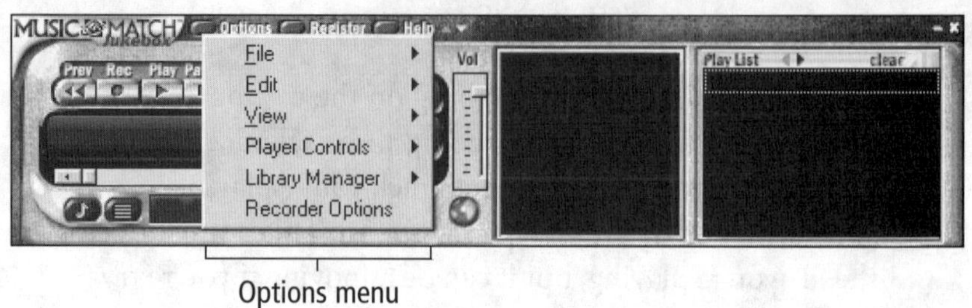

Options menu

TABLE 1.1: THE OPTIONS MENU

MENU SELECTION	WHAT YOU USE IT FOR
FILE	Add tracks to the Music Library, create, open, and save playlists, export playlists, convert files. (See Chapter 2, "Creating and Using Playlists," for information on the playlist options and Chapter 4, "Creating Your Own MP3 Files," for information on converting files.)
EDIT	Clear or delete playlists, delete individual tracks from the Play List window, edit the information for a specific track. (See Chapter 2, "Creating and Using Playlists," for information on these options.)
VIEW	Display a track's cover art, display the Track Info, Play List, or Music Library windows, display the Recorder. (See Chapter 2, "Creating and Using Playlists," for information on these options.)
PLAYER CONTROLS	Change the play cycle and play order, change the default player used in MusicMatch. (See Chapter 2, "Creating and Using Playlists," for information on the play cycle and play order options and see the "Using Other MP3 Players with MusicMatch" section later in this chapter for information on changing the default player.)
LIBRARY MANAGER	Clear the tracks from the Music Library, load a predefined set of tracks, save a database of tracks. (See Chapter 2, "Creating and Using Playlists," for information on these options.)
RECORDER OPTIONS	Set recorder options and record tracks. (See Chapter 5, "Recording from Your Computer to Your Audio System," for information on these options.)

You'll see how to use all of these commands and options in this and subsequent chapters.

USING OTHER MP3 PLAYERS WITH MUSICMATCH

If you've already been doing a little experimenting with MP3 files, you may have tried another MP3 player called Winamp. Winamp is a very good (and very popular) MP3 player. You'll be pleased to know that you don't need to give up using Winamp to take advantage of the features of MusicMatch Jukebox. Although the default settings for MusicMatch Jukebox use the MusicMatch player, you can also designate Winamp as your default player.

To set Winamp as your default player, do the following:

1. Click Options on the main MusicMatch screen.

2. Select Player Controls, then choose Use Winamp Player. MusicMatch will display a dialog box for you to specify where to find the Winamp player.

3. When you are satisfied with your entry, click OK. Music-Match displays a message in the main screen that shows you that the active player is now Winamp, as you can see in Figure 1.6.

Now, when you play a track, MusicMatch will use Winamp as the player. As you can see in Figure 1.7, the Winamp player window appears in place of the MusicMatch player when it's playing a track.

You can use this feature to specify players other than Winamp as the default, too, but only if you're sneaky. For example, suppose you want to use Sonique (another popular player). When you select

FIGURE 1.6:
MusicMatch main screen with the default player set to Winamp.

Winamp player

FIGURE 1.7:
Winamp playing an MP3 file.

Player Controls from the Options menu, then choose Use Winamp Player, MusicMatch asks you to specify where to find the Winamp player. You can't tell MusicMatch you want to use a player with a name other than WINAMP.EXE, but you can copy the SONIQUE. EXE file to WINAMP.EXE and then tell MusicMatch to use *that* file. Lo and behold, when you play a file, MusicMatch will use the file it thinks is Winamp. Sneaky? You bet. But it works.

To go back to the way things were, you can switch back by choosing Use MusicMatch Player from the Player Controls menu. If you ever move Winamp from its current location on your computer, you can use the Change Winamp Path option to tell MusicMatch where to find Winamp. You can also use this to switch between alternate players.

A WORD ABOUT FREEWARE AND SHAREWARE

Freeware is software that's been developed and released to the public at no charge, such as Sonique. Freeware may not always have everything you want, but you don't pay anything for it, so what the heck? Other programs are *shareware*. Shareware lets you try the software before you buy it. If you like it, you pay a nominal fee (usually less than $40) for the right to keep using it. The shareware system works because there's no cost of goods or cost of distribution for the shareware version of the product.

Registration can usually be done by mail, phone, and the Internet. Some programs (such as MusicMatch Jukebox) give you additional features when you register. Registering a program like this will get you a registration key of some kind that you enter in the program to unlock the additional features, including unlimited recording capabilities and converting WAV files to MP3. Other programs (like Winamp) work exclusively on the honor system: you don't get anything extra in the program for registering, although you may get free updates, documentation, or support, as well as the warm glow of having done the right thing.

Generally, if you use a shareware program for more than 30 days, you're expected to pay for it. If you don't like it, remove it from your computer and try something else. The cost of registering your shareware is minimal. Check the documentation and the help files for each of the programs for information on how much they cost to register and what you'll get for it.

This chapter introduced you to the basics of MP3 files, what you need in the way of hardware and software, and how to play MP3 files using the standard Windows Media Player. You also installed Music-Match Jukebox on your computer, saw how to play a single track, and were introduced to the basic features and options in MusicMatch Jukebox. Finally, you saw how to use a different MP3 player. In the next chapter, you'll explore the Music Library and the Play List features in MusicMatch Jukebox, learn how to create databases of music, and see how to create and use playlists of tracks.

Creating and Using Playlists

In the preceding chapter, you were introduced to the basics of MP3 files, saw how to install and use Music-Match Jukebox to play a single track, and learned about MusicMatch's basic features and options. In this chapter, you're going to learn more about two of those features: the Play List window and the Music Library. You'll see how to create and use playlists of tracks and databases of music.

CREATING A PLAYLIST BY DRAGGING AND DROPPING TRACKS

As you read earlier, a playlist is a list of the tracks you want to play in the order you want to play them. If you were just going to play tracks by double-clicking them in the Windows Explorer or loading them one at a time, you could just use the Windows Media Player that's part of Windows 95 and Windows 98. But playing tracks one at a time is a nuisance. Just like playing a CD, you'll want to cue up a whole album's worth of tracks at once.

Before you create a playlist, take a moment to look at the Play List window shown in Figure 2.1.

The Play List window in Figure 2.1 is the one you see when you start MusicMatch Jukebox. It's good for seeing what you have playing, but it's no good for creating playlists. To see the full Play List window, click the Play List maximize button, or choose Show Playlist Control from the View menu on the Options list. The full Play List window appears, as shown in Figure 2.2.

The left side of the Play List window shows the tracks in the playlist currently open or under construction. The

FIGURE 2.1:
The MusicMatch Jukebox main screen with the standard Play List window.

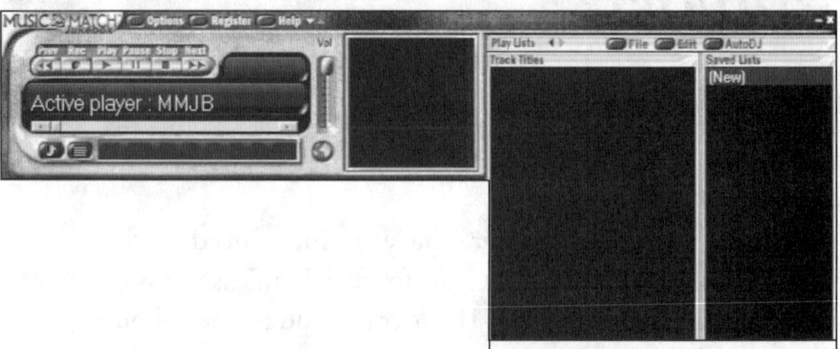

FIGURE 2.2:
The MusicMatch Jukebox main screen with the full Play List window displayed.

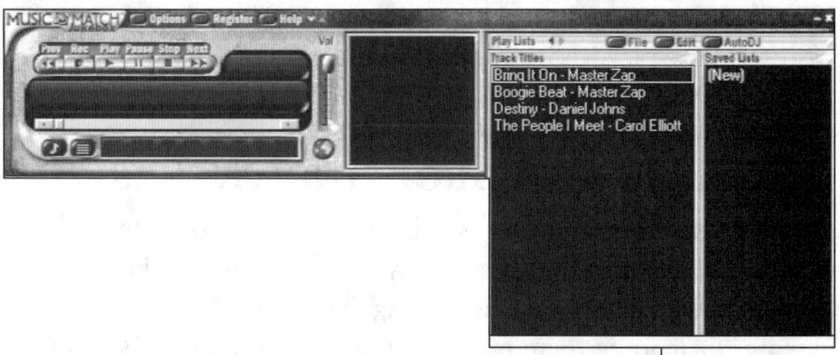

FIGURE 2.3:
The Play List window with several tracks added.

right side of the Play List window shows the playlists you can choose from.

The simplest way to create a playlist is to open the Play List window, then open Windows Explorer, and drag and drop MP3 files from the Windows Explorer to the left side of the Play List window. As you drop each file into the Play List window, you'll see an entry for the track appear on the left side of the Play List window. Figure 2.3 shows a playlist under construction with several tracks already added.

If you're not sure what a single track sounds like, you can double-click the track in the playlist to start playing it. To delete a single track, highlight the track and either press Delete or select Delete Track from the Play List window's Edit menu. (Actually, the Edit menus on the Play List window and on the MusicMatch Jukebox main screen are identical so it doesn't matter which of those two Edit menus you use.) You can delete the entire list of tracks and start over by selecting Clear Playlist from the Play List window's Edit menu. If you want to change the order of the tracks (remember, MusicMatch plays the tracks in the order they appear in the playlist), you can highlight a track and drag it to the place you want it to appear in the playlist.

You can add as many tracks as you like to the playlist. When you're satisfied with your selections and want to hear what you've done, you can play the tracks you've assembled by clicking Play (▶) on the Player. MusicMatch Jukebox will start playing the first track in the list. You can skip to the next track by clicking Next (▶▶). Looks like MusicMatch Jukebox is beginning to act a little more like a regular CD player now!

As a matter of fact, you can make MusicMatch Jukebox act even more like a regular CD player with a few of the Player Control commands. You can have MusicMatch Jukebox play a playlist continuously by going to the main screen's Options menu, selecting Player Controls, then choosing Play Cycle, and then choosing Continuous (the default is Once). You can also have MusicMatch Jukebox play tracks at random (rather than in order) by selecting Player Controls again, then choosing Play Order, and then choosing Shuffle (the default is In order).

The playlist you've created isn't saved anywhere yet. If you like it and want to save it, select Save Playlist from the Play List window's File menu and enter a name to save the playlist as. The saved playlist appears on the right side of the Play List window. You can start building a new playlist by clicking [New] on the right side of the Play List window or by selecting New from the Play List window's File menu. MusicMatch clears the tracks from the left side of the Play List window, and you're ready to go. Figure 2.4 shows the Play List window with a couple of playlists already saved and a third playlist being created.

By saving playlists, you're creating albums of tracks to play for whatever occasion you like. To cue up a saved playlist and start play-

FIGURE 2.4:
The Play List window with saved playlists.

Saved playlists

ing the tracks, double-click the name of the playlist in the right column of the Play List window. (You might think you can select Open Existing Playlist from the main screen's File menu, but this just brings up the Play List window so you can double-click the playlist, so save time and go there first.) When you open a playlist, the tracks in the playlist appear on the left side of the Play List window.

If you're tired of a playlist, you can delete it by highlighting the playlist in question and either pressing Delete or selecting Delete Playlist from the Play List window's Edit menu.

USING THE MUSIC LIBRARY

Dragging and dropping files from the Windows Explorer is an acceptable way of creating a playlist, but it doesn't take advantage of sorting and classification information that can be embedded in MP3 files. To do this, you need to use MusicMatch Jukebox's Music Library.

ADDING TRACKS TO THE MUSIC LIBRARY

As you saw briefly in Chapter 1, the Music Library displays a group of tracks (also known as a *database*). The contents of the Music Library isn't a playlist; it's more like a collection of singles you can select from. The Music Library lets you see the tracks you have in your collection and provides you with some fancy ways of sorting and classifying tracks.

The first thing you need to do to use the Music Library is to add tracks, as follows:

1. From the Music Library, click Add. The Add Songs window (shown in Figure 2.5) appears.

2. Select the drive and directory you want to add files from. (You can select MP3 files from the CD accompanying this book by inserting the CD in your CD-ROM drive and selecting the appropriate drive and the TRACKS directory.) The MP3 files in the directory appear in the lower window.

3. Select the tracks you want to add to the Music Library. You'll usually want to click Select All to add all the tracks in the directory. You can select a single file by highlighting it. If you want to select several files, hold down the Ctrl key and click the files you want to add. If you're not sure if you want to add a track, you can get information about the track by highlighting the file. The name, artist, album, and album cover art (if any) will appear on the right side of the Add Songs window as shown in Figure 2.6.

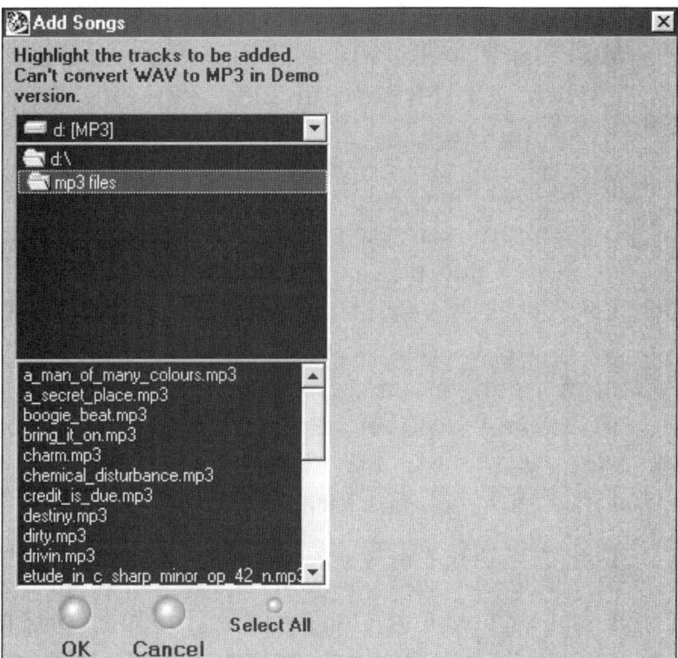

FIGURE 2.5:
The Add Songs window.

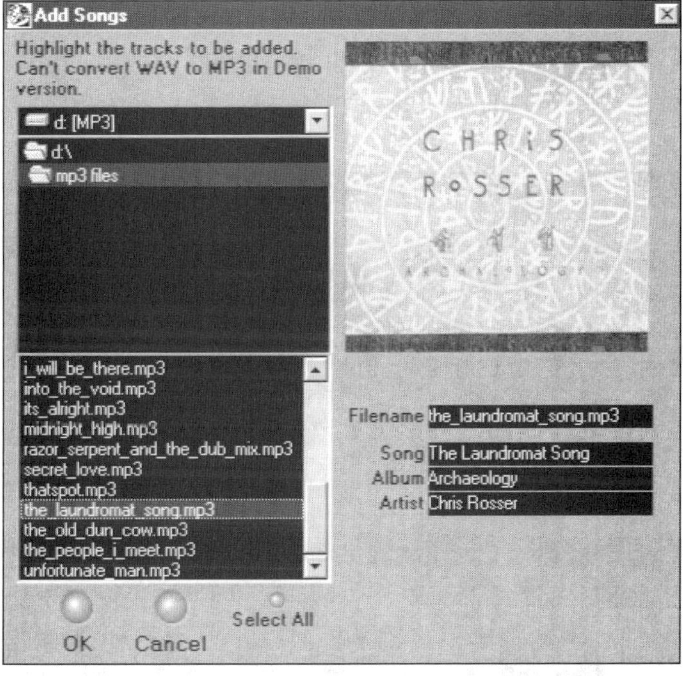

FIGURE 2.6:
The Add Songs window with basic track information displayed.

4. When you are satisfied with your entries, click OK. Music-Match starts adding files to the Music Library. If there's a duplicate track already in the Music Library, MusicMatch will ask you if you want to replace the existing record. You can click Yes to replace the existing track with this track,

Yes to All to replace any tracks automatically, No to skip this track, and No to All to skip any duplicate tracks. When MusicMatch is finished, the Music Library will show the tracks you've added, as shown in Figure 2.7.

You can click the maximize button on the Music Library window (![]) to expand the Music Library window. Not only do you see all the columns of information, but expanding the Music Library window lets you see twice as many tracks, as you can see in Figure 2.8. You can click the minimize button (![]) to return the Music Library window to its original size.

You can adjust the size of the columns by moving the mouse pointer up to the space between the column headers. When you see the double-headed arrow appear, click and drag. The column to the left of the mouse pointer will expand or contract. Figure 2.9 shows the Music Library window in Figure 2.8 with the first two columns expanded.

You can remove individual tracks by highlighting the track and pressing Delete on your keyboard or clicking Delete on the Music Library window. You can remove everything in the database by selecting Clear Database from the Music Library's Options menu. (The database commands on the Music Library's Options menu are the same commands as appear in the Library Manager option of the

FIGURE 2.7: The Music Library window with tracks added.

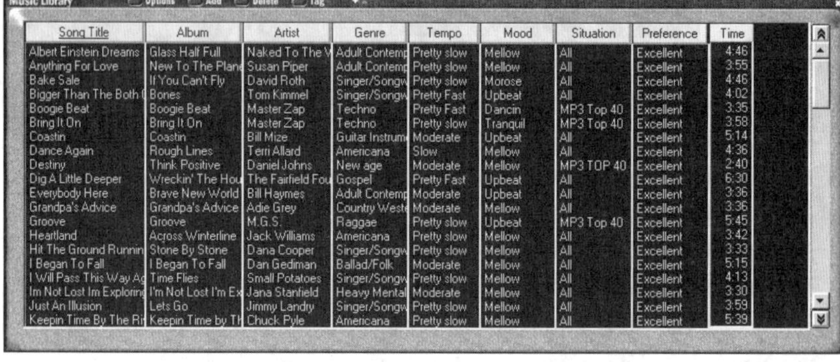

FIGURE 2.8: The Music Library window with all the columns displayed.

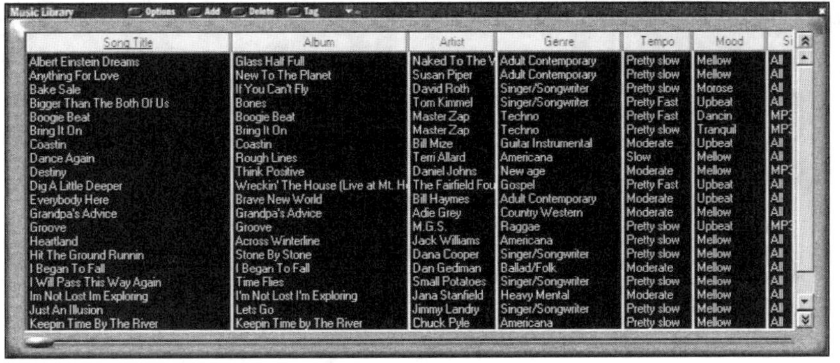

FIGURE 2.9:
The Music Library window with some of the columns expanded.

Options menu on the MusicMatch Jukebox main screen.) Removing the tracks from the Music Library doesn't delete the actual files, just the entries for them in the database.

After you've been collecting MP3 files for a while, you may have collected enough that you'll want to save different volumes of them in separate databases. For example, you might have a large collection of upbeat music, one of comedy tracks, and so on. You can save a database of tracks in the Music Library by selecting Save Database (or Save Database As) from the Music Library's Options menu. Music-Match Jukebox saves the list of tracks in a file. To load a new database, select Load New Database from the Music Library's Options menu and specify the database you want to load. The tracks in the database will appear in the Music Library, sort of like opening a different cabinet of CDs to choose from.

CREATING A PLAYLIST WITH THE MUSIC LIBRARY

Once you've added songs to the Music Library, you can play tracks and create playlists from the Music Library database. The advantage of using the Music Library to create playlists as opposed to dragging and dropping files in the Play List window as you saw earlier is that you can see information about the tracks and even hear the track before adding it to the playlist.

Playing a single track from the Music Library is simple:

1. Highlight a track in the Music Library. As you can see from Figure 2.10, a track indicator (▶) appears to the left of the track you've highlighted.

2. Click the track indicator. The track information appears in the Play List window and MusicMatch Jukebox starts playing the track.

You can add tracks to the Play List window (without playing them) by double-clicking the track in the Music Library or by highlighting the track and then dragging it to the Play List window. You can put a block of files into the Play List window by doing the following:

1. In the Music Library, highlight the first track you want in the block.

2. Hold down the Shift key and then click the last track you want in the block. The files between the first and last tracks will also be highlighted.

3. Without releasing the mouse button, drag the files up to the Play List window and drop them. The tracks appear in the Play List window.

An even slicker way of adding tracks is to right-click once in the Music Library window when you have the files highlighted. A floating menu appears. Select Add songs to playlist to move the songs to the Play List window. (If you select the other option on the floating menu, Delete, MusicMatch Jukebox deletes the highlighted songs from the Music Library. This is convenient but it can be slightly dangerous, so be careful.)

You can also add a number of files that don't appear one after another in the Music Library by doing the following:

1. In the Music Library, highlight the first track you want.

2. Hold down the Ctrl key and then click the tracks you want to add to the playlist. As you click each track, it's highlighted.

3. Once you've highlighted the tracks you want to add, you can either right-click and select Add songs to playlist or drag and drop them as you did in the previous procedure. The tracks appear in the Play List window.

FIGURE 2.11:
The Music Library sorted by Artist.

Once the files are in the Play List window, you can then rearrange the playlist, add and delete tracks, and save the playlist as you saw earlier in this chapter.

SORTING YOUR COLLECTION OF TRACKS

One of the really cool things about using the Music Library is that you can sort the music any way you want. This makes it much easier to find the tracks you want to play. If you look at Figures 2.7 and 2.8, you'll see that the Song Title heading is underlined, showing that the tracks are sorted by song title. To sort by another category, click on a column heading to sort the list by that category. Figure 2.11 shows the entries in the Music Library sorted by Artist.

You can use this feature of the Music Library to look for the artist or type of song you'd like to hear. Once you've sorted the tracks, you can easily select all the tracks by one artist or of one type and move them all to the playlist. For example, if you feel like listening to low, depressive stuff, look for songs labeled "Morose" in the Mood column. Or you might want something for the holidays: select "Seasonal" in the Situation column. As you'll see a little later, you can edit the information for a song and use your own descriptions in the columns such as "Novelty Tune," "Ragtime," or "Sing-along."

EXPORTING A DATABASE

You can export a database in a tab-delimited text file: the column information is separated by tabs. This is useful for seeing what you've got and identifying changes you'd like to make. The tab-delimited format can be used by databases, spreadsheets, and word processing programs.

To export a database:

1. Select Export Database to Tab-delimited File from the Music Library's Options menu.
2. Enter the name of the file in the File Save dialog box and click OK.

MusicMatch Jukebox will export the database information to the text file.

EDITING TRACK INFORMATION

Tracks will usually come to you with at least some of the information entered—the song title, the artist—but even if information is entered for every column in the Music Library, you may want to change or expand some of the information that appears in the Track Info window. And if you're creating MP3 files of your own for distribution, you'll definitely need a way to enter and edit the information for your MP3 files. The process of saving information in an MP3 file is known as *tagging*.

There are two kinds of tagging that are in common use: MusicMatch and ID3 tagging. These two types use a different format. Versions of MusicMatch Jukebox prior to v3.05 used the MusicMatch format; versions of MusicMatch Jukebox from 3.1 on use ID3 tags. (The newer versions of MusicMatch Jukebox also recognize the older MusicMatch tags as well.) When you change tag information for an MP3 file that already has a MusicMatch format tag, MusicMatch Jukebox asks if you want to use the MusicMatch tag, the ID3 tag, or Cancel. Whenever you make changes to an MP3 file's tag information, the newer versions of MusicMatch Jukebox always save the tag information in ID3 format.

If you have a lot of MP3 files that use the older MusicMatch format, you can select Convert ID3 Tags from the Options menu in the Music Library to convert the tags to ID3 tag format. If you are just using MusicMatch Jukebox for your files, the tagging format really won't matter much, but using ID3 tagging will make your files more compatible with other MP3 players and products.

Most of the time, you'll probably just want to change some of the entries in the columns appearing in the Music Library so you can use different sorting criteria. Occasionally, you'll want to add or change information such as the lyrics, cover art, and bio entries. Both of these types of changes require you to use the Track Information screen for making entries and changes, as follows:

1. Highlight a track in the Music Library and click Tag. (You can also click Tag in the Track Info window, or highlight a track in Play List window and select Edit Track Info from the menus in the Player or Play List windows.) The Track Information screen (shown in Figure 2.12) appears.
2. Enter information in the fields as follows:

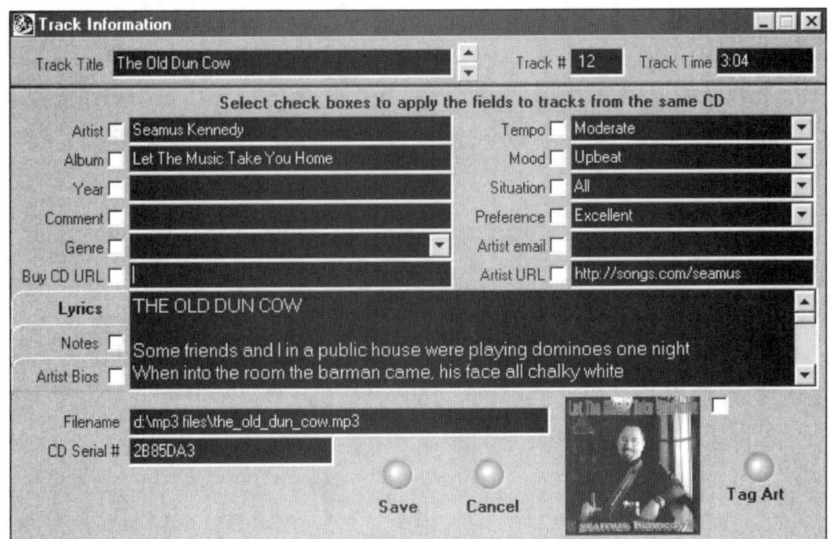

FIGURE 2.12:
The Track Information screen.

TRACK TITLE

Enter the title for the track. (This information shows up in the Song Title column in the Music Library.) Use the up and down arrows to show other track titles you've entered in this session.

TRACK

Enter the track number. This number comes from the CD from which the track was recorded. If you're listening to a group of songs, you can identify the order in which the songs appear on the original CD. You probably won't want to change this.

TRACK TIME

Track time is calculated when the MP3 file is created. You can change this if you want, but it's probably a good idea not to. (This information shows up in the Time column in the Music Library.)

ARTIST

Enter the artist's name. (This information shows up in the Artist column in the Music Library.)

ALBUM

Enter the album name. (This information shows up in the Album column in the Music Library.)

YEAR

Enter the year the track was recorded.

COMMENT

Enter a comment of up to 40 alphanumeric characters about the track in this field. This is for informational purposes only and does not appear anywhere else.

GENRE

Select the genre information for the track from the drop-down list. (This information shows up in the Genre column in the Music Library.) There are 126 entries to select from for Genre, as shown in Table 2.1. You can also add your own categories to this list, as described later in this chapter.

BUY CD URL

Enter the URL to go to for buying the CD. Again, this appears on the screen for reference only. If you want to visit this web site, you'll have to open your browser and enter this URL.

TABLE 2.1: SELECTIONS IN THE GENRE DROP-DOWN LIST

Acapella	Christian Rap	Fast Fusion	Jazz	Power Ballad	Slow Jam
Acid	Classic Rock	Folk	Jazz+Funk	Pranks	Slow Rock
Acid Jazz	Classical	Folk-Rock	Jungle	Primus	Sonata
Acid Punk	Club	Folklore	Latin	Progressive Rock	Soul
Acoustic	Comedy	Freestyle	Lo-Fi	Psychedelic	Sound Clip
Alternative	Country	Funk	Meditative	Psychedelic Rock	Soundtrack
AlternRock	Cult	Fusion	Metal	Punk	Southern Rock
Ambient	Dance	Game	Musical	Punk Rock	Space
Avantgarde	Dance Hall	Gangsta	National Folk	R&B	Speech
Ballad	Darkwave	Gospel	Native American	Rap	Swing
Bass	Death Metal	Gothic	New Age	Rave	Symphonic Rock
Bebob	Disco	Gothic Rock	New Wave	Reggae	Symphony
Big Band	Dream	Grunge	Noise	Retro	Tango
Bluegrass	Drum Solo	Hard Rock	Oldies	Revival	Techno
Blues	Duet	Hip-Hop	Opera	Rhythmic Soul	Techno-Industrial
Booty Bass	Easy Listening	House	Other	Rock	Top 40
Cabaret	Electronic	Humour	Polka	Rock & Roll	Trailer
Celtic	Ethnic	Industrial	Pop	Samba	Trance
Chamber Music	Euro-House	Instrumental	Pop-Folk	Satire	Tribal
Chanson	Euro-Techno	Instrumental Pop	Pop/Funk	Showtunes	Trip-Hop
Chorus	Eurodance	Instrumental Rock	Porn Groove	Ska	Vocal

TEMPO

Select the tempo information for the track from the drop-down list. (This information shows up in the Tempo column in the Music Library.) You can select from Fast, Pretty Fast, Moderate, Pretty Slow, Slow, and None. You can also add your own categories to this list, as described later in this chapter.

MOOD

Select the mood information for the track from the drop-down list. (This information shows up in the Mood column in the Music Library.) You can select from Wild, Upbeat, Morose, Mellow, Tranquil, and Comatose. You can also add your own categories to this list, as described later in this chapter.

SITUATION

Select the situation information for the track from the drop-down list. (This information shows up in the Situation column in the Music Library.) You can select from Dance, Party, Romantic, Dinner, Background, Seasonal, Rave, and Drunken Brawl. You can also add your own categories to this list, as described later in this chapter.

PREFERENCE

Select the preference information for the track from the drop-down list. (This information shows up in the Preference column in the Music Library.) You can select from Excellent, Very Good, Good, Fair, Poor, and Bad Taste. You can also add your own categories to this list, as described later in this chapter.

ARTIST EMAIL

Enter the artist's e-mail address.

ARTIST URL

Enter the URL of the artist's web site. This appears only on this screen for reference purposes. If you want to visit this web site, you'll have to open your browser and enter this URL.

LYRICS/NOTES/ARTIST BIOS

Enter the lyrics, any notes about the track or the album, and the artist bios. When you first open this window, the lyrics information appears in the field. You can display and edit each of the types of information by clicking the category name to the left of this field.

Unless you're the artist, you probably won't need to make an entry in this field or in the Artist e-mail or Artist URL fields.

FILENAME

Enter the filename for the MP3 file. This is generally for information purposes only, but if you've moved the MP3 file to another location on the hard disk since you've added this, you'll need to change this filename so the Music Library knows where to look for the file.

CD SERIAL

This display-only field is the unique CD identifier used by sites such as *http://www.CDDB.com* to identify the CD and look up information for it. This information is automatically pulled off a CD when the MP3 files are ripped. The serial number frequently can be found on the CD jacket or insert.

3. If you are going to add or change the artwork associated with the file, click Tag Art. The MusicMatch-Art screen appears, as shown in Figure 2.13.

4. Using the directory and file windows on the left side of the screen, select a *bitmap file* (BMP) or a *JPEG file* (JPG) to use as the cover art. The selected bitmap will appear in the cover art window. As you can see from Figure 2.13, if there's already a bitmap or JPEG file associated with the MP3 file, it will appear on the MusicMatch-Art screen. When you are satisfied with your selection of cover art, click Done to return to the Track Information screen. If

FIGURE 2.13:
The MusicMatch-Art screen.

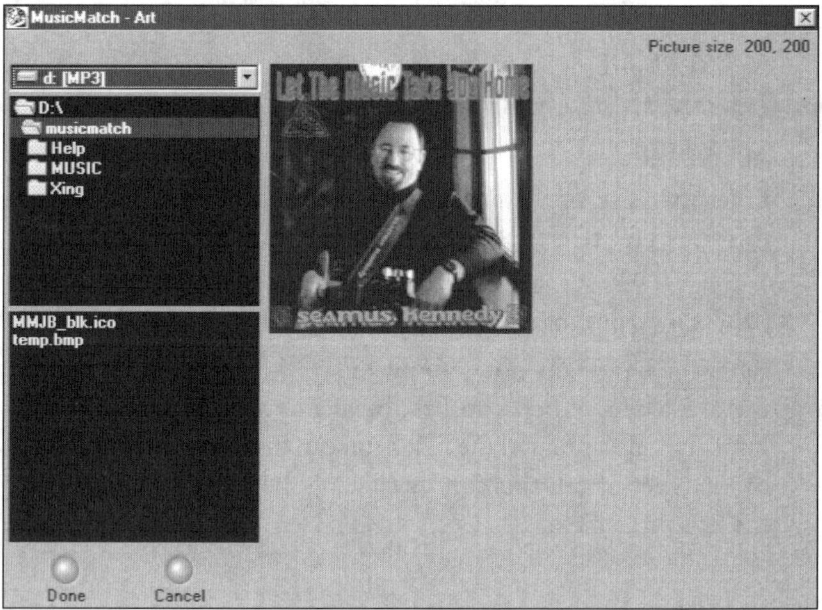

you have a scanner, you can scan album covers or other artwork to add to your MP3 files. As an alternative, you could create a bitmap and use it for your artwork. The only requirements are that the files must be in bitmap or JPEG format. MusicMatch Jukebox will automatically scale the picture so that it appears in a file format of up to 200x200. You can create and edit bitmap files with Microsoft Paint or dozens of other art and graphics programs.

5. When you are satisfied with your entries on the Track Information screen, click OK to change the information for the MP3 file or Cancel to leave things as they are.

Where there are no drop-down lists to select from on the Track Information screen, you'll need to type each entry. To save time when entering track information, MusicMatch Jukebox has a handy technique for carrying information over from one file to the next when you're tagging a group of files from the same album, as follows:

1. Highlight a track in the Music Library and click Tag. The Track Information screen (shown earlier in Figure 2.12) appears.

2. Enter information in the fields as described earlier.

3. Check the boxes by the side of the fields that you want all the other tracks from the album to have. Figure 2.14 shows the Track Information screen with several fields selected for carrying over to other tracks.

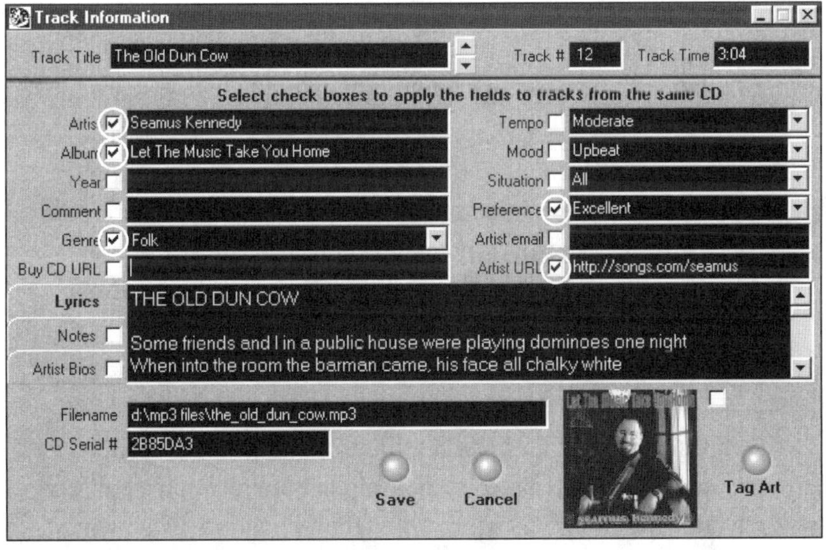

FIGURE 2.14:
The Track Information screen with fields selected for other tracks. *(Selected fields are circled in white.)*

4. When you are satisfied with your entries, click Save. Music-Match Jukebox will save the information for this track and will also modify the track information for all other tracks with the same CD serial #.

MODIFYING THE TRACK INFORMATION DROP-DOWN LISTS

You saw earlier how to use the drop-down lists in the Track Information screen to enter such information as Genre, Tempo, and Mood. As you do more cataloging, you'll probably want to add items to the drop-down lists that reflect your own music preferences. For example, you may want to create a new category of music in your database, such as "Housecleaning" or "Rude Comedy."

Here's how to change the selections available to you in the drop-down lists:

1. Open the Windows Notepad (open the Windows Start menu, go to Programs, Accessories, and select Notepad from the list).

2. In Notepad, open the ID3V1.CAT file, which is in the MusicMatch folder (or the folder you installed Music-Match in). The ID3V1.CAT file contains the default entries for the Genre category. If you want to change the entries for Tempo, Mood, Situation, or Preference, open the BRAVADJ.CAT file. The categories appear at the start of each list of entries in [brackets].

3. You can add, change, or delete entries. The ID3V1.CAT file has each entry numbered. If you add entries to the ID3V1.CAT file, you'll have to add a number for them, too. (Don't change any of the numbered entries that are already there, as these are standard ID3V1 categories.) Whatever you enter in the files will appear in the appropriate drop-down menu. Table 2.2 shows the default entries for the Situation category and a customized Situation list with entries changed and a couple of additional entries added.

4. When you are satisfied with your entries, save the file. (If you opened the file in something other than Notepad, be sure to save the file as a text document with no formatting). The next time you open MusicMatch, you'll be able to use the new drop-down list. Tempo, Mood, Situation,

and Preference entries appear in the order they appear in the list; the Genre entries are automatically alphabetized for you, so you don't need to enter the new entries in alphabetic order.

TABLE 2.2: SAMPLE DEFAULT AND CUSTOMIZED ENTRIES FOR A DROP-DOWN LIST

ORIGINAL LIST	CUSTOMIZED LIST
[Situation]	[Situation]
Dance	Dance
Party	Party
Romantic	Romantic
Dinner	Dinner
Background	Light
Seasonal	Yule
Rave	Poker night
Drunken Brawl	Housecleaning
	Bedtime
	Kids

CREATING AUTOMATIC PLAYLISTS

So far in this chapter you've seen a couple of ways to create playlists. All these methods have one thing in common: they require you to select the tracks you want to play and put them into the Play List window. You're now going to see how you can make MusicMatch Jukebox do a lot of the work for you and create automatic playlists.

Automatic playlists are playlists that you create by specifying the length of the playlist you'd like and defining the types of music you want in your playlist. MusicMatch Jukebox runs through the songs in the database and creates a playlist from the tracks that meet the criteria.

To create an automatic playlist:

1. Click AutoDJ in the Play List window or select the AutoDJ: Auto-Create Playlist option from the File menu on the Options menu of the MusicMatch Jukebox main screen. The Auto DJ screen appears (as shown in Figure 2.15).

2. Enter the desired playing time in the Enter Play Time field. MusicMatch will try to find enough tracks to play for this time. The default is eight hours.

FIGURE 2.15:
The Auto DJ screen.

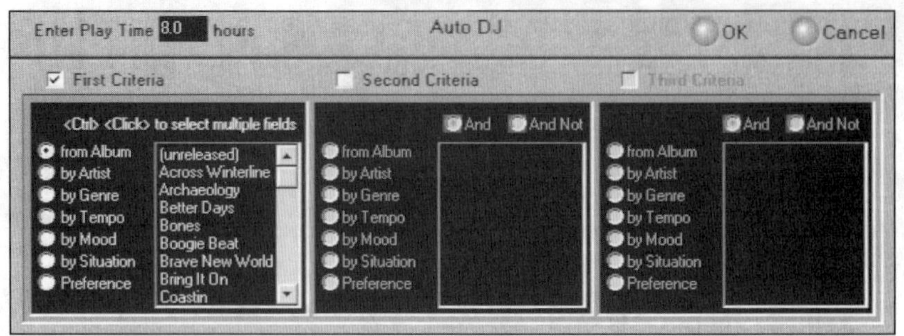

3. Enter the first criterion to select from the Music Library's database with. For example, you might want to select all tracks that have a Mood of "Mellow." You can select multiple items by holding down the Ctrl key and clicking the individual items to highlight them. You can select a range of items by holding down the Shift key and clicking the first and then the last items in the range.

4. Check the Second Criteria box if you want to refine your list by specifying a second criterion. You can now select items in the Second Criteria window. You'll see that the criterion you used for the first criterion is grayed out. One of the cool features here is that you can select for or against a criterion by selecting the And or And Not radio button at the top of the selection criterion window. For example, if your first criterion is Mellow tracks and the second criterion is MP3 Top 40, and you check And, MusicMatch will select all Mellow tracks that are MP3 Top 40. On the other hand, if you check And Not, MusicMatch will select all Mellow tracks except for those that are MP3 Top 40.

5. If you'd like to further refine your selection, you can check the Third Criteria box. The criteria you selected earlier are grayed out in the Third Criteria window. Figure 2.16 shows you the Auto DJ screen with first, second, and third selection criteria selected.

6. When you are satisfied with your entries, click OK. MusicMatch Jukebox selects the tracks in the Music Library that meet the criteria you've specified. You'll see a dialog box like the one in Figure 2.17 that tells you how many tracks were selected and their total playing time.

> **NOTE**
>
> *The entries that appear in the selection window are the entries that you have for the tracks in your database, rather than the selection criteria in the Music Library's drop-down lists.*

FIGURE 2.16:
The Auto DJ screen with criteria selected.

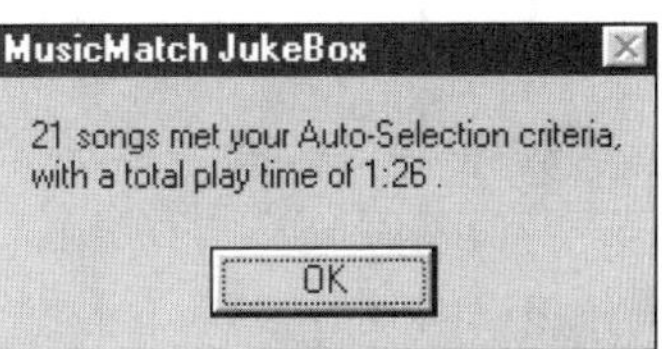

FIGURE 2.17:
The dialog box showing the number of tracks selected.

FIGURE 2.18:
The Play List window showing the tracks selected.

7. When you click OK in this dialog box, the selected tracks appear in the Play List window, as shown in Figure 2.18. You can then edit and save the playlist as you saw how to do at the beginning of this chapter.

If you have specified less time than the total playing time of the tracks available, MusicMatch Jukebox will select as many as will fit in the playing time in the order they appear in the Music Library.

TROUBLESHOOTING

Not everything works every time. Here are some common problems and how to solve them:

Problem: There's an entry in the database, but MusicMatch Jukebox can't find the track.

Solution: When you add tracks to the Music Library, Music-Match Jukebox builds a list of entries in the database. As you saw earlier in Figure 2.12, the file's location is stored in the database. When you try to play that track, the Music Library can't find the file. If the files corresponding to the tracks have been deleted, you'll need to delete the tracks from the Music Library as well. If you've only moved a couple of tracks, you can correct the filenames in the Track Information screen. If you've moved a large number of tracks (for example, you moved all your MP3 files to another disk drive with more room), you'll probably find it easier just to delete the database entries for the tracks and then add them again to the Music Library.

Problem: The song is playing (you can see the time indicator changing) but there's no sound.

Solution: Start by checking the volume control to the right of the MusicMatch player to make sure that the volume isn't turned all the way down. Also check the Volume Control by going to the Windows Start menu, then select Programs, Accessories, Multimedia, then selecting Volume Control. Make sure that none of the "Mute" or "Mute All" boxes are checked and that the volume levels are set appropriately.

If neither of these solutions work, make sure that you can play any sounds by opening a WAV file in the Windows Media Player. (There are a number of WAV files in the \Windows\Media directory that will do for this experiment.) If you can't, try rebooting the computer—Windows may have gotten confused for some reason. And if nothing else works, check that your speakers are plugged into the right jack on the sound card, and that (if necessary) the power's on to the speakers.

This chapter showed you how to use the Play List window to create and use playlists of tracks. You also saw how to use the Music Library to create and maintain databases of tracks that you can sort by different criteria to find just the right track. Finally, you saw how to edit track information and add your own categories. In the next chapter, you'll see how to get more MP3 files from newsgroups, web sites, and other sources.

Getting More MP3 Files

The previous chapter showed you how to use the Play List window to create and use playlists of tracks. You also saw how to use the Music Library to create and maintain databases of tracks and how to edit track information and add your own categories. In this chapter, you'll see how to get MP3 files from the Internet. You'll also see how to upgrade your computer to accommodate the vast numbers of MP3 files you'll be getting.

"AVAST, ME HEARTIES!" PIRACY AND COPYRIGHT LAW

There's something you should know about some of the MP3 files you're likely to run into online: they may be illegal. That's right, if someone creates an MP3 file of a song and posts it to the Internet without the permission of the owner of the music, then they've committed a crime; specifically, a violation of federal copyright laws and also of the No Electronic Theft, or NET, Act of 1997, which makes it a felony to create or distribute unauthorized digital music. Such felonies aren't cheap, either: even if there is no financial gain, the potential penalties are up to 3 years in jail and $250,000 in fines.

The *Recording Industry Association of America (RIAA)* has been keeping an eye on what's being distributed. When MP3 files were first being distributed on the net, they were mostly illegal. However, in the last year a lot of the MP3 sites have cleaned up their acts and are only distributing authorized MP3 files.

The issue of creating MP3 files at home is still under discussion. While the Supreme Court has ruled that you can record your own videos at home for purely personal use without violating the copyright laws relating to the copying of a copyrighted film, there is no clear ruling yet on whether it's legal to create MP3 files from CDs or albums that you own. The RIAA contends that it is illegal to do so and is a violation of the Audio Home Recording Act of 1972. They could be right, too.

Isn't this like the flap in the early 1970s over people owning cassette recorders that would let them duplicate vinyl albums and distribute cassette copies? No, not really. With your own cassette recorder, you could only make copies by recording the album onto a cassette, which would get you perhaps one cassette every 45 minutes or so. It definitely violated the copyright of the music but the quantity was relatively small. There was some signal loss, too: a cassette tape you recorded off an album wouldn't be quite as good as a commercial copy of the album on cassette (just like a video you taped off cable won't be quite as crisp as a commercial copy you rented). Moreover, the cassette would fade with time the more you played it. In contrast, you could rip the tracks from a new CD into MP3 format with virtually no loss of quality, upload them to a newsgroup or web site, and have thousands of people a day downloading them. Both kinds of piracy are illegal and cost the artists money in lost royalties, but MP3 files can be a lot more devastating. And this is what's causing concern with the RIAA and regulatory agencies.

"So what *is* legal about MP3 files, then?" I hear you cry. Well, a rapidly growing number of musicians and artists are releasing authorized MP3 tracks for distribution on MP3 web sites, newsgroups, FTP sites, and on collections of MP3 files on CD. You can also record and distribute MP3 files of anything you have the rights to, such as music your band has written and recorded. (It's worth noting that making copies of CDs or vinyl that you own onto cassettes that are intended for your own personal, noncommercial use is also legal.) Ripping MP3 files from your CDs and albums is a no-no, but I doubt you'll get busted for doing either one. But you should think twice before ripping the entire *Titanic* soundtrack and tossing it up on the net for several thousand of your closest friends to download, because you may find yourself in water that's surprisingly hot.

GETTING DIGITAL MUSIC ONLINE

The CD accompanying this book contains a number of MP3 files, but sooner or later you're going to want more files. The most effective way to do this is to download files from the Internet.

There are hundreds of web sites, newsgroups, and FTP sites devoted to distributing MP3 files. Many of the web sites are general covering a wide range of MP3 files, but others—particularly newsgroups—tend to focus on specific types of music, such as classical, 1960s, or Brazilian. There's something for everybody: you should be able to find something you like on the Internet, no matter what your musical tastes.

GETTING MP3 FILES FROM WEB SITES

The most popular way of finding MP3 files is through MP3 web sites. There are hundreds of MP3 web sites in existence that distribute MP3 files, software, news bulletins about MP3, and provide a forum for discussions by MP3 users. Many of these sites are listed in Appendix A, "Resources."

One of the most popular web sites for MP3 files is *http://www.mp3.com*. This site is probably the best-known MP3 site in existence. As you can see from Figure 3.1, there's an extensive free music section that is cataloged and cross-referenced in a variety of ways.

One really interesting feature of *mp3.com* is the Top 40 list, shown in Figure 3.2. The Top 40 list is the top 40 MP3 files being downloaded on the Internet. But perhaps equally interesting is the Bottom 40 list (shown in Figure 3.3), which shows you the 40 least popular MP3 files on the list. (You might think of listing the bottom 40 tracks as a way of "churning the stock;" people will perversely want to know what some of the least popular tracks sound like, download them, and presto! they're no longer the least popular songs.)

You can also select songs by category. For example, Figure 3.4 shows some of the songs in the Folk category. Songs in the list are sorted in order of popularity.

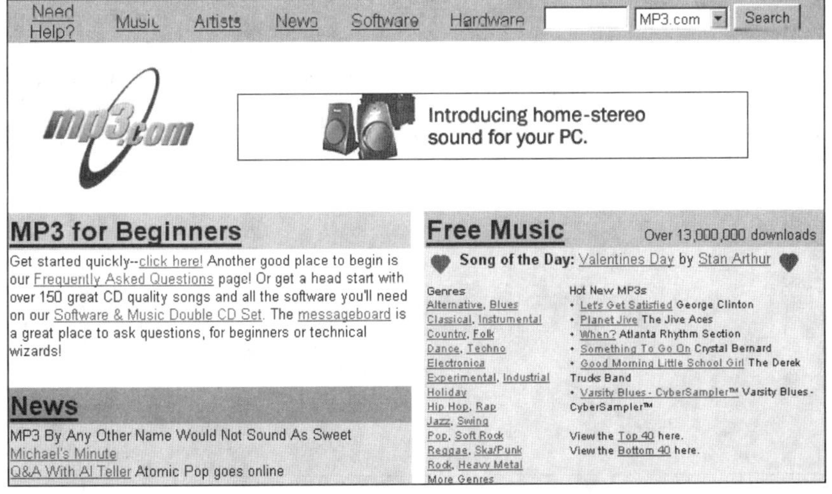

FIGURE 3.1:
The *mp3.com* main screen.

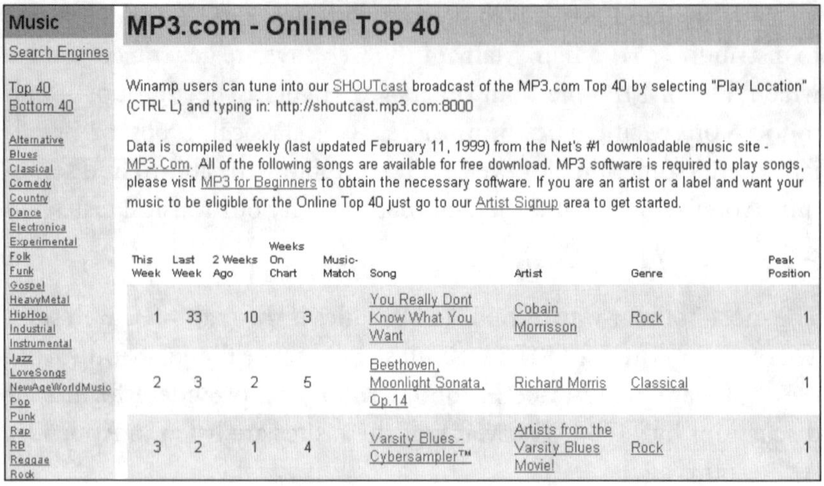
Music
Search Engines
Top 40
Bottom 40
Alternative
Blues
Classical
Comedy
Country
Dance
Electronica
Experimental
Folk
Funk
Gospel
HeavyMetal
HipHop
Industrial
Instrumental
Jazz
LoveSongs
NewAgeWorldMusic
Pop
Punk
Rap
RB
Reggae
Rock
MP3.com - Online Top 40
Winamp users can tune into our SHOUTcast broadcast of the MP3.com Top 40 by selecting "Play Location" (CTRL L) and typing in: http://shoutcast.mp3.com:8000
Data is compiled weekly (last updated February 11, 1999) from the Net's #1 downloadable music site - MP3.Com. All of the following songs are available for free download. MP3 software is required to play songs, please visit MP3 for Beginners to obtain the necessary software. If you are an artist or a label and want your music to be eligible for the Online Top 40 just go to our Artist Signup area to get started.
This Week | Last Week | 2 Weeks Ago | Weeks On Chart | Music-Match | Song | Artist | Genre | Peak Position
1 | 33 | 10 | 3 | You Really Dont Know What You Want | Cobain Morrisson | Rock | 1
2 | 3 | 2 | 5 | Beethoven, Moonlight Sonata, Op.14 | Richard Morris | Classical | 1
3 | 2 | 1 | 4 | Varsity Blues - Cybersampler™ | Artists from the Varsity Blues Movie! | Rock | 1

FIGURE 3.2: *mp3.com's* Online Top 40 list.

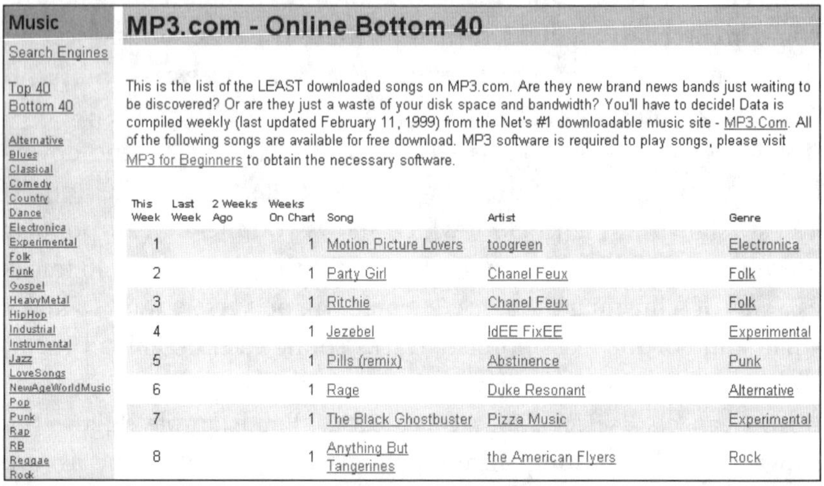
Music
Search Engines
Top 40
Bottom 40
Alternative
Blues
Classical
Comedy
Country
Dance
Electronica
Experimental
Folk
Funk
Gospel
HeavyMetal
HipHop
Industrial
Instrumental
Jazz
LoveSongs
NewAgeWorldMusic
Pop
Punk
Rap
RB
Reggae
Rock
MP3.com - Online Bottom 40
This is the list of the LEAST downloaded songs on MP3.com. Are they new brand news bands just waiting to be discovered? Or are they just a waste of your disk space and bandwidth? You'll have to decide! Data is compiled weekly (last updated February 11, 1999) from the Net's #1 downloadable music site - MP3.Com. All of the following songs are available for free download. MP3 software is required to play songs, please visit MP3 for Beginners to obtain the necessary software.
This Week | Last Week | 2 Weeks Ago | Weeks On Chart | Song | Artist | Genre
1 | 1 | Motion Picture Lovers | toogreen | Electronica
2 | 1 | Party Girl | Chanel Feux | Folk
3 | 1 | Ritchie | Chanel Feux | Folk
4 | 1 | Jezebel | IdEE FixEE | Experimental
5 | 1 | Pills (remix) | Abstinence | Punk
6 | 1 | Rage | Duke Resonant | Alternative
7 | 1 | The Black Ghostbuster | Pizza Music | Experimental
8 | 1 | Anything But Tangerines | the American Flyers | Rock

FIGURE 3.3: *mp3.com's* Online Bottom 40 list.

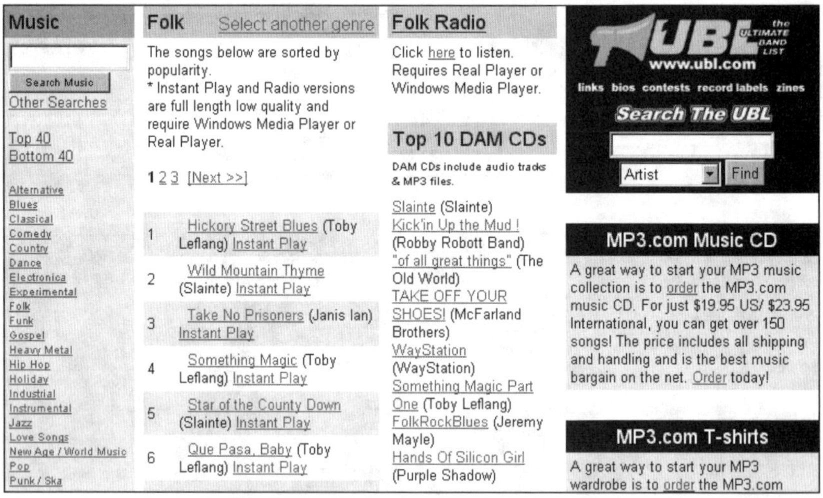
Music
Search Music
Other Searches
Top 40
Bottom 40
Alternative
Blues
Classical
Comedy
Country
Dance
Electronica
Experimental
Folk
Funk
Gospel
Heavy Metal
Hip Hop
Holiday
Industrial
Instrumental
Jazz
Love Songs
New Age / World Music
Pop
Punk / Ska
Folk Select another genre
The songs below are sorted by popularity.
* Instant Play and Radio versions are full length low quality and require Windows Media Player or Real Player.
1 2 3 [Next >>]
1 Hickory Street Blues (Toby Leflang) Instant Play
2 Wild Mountain Thyme (Slainte) Instant Play
3 Take No Prisoners (Janis Ian) Instant Play
4 Something Magic (Toby Leflang) Instant Play
5 Star of the County Down (Slainte) Instant Play
6 Que Pasa, Baby (Toby Leflang) Instant Play
Folk Radio
Click here to listen. Requires Real Player or Windows Media Player.
Top 10 DAM CDs
DAM CDs include audio tracks & MP3 files.
Slainte (Slainte)
Kick'in Up the Mud ! (Robby Robott Band)
"of all great things" (The Old World)
TAKE OFF YOUR SHOES! (McFarland Brothers)
WayStation (WayStation)
Something Magic Part One (Toby Leflang)
FolkRockBlues (Jeremy Mayle)
Hands Of Silicon Girl (Purple Shadow)
UBL the ULTIMATE BAND LIST
www.ubl.com
links bios contests record labels zines
Search The UBL
Artist
Find
MP3.com Music CD
A great way to start your MP3 music collection is to order the MP3.com music CD. For just $19.95 US/ $23.95 International, you can get over 150 songs! The price includes all shipping and handling and is the best music bargain on the net. Order today!
MP3.com T-shirts
A great way to start your MP3 wardrobe is to order the MP3.com

FIGURE 3.4: A specific category of MP3 tracks on *mp3.com.*

You can also search for specific artists or songs in the site by entering the artist or name in the Search field (shown in the upper left corner of Figure 3.4). Figure 3.5 shows the results of a search for "Squirrel" to see if there are any tracks by the Squirrel Nut Zippers. As you can see, the search turned up tracks by six different artists and one song match. Clicking the "Under the Attic" artist name displays the information shown in Figure 3.6, which contains a reference to the Squirrel Nut Zippers in the "Similar Artists" section of the band's information.

Once you've found an artist or band you like, you can read more about them, download MP3 files for that artist, send e-mail, or go to the artist's web site. All of this is designed to help you find both the MP3 files you're interested in and enough information to find other artists you might also enjoy.

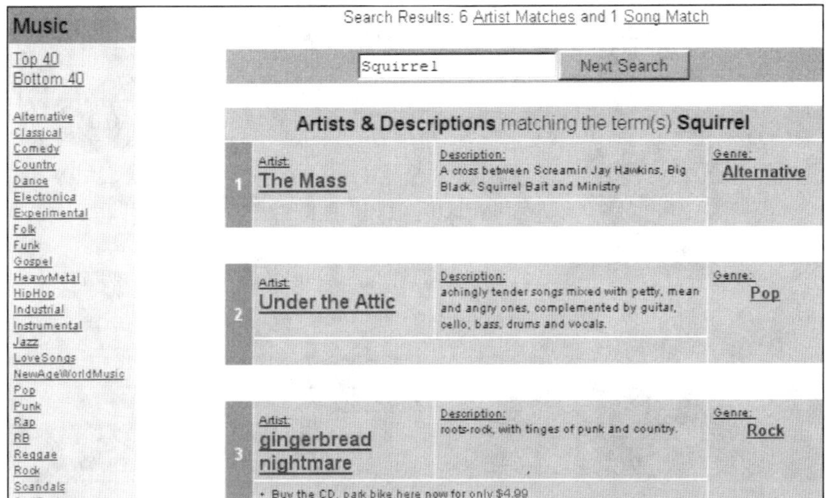

FIGURE 3.5:
Searching for MP3 files on *mp3.com.*

FIGURE 3.6:
Examining a file in detail on *mp3.com.*

The search item

Another very popular web site is *http://www.songs.com* (shown in Figure 3.7). *Songs.com* is a web site based in Nashville, TN, for several hundred independent musicians who are jointly promoting their work online. Many of the artists are popular and tour regularly but may not be as recognizable as some of the stars in their genre.

Songs.com features more than MP3 files; it's also a promotional venue for the artists themselves. Most of the artists have web sites and e-mail. You can search for a category of music by selecting the category from the drop-down list. Figure 3.8 shows the results of searching for Novelty tunes. As you can see, the results are similar to the search shown earlier in Figure 3.4.

FIGURE 3.7: Main screen for *songs.com*

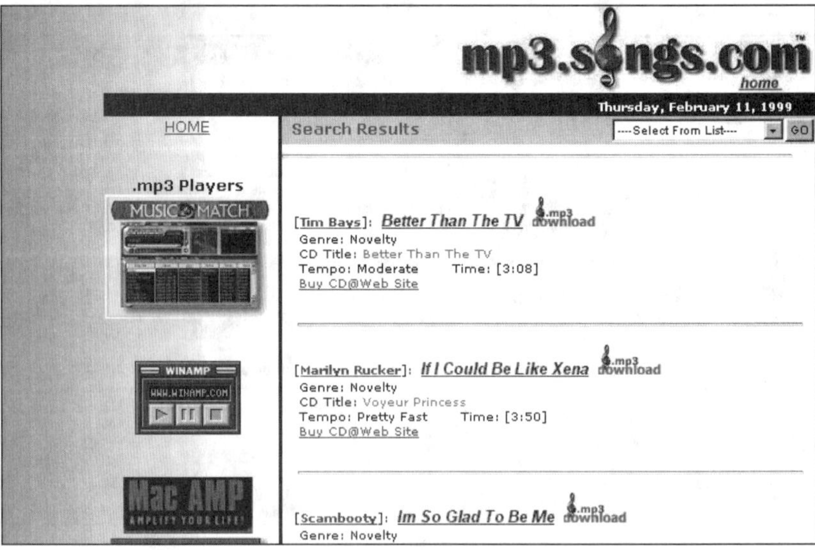

FIGURE 3.8: Displaying a category on *songs.com*.

Clicking on the artist's name will display masses of information about the artist: pictures, bios, concert dates, CDs and how to order them, fan club info... everything you might like to know about the artists and their music. Clicking on the MP3 download logo will let you download the track. Figure 3.9 shows an MP3 file ready to be downloaded.

You can search by artist name, category, and other criteria just like you did on the *mp3.com* web site.

There are a number of other excellent MP3 sites. Dimension Music (*http://www.dmusic.com*) focuses on providing artists with the tools they need to survive and thrive in the digital music arena. Dimension Music gives artists the ability to reach their fans though mailing lists, web pages, and help with creating MP3 files. They also can provide assistance with other marketing tasks such as designing logos and T-shirts as well as burning custom CDs. In addition to artist support, the web site showcases popular bands and maintains a large library of MP3 files for downloading. The Dimension Music main screen appears in Figure 3.10.

MP3-2000 (*http://www.mp3-2000.com*) features a variety of MP3 files, news, and software. The main screen appears in Figure 3.11.

Still other sites worth checking out include *http://www.mp3place. com* and *http://www.audiodreams.com.* For a more complete list of MP3 web sites, look at Appendix A, "Resources." Most of the larger web sites will also have links to other web sites themselves. Be sure to look for links to other MP3 web sites.

FIGURE 3.9:
Downloading an MP3 file on *songs.com.*

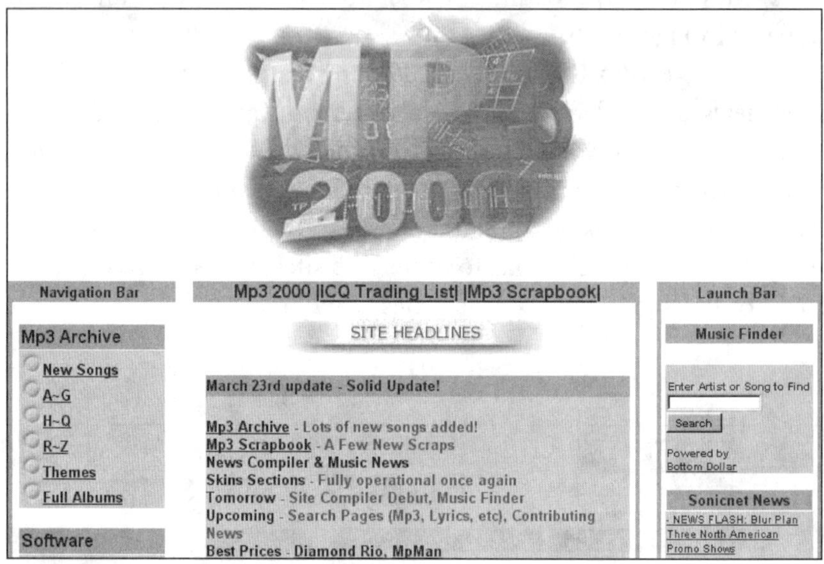

It's worth noting that the MP3 web sites aren't just repositories of MP3 files. Besides MP3 files, you can get all sorts of other things at MP3 web sites, including:

✦ **Software**—You can find every kind of MP3 software imaginable on web sites. Some of them have so much software that it's arranged by type and operating system.

✦ **Hardware**—Many of the MP3 web sites sell the Rio (a portable MP3 player) as well as other MP3 players. Some of them also sell equipment such as cables so you can hook your computer up to your sound system and play MP3 files through a really good set of speakers.

✦ **Newsletters**—There are half a dozen e-mail newsletters about MP3 that you can sign up for through the sponsoring web site.

✦ **Reviews**—Web sites have reviews of MP3 tracks, software, hardware.

✦ **FAQs and technical info**—There is a wealth of background information for all expertise levels, from the beginner to the serious audiophile.

✦ **Message forums**—Some of the larger MP3 web sites have bulletin boards and other message forums where you can post comments, swap opinions, and ask questions.

✦ **Breaking news**—There are lots of developments in MP3 technology, legislation, and policies. Most of the sites have some kind of daily news column; many also have regular editorials and feature articles.

One final tip about downloading MP3 files from web sites: it's not always possible to tell if a track is legal or illegal. Some unabashedly illegal MP3 files are often recognizable by being referred to as *warez* (slang for pirate software of any kind) or simply *MP3z*. But most illegal MP3 files don't advertise that they're illegal. They just are.

GETTING MUSIC FROM NEWSGROUPS

Although most people tend to think of the Internet as being web sites and e-mail, there are other ways of getting information, such as newsgroups. *Newsgroups* (also known as *Usenet groups*) are a bit like large cork bulletin boards on a wall on which you can post messages (known in newsgroup parlance as *articles*), ask questions, and get files, including the latest versions of MP3 software, files, and other information.

Newsgroups provide an enormous amount of information. There are more than 30,000 newsgroups on virtually any subject you can imagine (and a lot you probably can't), with new newsgroups being created all the time. There are currently several dozen newsgroups that focus specifically on MP3 files and information. (Appendix A, "Resources," lists a number of newsgroups that contain MP3 files and information.)

To explore newsgroups, you'll need a *newsreader*, a program that lets you read newsgroups and post articles to them. The newsreader will display the newsgroups in one window and the articles within the selected newsgroup in another. The content of the selected article

Web sites change, move, and go out of existence all the time. It's a good idea to check your favorite MP3 sites regularly as well as be on the lookout for new MP3 sites.

will appear in a third window. Most newsreaders will have features that let you search and sort newsgroups and individual articles.

Both the Netscape Navigator and Internet Explorer browsers already have adequate newsreaders built into them that will let you explore newsgroups and post articles. In Netscape Navigator 4.5, look for the Newsgroups option on the Communicator menu. In Internet Explorer 4.0, selecting News from the Go menu will start Microsoft Outlook Express. Similarly, if you're using AOL for your Internet access, you can use the AOL newsgroup reader at Keyword: Newsgroups. All of these newsreaders are adequate, but you may want to consider getting one of the best newsreaders out there, Free Agent from Forté, Inc.

In addition to being a very good program, one of Free Agent's major advantages is that it's free. (Agent, the registered version, has more features and options.) You can download both from the Free Agent web site (*http://www.forteinc.com*). You'll also find a lot of FAQs, tips, and information about the products. Free Agent and Agent also provide you with extensive options for sorting and filtering to keep you from being overwhelmed by useless or irrelevant information. Figure 3.12 shows the Agent main window with a number of sample MP3 newsgroups displayed.

Take a look at the Agent main window for a moment. On the left side of this window, you can see the newsgroups that are selected for monitoring. The number of articles in each newsgroup appears to the left of the newsgroup's name. On the top right of the window are the articles in the newsgroup. The articles in this group have been downloaded for reading. The number of lines in each article appears to the left of the article's subject. You can see that the first article, "Hottest new music out of Detroit!!!" is displayed in the bottom of the win-

FIGURE 3.12:
Agent main window

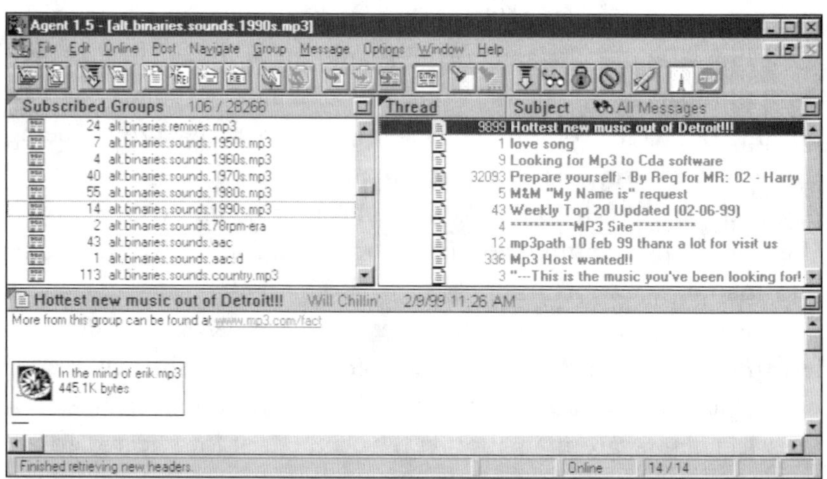

dow. As you can see, this article has an attached file, an MP3 file called "In the mind of erik.mp3" that's 441.5K.

Articles posted to a newsgroup have a lot in common with e-mail. They can be as simple as a few lines of text, or they can contain attached files. Like files attached to e-mail, files attached to newsgroups are encoded. The articles with attached files will have a large number of lines. For example, the "Prepare yourself" article in Figure 3.12 has 32093 lines in it, which will probably be a file of about 3 times the size of the one shown in the message window in Figure 3.12. Free Agent is pretty slick software; once you've downloaded the article, all you need to do to save the attached file is select Save All Attachments from the File menu and the file is yours.

By the way, you may see ostensibly the same MP3 file from two different sources that comes in two slightly different sizes. This can be because different settings in ripping options or minor variations in the actual ripping process created files of different sizes. In general, if you select the larger of the two files, you'll usually have the file with the better sound quality.

MP3 newsgroups let you ask questions about MP3 files and software, download MP3 files and software, read announcements about MP3 technology, and meet other MP3 users. However, it should be noted that most of the files that appear in MP3 newsgroups are... well... illegal. People will frequently rip tracks from CDs and upload them to a newsgroup just because they like the track. This is deplorable, but it's the way things are right now. The RIAA and a lot of music companies are very unhappy about newsgroups, because they're harder to monitor. Web sites are stationary and easy to shut down, but anyone can post anonymously to a newsgroup if he or she wants to.

There are some tricks to downloading files from newsgroups. For example, large tracks may be split into several articles, all of which must be downloaded and saved to have the complete track. Some files will be in a format that you can't read automatically, and you'll have to use a decoding utility such as WinCode. And never post marketing or advertising information to a newsgroup before you find out if it's OK. (This kind of behavior is usually frowned on.) Finally, it's always a good idea to read the newsgroup for a while first before posting questions. See if the newsgroup has a list of frequently asked questions (also known as a FAQ); these will provide a wealth of information.

USE FTP TO FIND DIGITAL MUSIC ONLINE

So far, you've seen how to use web sites and newsgroups to get MP3 files and information. Now, you're going to learn about the third way to get files online: from FTP sites.

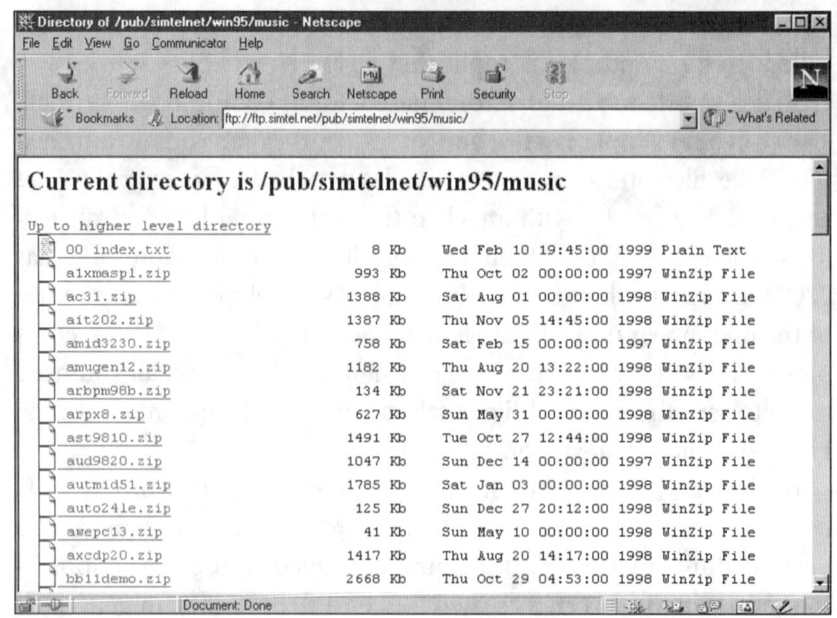

FTP (an acronym for *File Transfer Protocol*) is the general way for transferring files online. An FTP site is sort of a no-frills stack of files you can download. There are lots of FTP sites for MP3 software and tracks. Many of these are actually accessed directly through a web site: when you click on a specific file in a listing, you may be routed seamlessly to an FTP site maintained or accessed by the web sites.

FTP sites have an easily recognizable "no-frills" look. Figure 3.13 shows a popular FTP site for software, *ftp.cdrom.com*. Most directories in an FTP site will have an index file at the start of the files. These index files list the files in the directory and generally provide a brief description of what the files are. You can view this by double-clicking the file icon to the left of the file. (You can download any of the files in the directory in the same fashion.)

As you can see from Figure 3.13, the FTP site will look very much like a directory on your own computer. You can navigate between folders by double-clicking a folder icon to drill down a level or on the "Up to a higher level directory" link to move back up a level.

You don't need to have a special tool for accessing FTP sites. You can open FTP sites in your browser simply by entering the name of the FTP site. However, you can use FTP software such as Ipswitch's WS_FTP (available from *http://www.ipswitch.com*) or CuteFTP (*http://www. cuteftp.com*) to access FTP sites. Figure 3.14 shows *ftp.cdrom.com* opened using WS_FTP.

FTP sites will frequently have an array of MP3 software and utilities as well, but some are just MP3 files. Like MP3 web sites, FTP sites

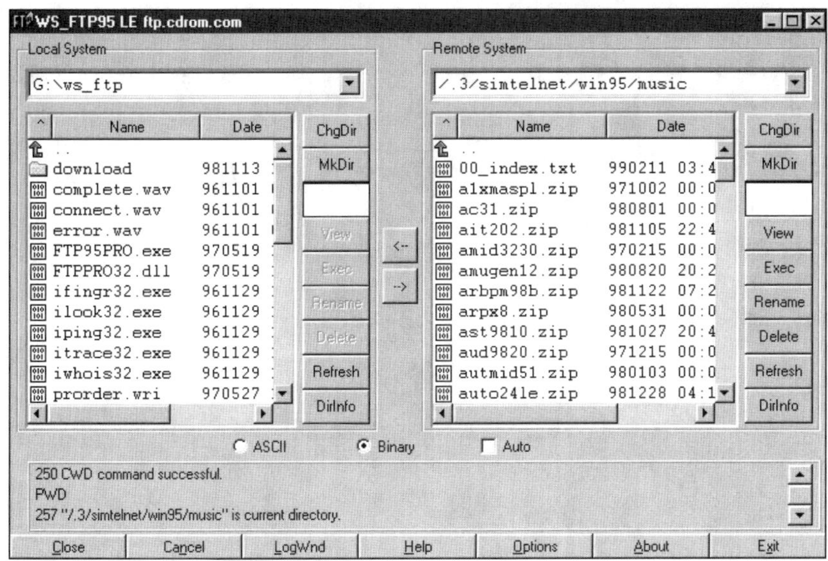

FIGURE 3.14:
FTP site displayed in WS_FTP.

vary in the level of legitimacy of the MP3 files you're likely to find there, from the absolutely legal to the latest MP3 files from Rusty Cutlass Productions. Be careful if you're concerned about downloading illegal or unauthorized files.

SEARCHING FOR SPECIFIC TRACKS

All the methods described so far will get you more MP3 files than you could possibly download, but what if you're after a specific track? You'll need to use a search engine for this. Search engines are nothing new to the Web; however, there are specialized search engines for MP3 files. One of the most effective search engines is the Lycos MP3 search engine at *http://www.lycos.com,* shown in Figure 3.15.

The Lycos search engine currently lists well over 500,000 MP3 files. To use it, you simply enter the name of the artist or the song and then click Go Get It! Lycos returns a list of the MP3 files that meet the criteria you entered. Figure 3.16 shows the results of a typical search for George Clinton's work.

As cool as the Lycos search engine is, you may actually want to use the search engine page in *http://www.mp3.com* (shown in Figure 3.17). You can enter your search criteria in the field for the appropriate search engine—there are about a dozen on this page—and then click Search. You'll be routed to the appropriate search engine, which will look up the MP3 files that match your criteria.

Another first-rate search engine is the *Scour.net* web site (*http://www. scour.net*). The main *Scour.net* screen appears in Figure 3.18.

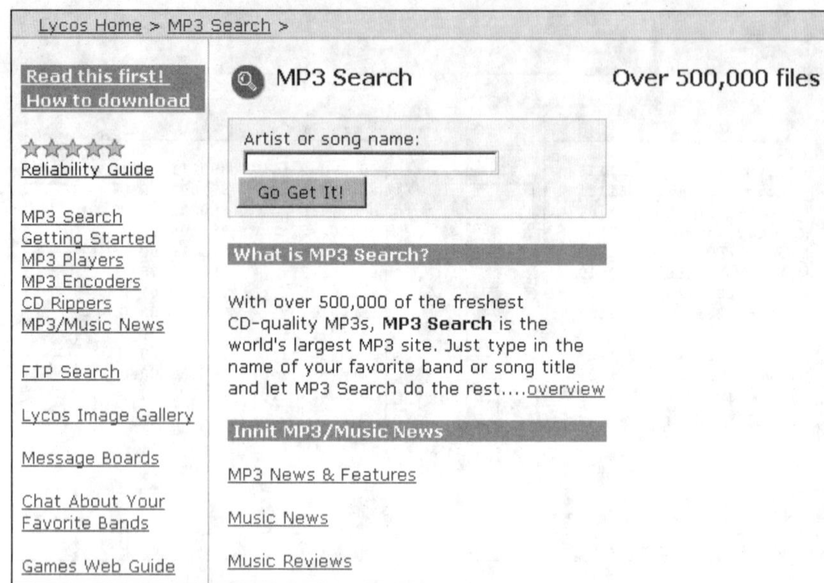

FIGURE 3.15: The Lycos MP3 search engine.

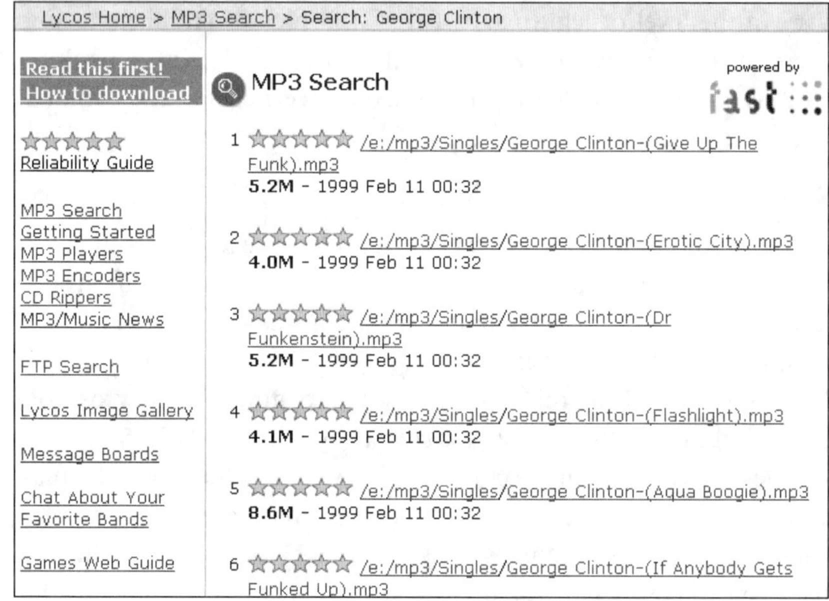

FIGURE 3.16: Results of a typical Lycos MP3 search.

You can use *Scour.net* to search for MP3 files as well as a wide variety of other audio, video, and graphics formats. Figure 3.19 shows a portion of the results for a search for Randy Newman MP3 files.

BUYING DIGITAL MUSIC ONLINE

One of the advantages of MP3 files, both to you and to the artist, is that you can order a CD online with the click of a button. For example, if the MP3 track has a URL entered in the Buy CD URL field on the Track Information screen (shown in Chapter 2 in Figure 2.12),

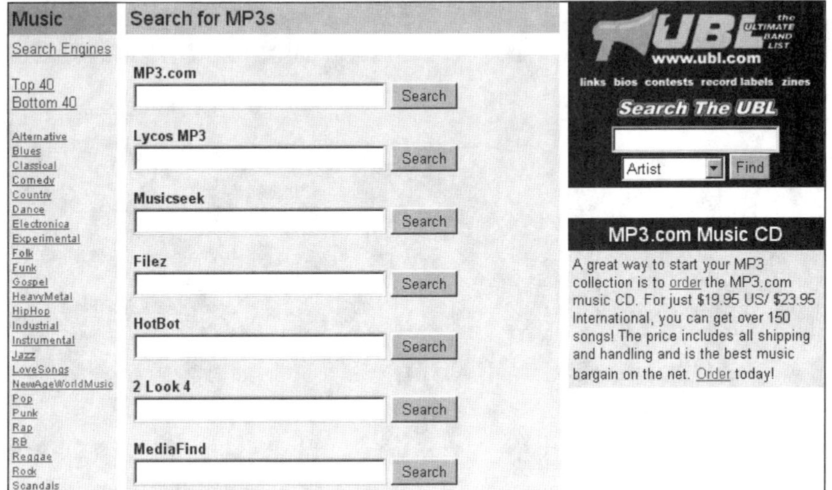

FIGURE 3.17:
The search engine page on *mp3.com*.

FIGURE 3.18:
The *scour.net* main screen.

clicking Buy CD on the Track Info window will take you to the specified URL where you can order the CD. If there's no specific URL set up to let you buy the CD, you can also use any of the large book and CD web sites to search for and purchase a CD.

Some web sites are set up on the principle of paying for the music you download at a nominal fee (usually around 99 cents) and letting you buy the CD directly. A good example of this kind of web site is *http://www.goodnoise.com,* shown in Figure 3.20.

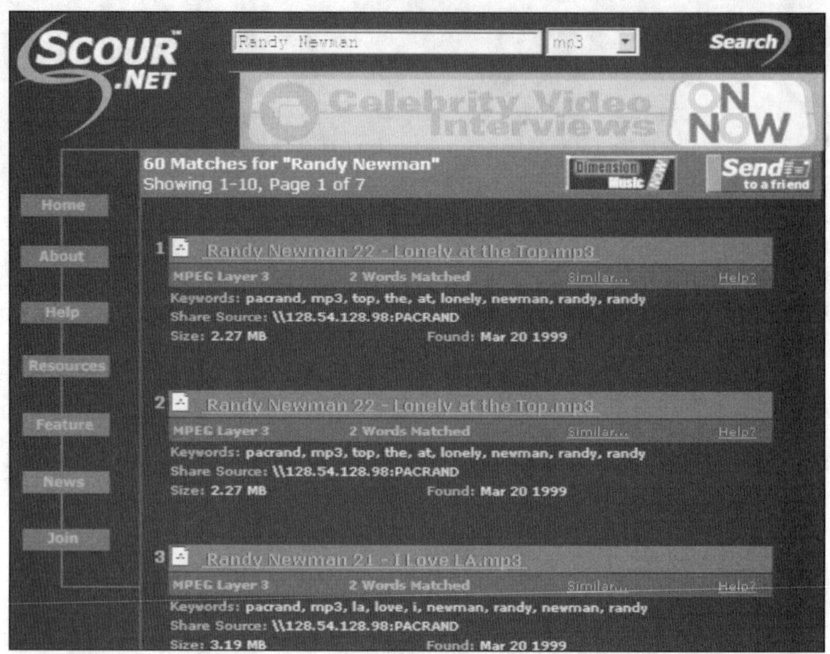

The idea behind *GoodNoise.com* and other sites is that you buy the right to download a single track in MP3 format for a small fee or an entire CD for much less than you'd pay for it in the store. The advantages to this are:

- ✦ **You can try before you buy.** You can listen to a track or two of a CD before you buy the whole thing.
- ✦ **You don't have to buy the whole album.** If you like just one or two tracks on the CD, you don't have to buy the whole album.

- ✦ **You can get tracks you wouldn't otherwise be able to get.** There are a number of artists whose work isn't available as free files but that you can buy online.
- ✦ **It's cheaper than buying a CD.** You're buying the album online rather than on a CD, so you're not paying for the costs of distribution.

The only disadvantage to this system may be that there's a lot of competition with free MP3 files, but web sites such as *http://www.goodnoise.com, http://www.nordicdms.com,* and others have been making a go of it so far, so time will tell.

UPGRADING YOUR COMPUTER

As you add more MP3 files, you're going to want to consider getting a faster Internet connection and adding more disk space. This section will outline a few of the options.

GETTING A FASTER INTERNET CONNECTION

As you read in Chapter 1, one of the biggest reasons MP3 files are so popular is that they're relatively small compared to CD-DA or WAV files. In particular, they're small enough (3–5 MB) to send at current speeds over the Internet. But even at this size, if you have a 28.8K modem connection, a 3 MB MP3 file will take around 18 minutes to download; slightly faster if you are using a 33.6K modem. If you download a lot of MP3 files, you may want to consider increasing the speed of your Internet connection.

Possibly the easiest thing to do if you're using a 28.8K or a 33.6K modem is to upgrade to a 56K modem. This will cut your download times by about 40% (most phone lines will not support true 56K connectivity even if the modem will; the fastest connection is rarely better than about 40K). If you're just buying a modem now, buy a 56K modem. 56K modems are only about $20 to $50 more than a 28.8K modem. The cost difference will be recouped in time savings in the first month you own it.

For something even faster, you might want to consider one of the cable modems from your local cable provider (such as TCI's "@Home" service). These can give you much higher download speeds. Installation is handled by the cable company providing the service, and you don't need to install a second phone line for your computer, which can underwrite a substantial portion of the monthly cost (around $40/month).

For the most in residential Internet access, you should look at *Digital Subscriber Line (DSL)* service. DSL provides a direct 24-hour link to the Internet at speeds of at least 144K, six times the speed of the average modem. This kind of service is offered by phone companies in many cities as well as a growing number of *Internet service providers (ISPs)*. There are a number of varieties of DSL service, but they're all roughly similar in the way they work: a piece of hardware called a *digital modem* connects your computer to a separate phone line. Depending on the type of DSL service you've subscribed for, you can get speeds of up to 1.5 M, which is probably far more than you need: at 1.5 M, a 3 MB MP3 file would take 20 seconds to download. (At this rate, you could fill up a 2GB hard disk in a little under 4 hours!)

One of the most convenient and low-cost methods of downloading MP3 files is to use your company's Internet connection, which will usually be something much faster than you're likely to be able to afford for yourself. You'll have to figure out how to transfer files from work to home, though, probably using a Zip disk or by putting collections of MP3 files on a CD-ROM. (Make sure that you're not violating your company's policies on using the Internet before you download MP3 files. Many companies have rather strict policies with regard to personal use of the Internet and you might get into trouble by doing so.)

ADDING MORE DISK SPACE

MP3 files are relatively compact, but they aren't microscopic. There is probably nothing these days that will fill your computer's hard disk faster than downloading a bunch of MP3 files. (Trust me on this: in my first two weeks of exploring MP3 web sites, I downloaded a <u>gigabyte</u> of MP3 files from some of the larger web sites.)

The bottom line is that you're going to need a couple of gigabytes of hard disk dedicated to MP3 files. Fortunately, hard disks are absurdly cheap these days: 10 GB hard disks and larger can easily be had for less than $200. Even a $100 6.4 GB hard drive will hold over 100 hours' worth of MP3 files. Whenever you buy a hard disk, it's a good idea to figure out how big a hard disk you need—be generous in your estimates—and then buy the next size up from that. You'll still use up all that space, but it'll take a little longer.

In this chapter, you saw how to get MP3 files from the Internet from web sites, newsgroups, and FTP sites, and how to buy digital music online. You also saw how to speed up your Internet connection and increase your computer's hard disk capacity to store your growing collection of MP3 files. In the next chapter, you'll learn how to rip MP3 tracks of your own from CDs, cassettes, and albums.

Creating Your Own MP3 Files

The last chapter showed you how to get MP3 files from the Internet from web sites, newsgroups, and FTP sites and how to buy digital music online. In this chapter, you'll learn how to rip MP3 tracks of your own from CDs, cassettes, and albums.

HOW ARE SOUNDS AND MUSIC STORED ON YOUR COMPUTER?

Before you try ripping your own MP3 files, you should know more about how sounds and music are stored on your computer. This will help you set your recording options for the best results.

As you doubtless remember from high school science classes, all sounds are composed of waves. Waves are *analog*: they continuously vary in strength or quantity. An analog wave looks like the one shown in Figure 4.1.

Information stored on computers is in a *digital* format. Digital sounds are stored as a series of bits rather than by a continuously varying signal, as shown in Figure 4.2.

Computers can only store sound in a digital format. This means that any sound waves you store on the computer must be converted from their analog format (what you hear with your ear) to a digital format (what the computer can under-stand) using an *analog-to-digital converter*, which is part of your computer's sound card. During the conversion process, the sound card *samples* the sound waves at regular intervals and stores the information from the sample in a digitized file, as shown in Figure 4.3.

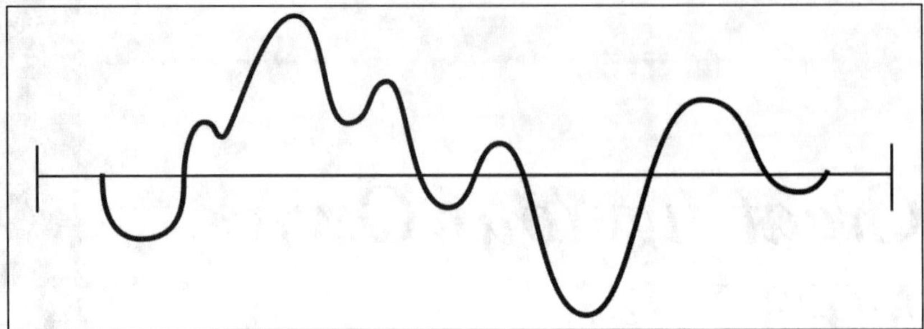

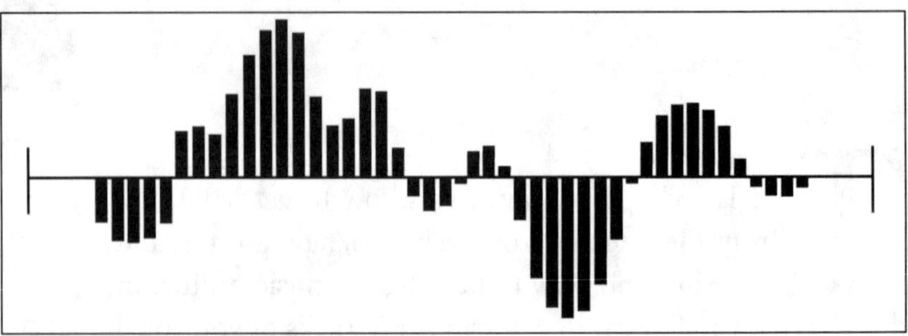

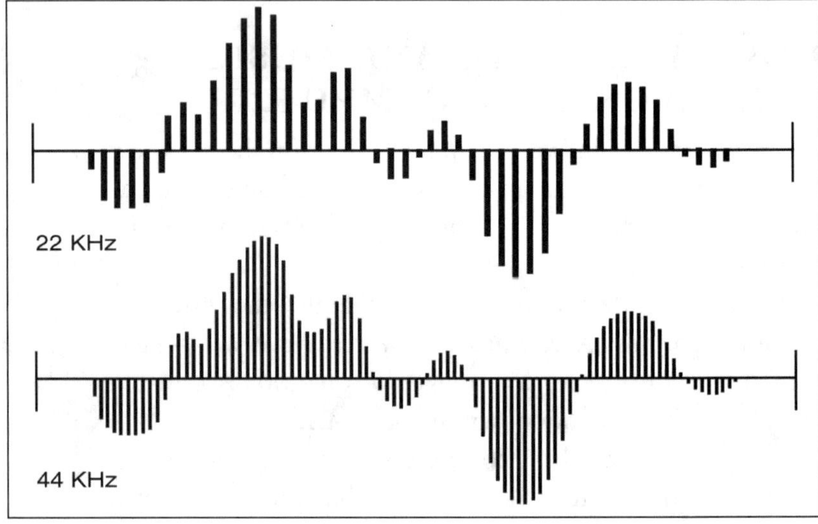

Whenever a signal is converted from analog to digital, digital to analog, or from one digital format to another, there will be some loss of quality. How accurately the conversion to digital works is determined by two factors: the *sampling rate* and the *sampling precision*.

The *sampling rate* is the number of times per second the sound card is sampling the sound being converted. Typical sampling rates for audio are 11 kilohertz, 22 kilohertz, and 44 kilohertz. One hertz (abbreviated Hz) is a single cycle per second, so a sampling rate of 44kHz means that the computer is sampling the sound 44,000 times every second. The more often the computer samples the sound, the more of the sound the computer 'hears'.

The *sampling precision* (also known as the *resolution*) is how much information is stored about the sample. Typical rates are 8-bit and 16-bit. 8-bit sampling will give up to 256 different levels, while 16-bit sampling gives up to 65,536 different levels. In general, the more frequently you sample and the greater the precision, the more closely the digital version will resemble the audio version.

WHAT ARE THE COMMON TYPES OF DIGITAL MUSIC FORMAT?

There are actually many different ways to store sound and music digitally. The most basic of these is the old familiar WAV (pronounced "wave") file. To create a WAV file, sounds are converted directly from the analog signal into digital sound and stored as the component waveforms. WAV files are *uncompressed*; that is, the computer doesn't do any additional processing to make the files more compact or to enhance the sound digitally. With WAV files, what you hear is what you get.

The digital audio files that appear on a CD are a different format from WAV files, but they're the same in a couple of important ways. First, they're digital. Second, they are uncompressed. And like WAV files, the sound you hear is exactly what went into them. When you play either of them, the digital information is converted to an audio signal you can hear after it goes through the speakers.

Because the data is uncompressed, WAV and CD-DA files (which are also known as "raw WAV files") have one other thing in common: they're big... really big. CDs are typically recorded at a sampling rate of 44.1 kHz with a bit rate of 16 bits (or 2 bytes) per sample. This means that a CD-quality digital audio file will require 88.2 kilobytes for each second of sound. Wait a minute, though; don't forget that this is only one channel. If you're recording in stereo, you'll need 176.4 kilobytes of storage for each second of sound. A typical three-minute CD track in stereo would require slightly over 31 megabytes of storage. CDs hold approximately 660 megabytes of data, so at around 11 megabytes for each minute of sound, a CD only holds about 60 minutes.

There are other popular kinds of digital music format, too. *MIDI* (an acronym for *Musical Instrument Digital Interface*) is a standard for connecting musical instruments and computers using a digital interface. You can play a MIDI instrument, record the output, and then play the resulting MIDI file very much like an old player piano roll. There are composing and editing tools that let you create MIDI files directly on the computer without having to play an instrument.

RealAudio files are another popular file format for sound. RealAudio files are compressed to minimize their size, but they are not as compressed as MP3 files. (There are also RealVideo formats for video files.) You can obtain a free player from Real Networks (*http://www.realnetworks.com*). RealAudio and RealVideo are aimed more at *streaming* (playing sounds and video in real-time while you download) than MP3 files. They're very useful, particularly for such things as reproduction and distribution of radio broadcasts. For example, the web sites for NPR (*http://www.npr.org*) and ABC News (*http://www.abcnews.go.com*) both have news articles and features available in RealAudio format.

AAC (an acronym for *Advanced Audio Compression*) is a new audio format that has not yet gained acceptance. It's slightly more memory-efficient than MP3 files, but the source code has not yet been widely licensed from Fraunhofer (who controls the technology). The AAC format may eventually supplant MP3 or become part of the next generation of sound encoding, but it has only just recently become visible. There are relatively few files available in AAC format.

There are a number of other sound file formats you may encounter, including VQF, VOC, MTM, DSM, MED, MOD, XM, IT, S3M, STM, AU, and AIFF. All of them will have various features and compression rates, but none of them provide the features of CD quality and the small file size that you can obtain with MP3 files. MP3 also is the most popular format because of the huge installed base. Even if another format were to appear that is substantially better and more compact, the large number of MP3 files and programs would make it difficult for the new format to take over.

HOW DO MP3 FILES WORK?

As you read in Chapter 1, MPEG is a group of standards for compressing and storing audio and video in files.

MP3 files give CD-quality sound in a file that's only about an eleventh the size of a WAV or CD-DA file. This means that where a CD-DA file requires about 11 megabytes for each minute of stereo music, MP3 files require only 1 megabyte. This massive reduction in file size is because, unlike CD-DA or WAV files, MP3 files do not completely reproduce all the sounds in the original. When you convert CD-DA or WAV files to MP3 files using an *encoder*, the encoder only saves the sounds that are important (that the human ear will actually hear) and throws away the rest. For example, the MP3 encoder will automatically remove sounds above a predetermined threshold level (most people can't hear sounds above 16kHz).

Ripping files with an encoder produces vastly better results than using the Windows Sound Recorder to record tracks from a CD. If you did this, the Sound Recorder will play the CD, get the audio output from the CD as it plays, and then reconvert this to digital audio. This process will introduce distortion and errors into the resulting signal, very much like recording a song off the radio by holding up a microphone to the speakers. Using an encoder takes the digital signal directly from the CD, resulting in a much better signal.

The encoder will also remove sounds that are masked by louder sounds at or near the same frequency. This is done using a collection of principles known as *psychoacoustics* or *neuristic listening*, which are fancy names for identifying how humans hear and noting some of the things they won't miss hearing. People hear from about 20Hz (low) to 20kHz (high), with the most sensitivity between 2 to 4 kHz. Voices range from 500Hz to 2kHz.

For example, when you're talking to someone in a quiet room, you can hear each other easily, but if the TV is playing or someone's vacuuming, the additional noise will mask what you can hear. Similarly, when there are loud noises happening in the sound file, quieter noises at or near the same frequency will be masked, and you won't be able to hear them. As part of the MP3 encoding process, the weaker sounds that would be masked by louder sounds are discarded, creating a file that sounds the same but is smaller than the original CD-DA or WAV file.

Depending on how high the compression ratio is, the encoding process removes more or less of the information. If the compression ratio is very high, you'll create very small files, but you will hear a distinct difference and reduction in quality as compared to the original CD-DA file. On the other hand, if the compression ratio is low, the resulting MP3 file may be fairly large as MP3 files go, but you won't be able to tell the difference between the original CD-DA and the MP3 file. Note that different encoders produce different results, depending on the underlying formulas they use.

Depending on what you're encoding, you may be able to get even greater compression ratios than the typical "one megabyte per minute of song." Speech doesn't require the dynamic range of music, so it's possible for the encoder to remove a lot more information from the original file. For example, a comedy album may only require quality as good as something you might hear on FM radio, which would compress about twice as well as CD-quality music (or about 1/2 megabyte for each minute of sound). Even better, old 78-rpm records, speeches, newscasts, language practice tapes, and other spoken information could be compressed as much as 96 times from the original, making it possible to store up to 8 minutes of information in a 1-megabyte file!

RIPPING FROM A CD TO YOUR COMPUTER

Finally, you get to try your hand at ripping tracks yourself. This is the section that will add gritty to your nitty.

With MusicMatch Jukebox, the general process for ripping tracks is pretty simple, as shown in the following procedure:

1. Load an audio CD into your CD-ROM drive. Most people will have their CD-ROM set up to automatically play an audio CD when it's inserted in the CD-ROM drive. You can just close the Windows CD Player software if you want and then proceed with the ripping process, but if you're going to be ripping a lot of CDs, you may find it easier to turn this feature off as follows:

   a. Double-click the My Computer icon.

   b. Double-click the Control Panel icon.

   c. Double-click the System icon in the Control Panel.

   d. Click the Device Manager tab. You'll see a list of hardware devices.

   e. In the list of devices, click the plus sign to the left of the CD-ROM entry. The list will expand to show your CD-ROM.

NOTE

While you can play MP3 files on a lower-end computer, you must have a good CD-ROM drive and a computer with enough processing power (at least 166 MHz and 32 MB of RAM) for the best results when ripping tracks.

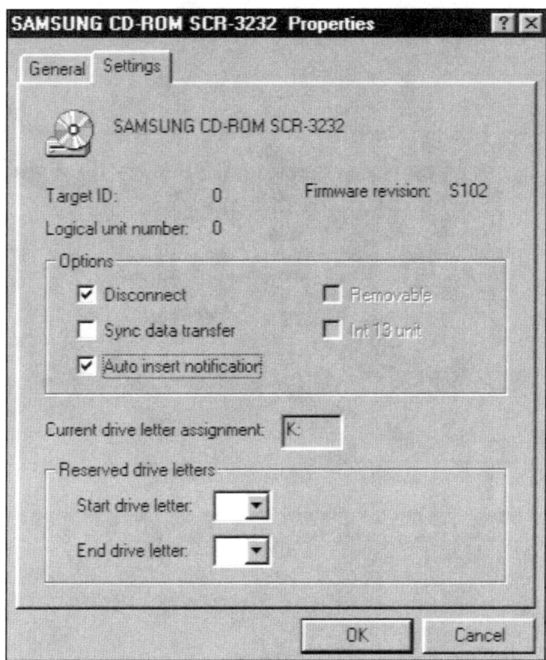

FIGURE 4.4:
Settings screen for a typical CD-ROM drive.

f. Double-click the listing for your CD-ROM. You'll see a general properties screen for the CD-ROM.

g. Click the Settings tab. You'll see a screen something like the one shown in Figure 4.4.

h. Uncheck the Auto insert notification box if necessary. (This tells Windows to automatically open the CD Player whenever it detects an audio CD.)

i. Click OK on the Settings screen, then click OK on the Device Manager screen. If you made any changes, Windows will ask if you want to restart your computer so that the changes can take effect. Click OK if you want to restart the computer at this point.

2. Start MusicMatch Jukebox and click Record ( ) on the main screen. The first time you do this, you will see the first Auto-Configuring screen, shown in Figure 4.5.

3. To let MusicMatch Jukebox determine the best settings for your CD-ROM drives (recommended), insert an audio CD in each of the CD-ROM drives in your computer and click OK. MusicMatch Jukebox will read the audio CDs in the CD-ROM drives and configure Music-Match Jukebox for the best settings for recordings. Once the configuration process is complete, MusicMatch Jukebox will display the first CDDB Preferences screen (shown in Figure 4.6).

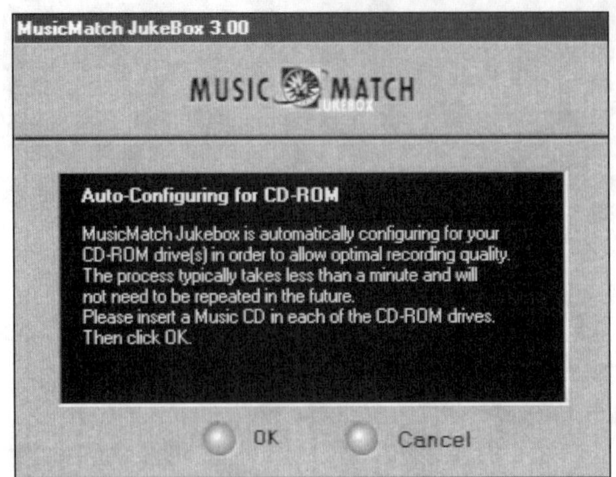

4. *http://www.cddb.com* is a free consumer-maintained online database of CD information with more than a quarter million CDs on file. Click OK to set up your CDDB preferences. The Second CDDB Preferences screen (shown in Figure 4.7) appears.

5. The first time you use the database, you need to enter a user name for yourself and tell the web site which server is closest to your location, as shown in Figure 4.7. By the way, once you have set up your CDDB preferences, the next time you go to record tracks, you won't see the CDDB screens shown in Figures 4.6 and 4.7. Instead, you'll see the CDDB Connect? screen shown in Figure 4.8.

6. When you click OK on this screen, you tell MusicMatch Jukebox to access *CDDB.com* (you'll need an Internet connection to do this). MusicMatch Jukebox passes the serial

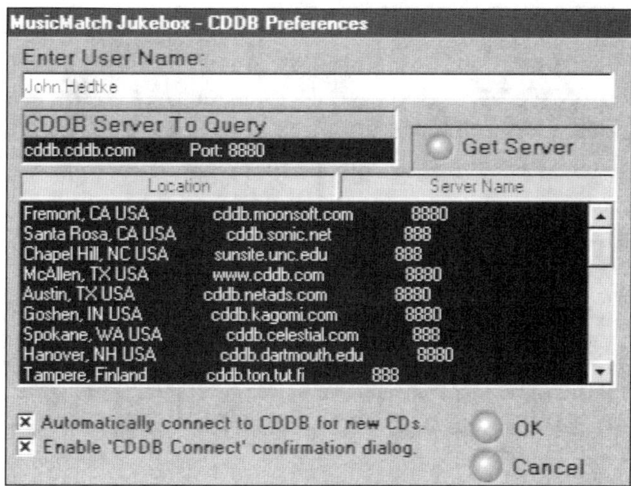

FIGURE 4.7:
Second CDDB Preferences screen.

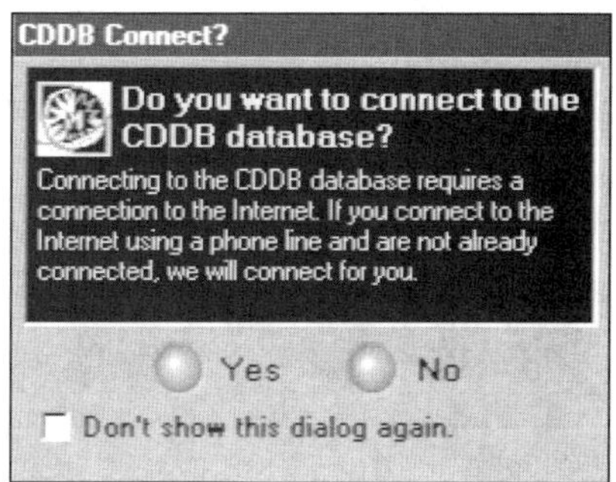

FIGURE 4.8:
The CDDB Connect? screen.

number of the CD you're ripping tracks from to the CDDB database, which then looks up the title, artist, and track information for your CD. (This information is also stored in the \Windows\CDPLAYER.INI file for future sessions. If you load the CD in MusicMatch Jukebox or in the Windows CD player thereafter, it will recognize the CD and display the track information automatically.) MusicMatch Jukebox then inserts the information into the appropriate fields of the Recorder screen, as shown in Figure 4.9.

If the CD is not found on *CDDB.com* or you don't look it up, the title and tracks appear simply as "Track 1," "Track 2," and so on, as shown in Figure 4.10. You can always enter album, artist, and track information manually. Once you enter information for a CD manually, MusicMatch Jukebox will save this and remember it the next time you insert the CD.

You can click CDDB in the Recorder screen to look up the CD in the *CDDB.com* database. This is useful if you switch CDs or you want to check the database after logging on to the Internet.

FIGURE 4.9:
The Recorder screen
with information
from *CDDB.com*.

FIGURE 4.10:
The Recorder screen
without information
from *CDDB.com*.

7. Select the tracks you want to record. You can click individual boxes to the left of individual tracks or click All above the track list to select all the tracks. (You can click None to clear your selections and start over.)

8. When you are satisfied with your selections, click Start (⏵). MusicMatch Jukebox will start the recording process for the selected tracks. A small histogram, or progress bar, will appear to the right of each track being ripped, showing the progress for the track. When Music-Match Jukebox completes a track successfully, a small green block appears in the histogram to show that the recording process completed successfully for that track. The progress for the specific track appears in the Record-

FIGURE 4.11:
Tracks being ripped from a CD.

FIGURE 4.12:
Newly created tracks added to the Music Library.

ing Status window at the bottom left of the Recorder screen. Figure 4.11 shows several tracks in the process of being ripped.

9. When the MusicMatch Jukebox is done ripping the selected tracks, you can play them as usual. Figure 4.12 shows the newly created tracks added to the Music Library.

As you can see from Figure 4.12, tracks created with MusicMatch Jukebox will have the song title, album, and artist information added to the MP3 file from the fields on the Recorder screen. If you like, you can add information to the track by using the Track Information screen (as described previously in Chapter 2, "Creating and Using Playlists") but the file's ready to play as is. And voila! that's all there is to it!

RIPPING BETTER MP3 FILES

The preceding section showed you just how easy it is to rip tracks from a CD. MusicMatch Jukebox offers a number of features to make your MP3 files better—higher quality, smaller size, faster recording—but you first need to learn a little more technical information to give you the background to make the best choices for what you'd like. You'll then see how to set specific options to make MusicMatch Jukebox give you exactly the MP3 files you'd like.

SETTING RECORDING OPTIONS

Now that you are a little more familiar with the kinds of recording, you're ready to look at how to set recording options in MusicMatch Jukebox. Follow this procedure:

1. Click Options at the top of the Recorder screen. The Record Options screen (shown in Figure 4.13) appears.

2. Select the options on the screen as follows:

DIRECTORY FOR NEW SONGS

Select the drive and directory for the completed MP3 files. The default drive and directory are C:\Program Files\Brava\MusicMatch Jukebox\Music; however, if you install MusicMatch Jukebox in another drive (as shown in Figure 4.13), the default directory will be the Music subdirectory under the MusicMatch directory under the new drive: (D:\MusicMatch\Music).

MAKE SUB-DIRECTORY USING

You can optionally create additional subdirectories using the artist's name or the album title. For example, if your basic des-

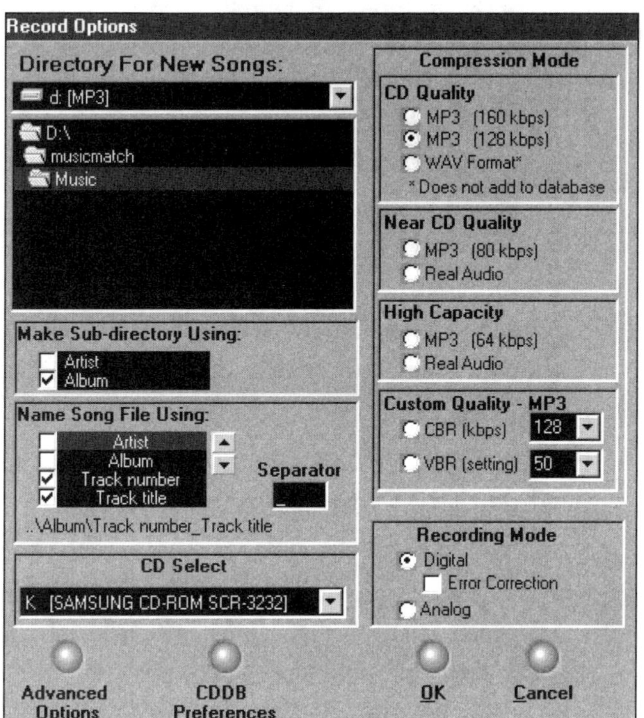

FIGURE 4.13: The Record Options screen.

tination directory is D:\musicmatch\music (as shown in Figure 4.13), clicking Artist and ripping tracks from Schmerdley's Greatest Hits would tell MusicMatch Jukebox to create a subdirectory D:\musicmatch\music\schmerdley and put all the ripped tracks into it. This option is very handy if you are doing a lot of ripping of a single artist's work and want to sort tracks by album, or you have many different artists who you want to keep separate. If you leave both the Artist and the Album fields unchecked, MusicMatch Jukebox will put the ripped tracks directly into the specified default directory.

NAME SONG FILE USING

This option lets you name the ripped tracks on the fly using information about the tracks. Check the items you want to include in the track name. (The default entries are Track Number and Track Title, separated by an underscore character.) You can change the order in which items appear in the name by highlighting an item and using the up and down arrows to reposition the item. You can change the separator character to any other printing character (you can't use spaces as a separator). The structure of the track title based on the options you've selected is displayed below the checkboxes.

For more information about digital and analog recording, or if you'd like to find out if your CD-ROM drive is able to digitally record, take a look at Stewart Addison's web site at http://www.tardis.ed.ac.uk/~psyche/cdda.

FIGURE 4.14: Example of changing track file naming convention.

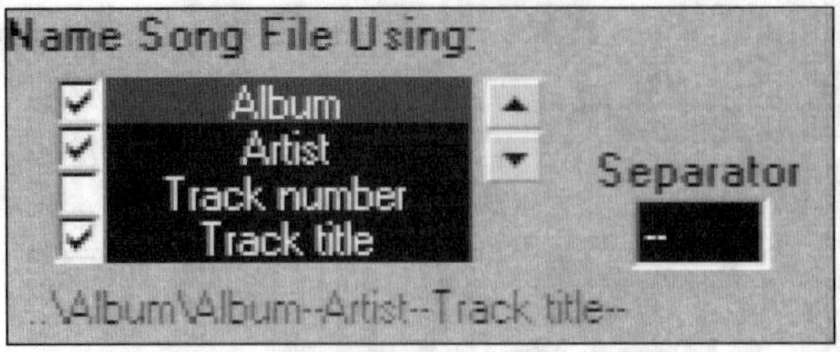

Figure 4.14 shows how this will look for a track title of Album, Artist, and Track Title with a separator of two hyphens.

CD SELECT

If you have multiple CD-ROM drives, choose the drive from the drop-down list you will use to record from.

COMPRESSION MODE

The *compression mode* determines the quality and format of the finished file.

There are four subclasses of compression mode:

- CD Quality
- Near CD Quality
- High Capacity
- Custom Quality-MP3

CD-Quality Recordings: Selecting one of the options in this subclass will give you the best-quality files from the CD. The compression ratio for CD-quality MP3 files is 12:1. Files recorded at 160kbps will be 25% larger than files recorded at 128kbps.

Selecting WAV format lets you create a WAV file from the CD file. (This file will not be added automatically to the Music Library as the MP3 files you create are.)

Near CD-Quality: Selecting an option in this subclass is good if you want an MP3 file that's "good enough" but that saves a lot of room on the disk. The reproduction quality is very close to CD-quality sound. The compression ratio for Near CD-quality MP3 files is 18:1. Near CD-quality recordings are added to your Music Library.

Selecting RealAudio format lets you create a RealAudio file. The compression ratio for this file is 17:1. RealAudio recordings are added to your Music Library.

> **NOTE**
> *You must use the MusicMatch Jukebox player or a RealAudio player to play a RealAudio file.*

High Capacity: Selecting an option in this subclass will minimize the resulting file size, but at the expense of quality. MP3 files created with this format are compressed at 70:1. (This option is also known as "FM radio quality.") This option should only be used for spoken words, low-fidelity recordings, or for ripping information from the radio.

Selecting RealAudio format lets you create a RealAudio file. The compression ratio for this file is about 80:1. RealAudio recordings are added to your Music Library.

Custom Quality-MP3: You can use this to set your own encoding rates. *Constant Bit Rate,* or *CBR,* records at a constant bit rate throughout the file, but this may reduce the quality of the resulting MP3 file as well as the efficiency of the encoder. Enter a setting in the CBR field of from 16kbps to 320kbps. Select this option when you want to limit the size of the resulting MP3 files or when you want to produce MP3 files that are have similar file sizes. Settings above 128kbps will probably not have much effect on the quality of the sound in the resulting MP3 file.

In contrast, *Variable Bit Rate,* or *VBR,* records at a variable bit rate that maximizes the quality of the audio but does not limit the size of the resulting MP3 files. Enter a setting in the VBR field of from 1 to 100. These settings correspond roughly to sampling rates. Table 4.1 shows some settings and the corresponding approximate sampling rates.

TABLE 4.1: VBR SETTINGS

VBR SETTING	APPROXIMATE SAMPLING RATE
25	80kbps
50	128kbps
75	160kbps

VBR settings above 50 will probably not have much effect on the quality of the sound in the resulting MP3 file.

MP3 files created with variable bit rate encoding will be larger than MP3 files created with constant bit rate encoding even when the sampling rates are the same: recording a track with a VBR setting of 50 will make a larger file than recording the same track with a CBR setting of 128 kbps. On the other hand, a variable bit rate file recording at an approximate sampling rate of 160kbps may well be smaller than a file

> **NOTE**
>
> *If you rip a track twice with different settings, you'll have two files with different sizes, but if you rip a track twice with the same settings, you'll still have two files with (slightly) different sizes. This is because minor variations in the way the CD is read each time will result in slightly different information being encoded during the ripping process. Don't worry; you won't be able to hear a difference when you play the two files.*

recorded using a standard CD-quality 160kbps setting: when you're recording at a variable bit rate, MusicMatch Jukebox won't generate a lot of bits if there's not a lot of sound to be sampled, whereas a file recorded with a 160kbps sampling rate will generate the same number of bits for each second of recorded MP3 file.

VBR is better than CBR for picking up high-frequency sound, but the resulting files are larger. Use VBR when you're recording something with a lot of high-frequency sounds such as cymbals or bells.

The size of the resulting MP3 files depends directly on the choice you make for compression ratio. A three-minute track that takes 32 MB in a WAV or CD-DA format will require slightly less than 3 MB in CD-quality format and about 1.8 MB in Near CD-quality.

RECORDING MODE

Although all the information on the CD is digital, there are actually two different types of recording that you can use when ripping tracks: *digital* and *analog*.

DIGITAL

Digital recording is a feature supported by about two-thirds of the CD-ROM drives on the market today. The ability to digitally record information from the CD is a feature built into the CD-ROM drive. The advantage to recording in digital mode is that it is up to five times faster than analog recording (the alternative) and it provides a slightly cleaner MP3 file. Analog recording "listens" to the CD as it plays and records from that via the sound card. Analog recording will only move as fast as the CD plays in the CD-ROM drive. You can see what type of recording MusicMatch Jukebox is doing by looking at the Recording Status field in the Recorder screen (as shown earlier in Figure 4.11).

ERROR CORRECTION

Check Error Correction to eliminate pops and clicks that may appear in the MP3 file. These can happen in digital recording mode when there are errors as the head seeks from one part of the CD to another as the CD-ROM drive reads the CD. Checking Error Correction will increase recording time slightly. (Depending on your CD-ROM drive, you may not need to do this. If you want, you can try digital recording both with and without this feature on several tracks to see what gives the best results, but MusicMatch Jukebox should configure this properly without you having to test it.)

ANALOG

Select analog recording if your CD-ROM drive doesn't support digital recording or it won't do so without lots of errors (even with Error Correction checked). The disadvantages of using analog recording are that it is much slower than digital recording—recording happens no faster than the actual playing time for the tracks—and that it's also not quite as accurate as digital recording. In addition, digital recording lets you specify which compression type and format you want to use, whereas analog recordings are automatically created as CD-quality MP3 files at 128kbps. And, as you'll see in the next section, you can fine-tune some of your recording options in the Record Advanced Options screen.

In general, you should start by selecting Digital as the preferred recording mode, if for no other reason than tracks are much faster to rip in digital mode. (Again, MusicMatch Jukebox should configure this for the most efficient recording options as part of the configuration process.) If your CD-ROM drive doesn't support digital recording at all, MusicMatch Jukebox will switch to analog and record the track in analog mode. Some CD-ROM drives are technically able to do digital recording, but they may not be able to do it well enough to produce a good track. If this happens, MusicMatch Jukebox may stop recording in digital mode after partially completing the ripping process for that track, reconfigure for analog recording mode for that track, and begin recording the track again.

Regardless of whether you use digital or analog recording, the actual difference in the resulting sound may not be substantial. You should experiment with digital versus digital with error correction versus analog versions of the same track and see what they sound like.

When you're satisfied with your entries, click OK. MusicMatch Jukebox saves the recording options.

SETTING ADVANCED RECORDING OPTIONS

If you're using digital recording, you can fine-tune some of the digital recording settings. Although you generally won't have to adjust any of these settings, you may need to to clear up some specific recording problems. Whenever you make an adjustment, it's a good

Some CD-ROM drives are technically able to record in digital mode, but the results will suffer from a problem known as jitter. Jitter sounds like there is a regular (and annoying) jitter in the file. It's caused by poor seeking accuracy when the CD-ROM drive is reading the track. If you're having problems with jitter in your MP3 files, you'll want to switch to analog recording mode.

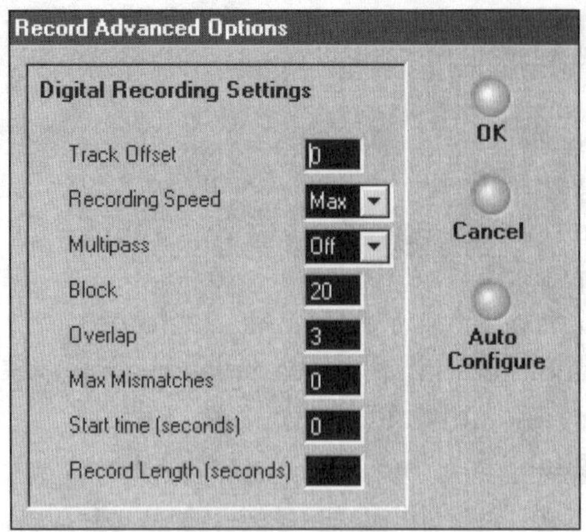

FIGURE 4.15:
The Record Advanced Options screen.

idea to make a note of what the settings were when you began so you can reset the settings to their defaults for your computer. Many of the settings interact, so you should experiment with small incremental adjustments when trying to eliminate recording problems.

To set advanced recording options, do the following:

1. Click Advanced Options at the bottom of the Record Options screen (shown earlier in Figure 4.13). The Record Advanced Options screen appears, as shown in Figure 4.15.

2. Select the options on the screen as follows:

TRACK OFFSET

This option adjusts the CD-ROM drive's position. (It doesn't change the start time of recording.) It is for those drives that cannot record either the first or last track because the CD-ROM drive inaccurately identifies the start and end times of the track by a small number of frames. (A *frame* is the smallest "slice" of data you can play or manipulate in a track being recorded. The term comes from movie and video production and frames of films.)

By making the offset value equal to something between 10 and 50, this problem will be eliminated. A higher number is not recommended, since you might cut out some of your song data. Some CD-ROM drives require this setting to be a negative value; in other words, the drive needs to be told to move back a certain number of frames to accurately be at the start of a track. Check your CD-ROM drive's documentation for more information about the preferred setting for this option. Experiment to see what works best for your drive.

RECORDING SPEED

Enter the speed to read information from the CD-ROM drive from the drop-down list. This is useful if your computer is using a lower-end processor that may not be able to encode as quickly as the CD-ROM drive can feed information to the MusicMatch Jukebox encoder. (The symptom is that your tracks will sound like they're playing too quickly.) You can step down the speed from the maximum speed your CD-ROM drive can handle (the default) to 4x, 2x, or even 1x.

MULTIPASS

As you read in the previous section, some CD-ROM drives have trouble with digital recording, resulting in jitter in MP3 files. Turning on error correction can solve some of this, but if you are still having problems with jitter, clicks, or pops, turn the Multipass feature on by selecting "On" from the drop-down list.

BLOCK

Set this option to determine the number of blocks to you want to read from the CD. Although this value can be increased up to 100 to correct jitter and speed problems in digital recording, you should start with a block value that, combined with the total overlap (twice the number in the Overlap field), is no higher than 26 blocks, which uses 64K of RAM.

OVERLAP

This option lets you specify how many blocks of data to overlap when MusicMatch Jukebox is reading data from the CD. Older drives will probably require an overlap of 3 blocks or more to make sure that there's no jitter, but newer drives may only need an overlap of 1 block. The smaller the overlap, the faster the CD will read data, but the greater the chance that there will be jitter. You can increase the Overlap to a maximum of 10, but this will slow down the recording process substantially. Because the overlap occurs at the start and end of the block, setting the Overlap to 10 would result in 20 blocks being reread each time MusicMatch Jukebox gets the next block of information.

Remember that your total Overlap plus the Block should be no greater than 26. (The default settings shown in Figure 4.15 have a Block setting of 20 and an Overlap of 3 for a total of 26.) It is possible that you may be able to use larger block and overlap totals than 26; however, you should experiment

with this to see how long the file takes to record and if you
have any problems with jitter.

MAX MISMATCHES

Like Multipass, you can increase Max Mismatches to up to
255 to eliminate jitter or poor digital recording quality.

START TIME (SECONDS)

Enter the time in seconds that you'd like to skip from the
beginning of a track. You can use this feature in conjunction
with Record Length (next feature) to create clips of sounds or
other tracks. This feature is also handy for cutting out intros,
clapping at the start of a track, and so on.

RECORD LENGTH (SECONDS)

Enter the time in seconds to record. Leave this blank to
record the entire track, regardless of length.

AUTO CONFIGURE

Click Auto Configure to tell MusicMatch Jukebox to automatically reconfigure itself when you run the program again.
Use this feature anytime you make changes to your computer's hardware.

3. When you are satisfied with your entries, click OK.

HOW LONG DOES IT TAKE TO RIP A TRACK?

The time it takes to rip a track depends on many different things,
including:

- ✦ How powerful your computer's chip is. A 266mHz chip
  will be much faster than a 166mHz chip.
- ✦ How much RAM you have.
- ✦ How fast your CD-ROM drive is.
- ✦ If you're recording in digital or analog mode.
- ✦ If you have error correction on.
- ✦ If the CD itself is in good condition and was recorded
  smoothly (surface blemishes on an older CD can add to
  the time it takes to correct errors).
- ✦ What compression level you're recording at (CD-quality,
  near CD-quality, and so on).

In general, if you're using a reasonably fast computer with a good
CD-ROM drive that lets you rip tracks in digital mode, you can
expect speeds of about 1/4 the playing time. This is best-case, how-

ever; if you're using analog mode, the time will be equal to the playing time for the track. Experiment with the settings and options, but don't be surprised if your mileage varies considerably.

SETTING CDDB OPTIONS

Earlier in this chapter, you saw how to set the CDDB options the first time you recorded something with MusicMatch Jukebox. At some point, you may want to make changes to this information, such as selecting a different server if your selected server is down. Click CDDB Preferences on the Record Options screen (shown in Figure 4.13) to display the two CDDB screens shown earlier in Figures 4.6 and 4.7.

GENERAL TIPS ON RIPPING

Here are some tips for ripping MP3 files successfully:

- ✦ Don't run other applications while ripping tracks. Ripping is a CPU- and memory-intensive process. If you're in the middle of ripping a bunch of tracks, then start another program, log on to the net, or scan a picture, it's the computer equivalent of driving uphill in high gear. The computer's CPU may not have enough power to handle everything, and the resulting MP3 file may suffer.

- ✦ Similarly, don't run other applications that are writing to the hard disk. (The most extreme example would be ripping tracks while defragmenting your hard disk.)

- ✦ Make sure you have enough memory (RAM) free. The more applications you have open, the less memory there is to go around. Furthermore, many Windows applications don't always do a good job of cleaning up after themselves when they close. At the very least, you should have most other applications closed when you're ripping so the maximum RAM is available. You might want to consider rebooting your computer before ripping tracks so that it's running as cleanly as possible.

- ✦ If you have several different files ripped by different people they'll be largely the same, but the file lengths will be slightly different because of the vagaries in each person's CD player.

- ✦ Finally, make sure you have enough hard disk space for the tracks you're ripping. Although this seems elementary, if you've been ripping a lot of tracks, it doesn't take many tracks at approximately 4 MB/track to fill up all the free space on your hard disk.

See the "Troubleshooting" section at the end of this chapter for other tips on how to improve your MP3 files and how to solve some of the more common problems.

RIPPING TRACKS FROM YOUR STEREO

The first half of this chapter dealt with ripping tracks from CDs in your computer's CD-ROM drive. Although this will give you the highest-quality MP3 files because of the high quality of the signal coming in from the CD, not everything you may want to turn into an MP3 file is available on a CD. This section will show you how to connect your stereo to your computer and how to rip MP3 files from cassettes, albums, and the radio.

CONNECTING YOUR STEREO FOR RECORDING MP3 FILES

The first step in ripping tracks from your stereo is to connect your stereo to your computer. To do this, you'll need a set of stereo cables with a pair of RCA plugs to plug into the line-out jacks of the cassette deck, the phono preamp, or the tuner, and a 1/8" 3-conductor (stereo) mini-plug to plug into the stereo input jack of your computer's sound card. Most headphones for portable radios, cassette players, and CD players use this plug. Some electronics stores may have a cable like this as a stock item, but you may need to look around for cables long enough to reach from your stereo to your computer. You can create your own with stereo cable, plugs, and a soldering iron if you're so inclined, but the most convenient way to go is probably ordering 100' and 300' cable sets from the *http://www.musicmatch.com* web site.

SOME BASICS OF CASSETTE DECKS

You may not have done much recording to or from cassette tape in the past. You may also only have a cassette player in your car and need to buy an inexpensive cassette deck for recording tapes. This section will give you some basic information about cassette decks.

When you are shopping for a cassette deck, you should look for one that has Dolby B and/or Dolby C recording. (Dolby C is better, but it's not accepted as a standard to the degree that Dolby B is.) Recording level meters on cassette decks aren't standardized from deck to deck. When recording to the cassette deck, you should set your input to the Dolby levels as described in the manual accompanying the cassette deck. You should also know that not all cassette decks are created equal, nor are they adjusted for optimal record and playback settings. If you want to squeeze every bit of fidelity out of your cassette deck, you'll need to use the cassette deck's bias-adjust control to adjust the tape bias. (The bias controls affect the amount of ultrasonic signal that is mixed with the recorded signal. The bias level has a significant effect on the recording fidelity of higher frequencies. When properly adjusted on a cassette deck with Dolby, you can eliminate almost all hiss from the tape.)

The best way to check that the bias is adjusted correctly is to tape the interstation hiss from your stereo's tuner (also known as "white noise") with the Dolby settings on. Adjust the bias about 1/8 turn or less every 10 seconds as you make the recording. When you're done, listen to the recording, then compare it with the white noise on the tuner. The optimal bias setting is the one that eliminates the most hiss from the recording. You'll quickly be able to get the optimal settings for the bias controls this way.

If you haven't got a stereo tuner, you can record from a CD that has a wide dynamic range, particularly in the high frequencies. Record a track, then listen to the tape and see how it sounds compared to the CD. Tweak the bias adjust very slightly, rerecord the track, and listen again. You won't have to tweak the bias control much—maybe as little as 1/8 or 1/6 of a turn—but your record and playback quality will change remarkably.

Whichever method you use for checking the bias control, when you finally get the setting just right, make pencil marks on the cassette deck to show where the optimal setting is so you don't have to do this more than once.

RIPPING TRACKS FROM A CASSETTE

With the cables set up, you're ready to begin recording from a cassette to a WAV file. Follow this procedure:

1. Start a suitable WAV recorder program. Windows comes with a standard program called the Sound Recorder that's probably worth skipping. It's okay for a quick and simple player and for recording voice, but it has no way to monitor recording levels, and there are very primitive editing features. Some of the WAV recorders that you might want to consider are Cool Edit 96 and Sound Forge XP. (Both Cool Edit 96 and Sound Forge XP are featured in Chapter 6, "Editing and Enhancing MP3 Files.") Figure 4.16 shows the main screen for Cool Edit 96.

2. Set the WAV recorder program for sampling rate and other options. For cassettes (and vinyl), you'll usually want to

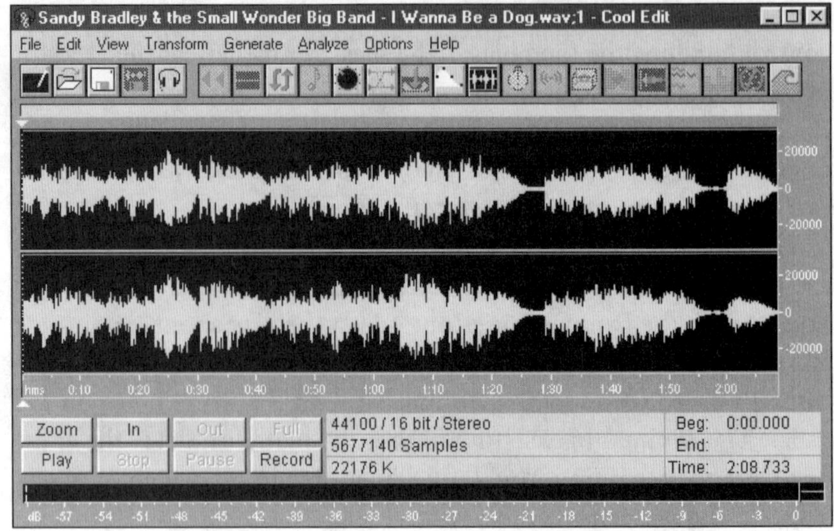

create 16-bit stereo sampled at 32k. Although most WAV files are created at 44k, 32k is adequate. Recording at 32k will give you a frequency range of 16kHz, slightly better than the frequency range you can get from cassettes and vinyl, which don't reproduce sounds above roughly 15kHz. Sampling at 44k will give you a larger file but won't give you any additional fidelity. Don't record at less than 32k, though, as you will lose fidelity in the recorded WAV file.

3. Start the WAV recorder program recording, then quickly start the cassette playing. (You want to get the cassette playing as quickly as possible so you have as little dead airtime at the beginning of the track as you can.)

4. When the cassette track is done playing, stop the WAV recorder, then shut off the cassette. The first few times you record from a cassette, you should listen to the WAV file all the way through to make sure there's no distortion and the sound is clear throughout.

5. As the final step in the WAV creation process, you should edit the WAV file to remove any blank time at the front of the file. You may also need to slice the WAV file into separate selections—if you recorded an entire side of the album, you'll have one big WAV file. You should also do any other editing: it's easier to edit WAV files than MP3 files and the tools for cleaning up and massaging the sound quality of WAV files are much better.

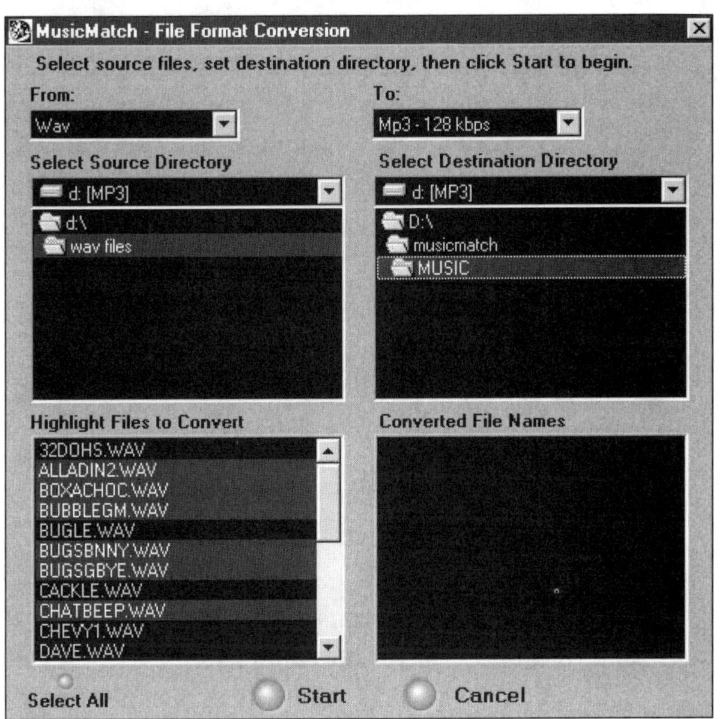

FIGURE 4.17:
The File Format Conversion screen.

You'll need to experiment with creating WAV files a few times to get the hang of it and to determine the optimal settings for your stereo. As you record, make sure that the record levels don't go too high, or you'll end up with distortion in the WAV file. You should probably not go above a -3 peak on the volume. Remember that you can use your WAV recorder/editor to clean up the resulting WAV file by normalizing it... but this may be more work than you really want to do, so it's better to get it right the first time.

Once the WAV file sounds right, you're ready to convert it to an MP3 file, as follows:

1. Click Options in the MusicMatch Jukebox Music Library and select Convert WAV files to MP3 from the menu. The File Format Conversion screen appears, as shown in Figure 4.17.

2. Make entries in the fields as follows:

FROM
Select WAV or MP3 from the drop-down list.

SELECT SOURCE DIRECTORY
Select the drive and directory to look for files of the type specified in the From field.

HIGHLIGHT FILES TO CONVERT

Select the files you want to convert. You can click Select All to convert all the files in the directory, or you can select a single file by highlighting it. If you want to select several files, hold down the Ctrl key and click the files you want to add one at a time.

TO

Select the format from the drop-down list to convert the files to. If you selected WAV in the From field, you can select MP3 files of 128 kbps, 80 kbps, or 64 kbps. If you selected MP3 in the From field, you can only select WAV format.

SELECT DESTINATION DIRECTORY

Select the drive and directory to put the converted files in.

CONVERTED FILE NAMES

This file is for display purposes only. It shows you the files in the conversion format already in the destination directory.

3. When you're satisfied with your entries, click Start to begin the conversion process. MusicMatch Jukebox will start converting the files you have selected. As each file is converted, it will appear in the Converted Files field.

4. When MusicMatch Jukebox is completed, click Cancel to close the File Format Conversion screen.

If you've spent a lot of time getting your cassette deck aligned and set for recording to MP3 files, one of the easiest ways to rip from vinyl is to make a good-quality tape copy of the album and then rip the track from the cassette tape. This might even provide an opportunity for cleaning up some of the hiss on some records with the cassette deck's Dolby features.

Try playing the converted files (you'll have to manually add them to the Music Library or Play List window) and see how they sound. If everything has gone smoothly, the final MP3 file should sound very close to the original cassette recording.

As before, once you've created a track, you can add tag information as described in the "Editing Track Information" section of Chapter 2, "Creating and Using Playlists." Be sure to update the track with information from web sites such as *http://www.cddb.com* and *http://www.lyrics.com*.

RIPPING TRACKS FROM VINYL

The process for ripping tracks from vinyl (the term "vinyl" actually covers standard LPs, 45s, and even old 78-rpm records) is similar to the process of ripping tracks from cassette tapes, but there are a few differences. The first thing you need is a phono preamplifier, which amplifies the output from the turntable to the level necessary to drive the sound card. An inexpensive phono preamp can be purchased at any discount electronics store.

You can simply hook up the turntable to the preamp and the preamp to the sound card if you wish; however, many sound cards will mute their output when you're recording so you can't hear what you've recorded until you play back the file. You can work around this by hooking the turntable to the preamp input, the preamp output into the stereo's phono input (or, if your amplifier doesn't have a phono input, you can plug the preamp into an auxiliary, tape, or CD input jack), and the RCA plugs from the sound card into the amplifier's Tape Out jacks. This lets you use the amplifier to play the record as you're recording it. It's worth noting that you can use this technique of hooking the sound card to the amplifier's Tape Out jacks to record anything that you can pipe in to the amplifier. All you need to do is to connect the device you want to record from to the input jacks on the amp. If it sounds good coming over the amp's speakers, then the Tape Out volume levels should be okay.

With the cables set up, you're ready to begin recording from the turntable to a WAV file. The process is very similar to recording from a cassette:

1. Start the WAV recorder program.

2. Set the WAV recorder program for sampling rate and other options. As with cassettes, the sampling rate will optimally be 16-bit stereo sampled at 32k.

3. Start the WAV recorder program recording, and then quickly start the record playing.

4. When the record is done playing, stop the WAV recorder, then shut off the turntable. The first few times you record from a turntable, you should listen to the WAV file all the way through to make sure there's no distortion and the sound is clear throughout.

5. Edit the WAV file to remove any blank time at the front of the file. You may also need to slice the WAV file into separate selections—if you recorded an entire side of the album, you'll have one big WAV file. Do any other editing necessary at this point, particularly pop and click reduction (many editors have pop and click filters that will help smooth out the sound quality).

As with recording from cassettes, you'll need to experiment with creating WAV files to check your recording levels and to determine the optimal settings for your stereo.

If you're recording from an old record with a lot of noise and hiss, or you're recording from a mono record, be sure to experiment with the noise-reduction and channel-switching options in your WAV editor. With judicious filtering and channel combination, you can dramatically improve the quality of the sound in the WAV file before you convert it to MP3. You should definitely see what you can do by playing with the equalization, as older records won't have a very good frequency range. (*Equalization* is the term for adjusting the relative output of frequencies in a given range to give a more even sound, such as dropping the output on frequencies around 10kHz to eliminate noise and hiss, or raising the output on the low frequencies up to 1000Hz.)

Once you're happy with the sound of the WAV file, you can convert it to MP3 as you did before with cassettes. Note that you may be able to use a lower sampling ratio that creates a smaller MP3 file for some vinyl; for example, comedy or spoken voice records can probably be compressed at 80 kbps or even 64 kbps without any noticeable loss of quality.

RIPPING TRACKS FROM RADIO

Once you've tried ripping tracks from cassettes and vinyl, there's not a lot new that you need to worry about to rip tracks from radio. You're probably not as likely to rip tracks from radio simply because of the generally lower quality of the signal compared to cassettes or vinyl, although you might do it if you're getting digital FM from a cable company.

The cables should be hooked up as described in the previous section, with the input to the sound card coming from the Tape Out jacks on the amplifier. Depending on what you're recording, you can probably use lower sampling rates (the frequency range of music played on FM radio is only about 14kHz).

RIPPING YOUR VOICE

As you've seen, anything that's in a WAV file can be turned into an MP3 file using the WAV-to-MP3 conversion feature of MusicMatch Jukebox. You can create MP3 files of your voice (or anything else you want) by plugging a microphone into your sound card's microphone input jack, then creating a WAV file using the Windows Sound Recorder. When you're happy with the way the WAV file sounds, convert it to MP3 format as described earlier.

SOME FINAL COMMENTS ON LEGALITY

According to the RIAA and the Audio Home Recording Act of 1992, you're legally allowed to make copies of albums, cassettes, and CDs that you own onto cassette tapes for your own personal, noncommercial use. However, it's currently illegal to rip tracks from albums, cassettes, and CDs into MP3 files unless you have the complete expressed right to do so both from the owner of the material and the artist performing the material. It is similarly illegal to distribute ripped tracks (even if you have the permission to rip them for your own use) unless you have the permission to do that as well. So just watch your step!

SELF-PROMOTION USING MP3 FILES

One of the real values of MP3 files is for self-promotion. This is one of the slickest ways of letting people know what you sound like. You can record yourself speaking, playing an instrument, or singing, create an MP3 file, and release it to the world. You should make sure that the track information in the Track Information screen is complete and correct. Include contact e-mail, CD prices, your web site's URL, lyrics, author bio, notes, mailing addresses—absolutely everything to make your MP3 file a self-contained advertising vehicle. Be sure to have a spiffy picture for the cover art, too. You might also want to put a notice in the "Notes" section saying that this file has been released for general distribution via MP3 provided that it's not changed or altered in any way.

Once you've created the MP3 file, you can release it to any or all of the web sites listed in Appendix A, "Resources." You can also upload it periodically to the relevant newsgroups. And always have the file available on your own web site so people who are already there can download the MP3 file.

TROUBLESHOOTING

The preceding parts of this chapter have told you about how things will work under optimal conditions. This section tells you what happens when things don't go as well as you'd like.

JITTER

As you've read earlier. one of the most common problems when ripping tracks from a CD is *jitter*. Jitter is caused because your CD-ROM drive is technically capable of doing digital extraction but isn't truly up to the job. It's important to note that this can be a problem even when the drive is within tolerances: according to the "Red Book" specification, an industry standard for CD-DA format and playback, a CD-ROM drive only needs to be able to position itself to read data within 1/75 of a second. The problem is that when you're reading

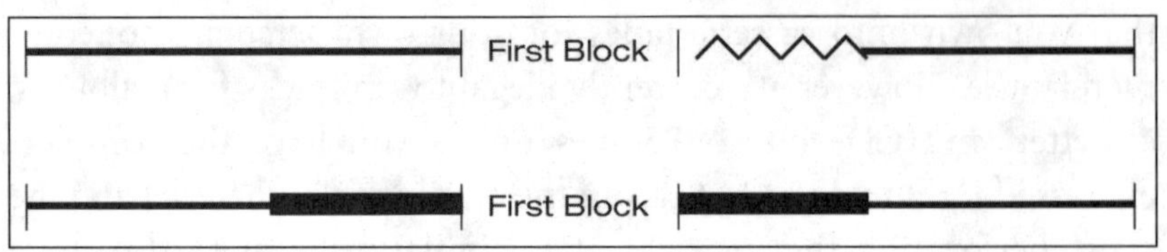

FIGURE 4.18: How overlapping works.

CD-DA in digital-extraction mode, the program will read a block of data from the CD and write it to the hard disk, then ask the CD-ROM drive for the next block of data. Meanwhile, the CD is spinning in the CD-ROM drive, and there may be a slight pause in the time it takes for the CD-ROM drive to get the next block of data. As a result, there may be very small pauses in the information written to the hard disk.

The first solution to try is to turn on Error Correction in the Record Options screen (shown earlier in Figure 4.13) and try ripping the track again. Error correction can frequently eliminate jitter entirely. However, you can also correct for digital seek errors by having the program read each block with a slight overlap of at least 1/75 second to allow for the CD-ROM drive's seek time, using the Overlap setting in the Record Advanced Options screen (shown earlier in Figure 4.15). The program will then match the bytes at the end of the first block with the bytes at the start of the second block, discard the duplicate bytes in the second block, and write the second block to the hard disk correctly. Figure 4.18 shows how this works.

GENERAL RIPPING PROBLEMS

This section discusses some of the general problems that can occur when you rip tracks, regardless of the format or source. All the problems underscore a basic principle: it's a good idea to listen to your tracks after you rip them to make sure they're okay.

If it looks like the ripping process went fine, but there's no sound when you play it, check the Windows Volume Control, as follows:

1. Select Programs from the Start menu.
2. Select Accessories.
3. Select Multimedia.
4. Double-click on the Volume Control. The Volume Control screen appears, as shown in Figure 4.19.
5. Make sure the Mute buttons are not checked (as shown in Figure 4.19). If they are, uncheck them. If this doesn't solve the problem, select Properties off the Options menu.
6. When the Volume Control Properties screen appears, click Recording, as shown in Figure 4.20.

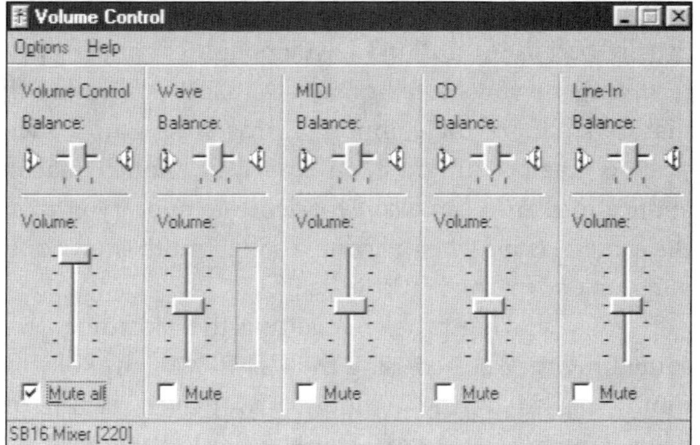

FIGURE 4.19:
The Volume Control screen.

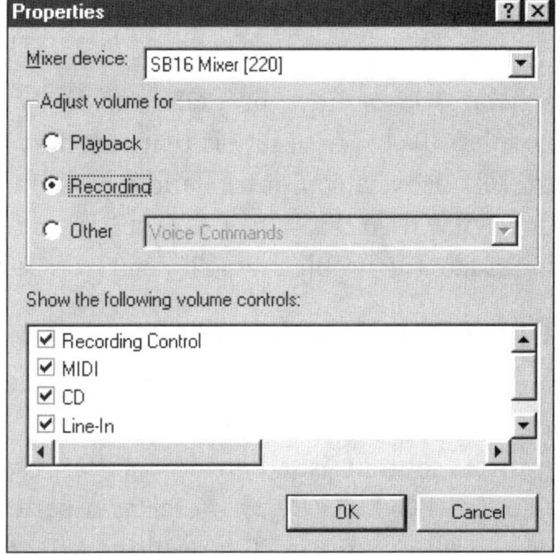

FIGURE 4.20:
The Volume Control Properties screen.

7. Make sure that the Line-in setting in the volume controls is not checked, and the CD or Mix-All settings are checked. When you are satisfied with your entries, click OK.

8. Close the Volume Control screen.

9. Rerecord the track. (Sorry, it had to be done.)

If a recorded track speeds up when you're playing it, it means that your computer isn't running fast enough to keep up with the data flow from the CD in the CD-ROM drive. You can change the speed of the CD-ROM drive by reducing the Recording Speed in the Record Advanced Options screen (shown in Figure 4.15).

If the recorded track is shorter than the actual song time, you may also need to reduce the Recording Speed, or you may have inadvertently made an entry in the Start time or Record Length fields in the Record Advanced Options screen (shown in Figure 4.15).

If a recorded track speeds up and slows down or warbles slowly, it's usually because you didn't have enough computer power to do the recording, or you started or used applications during the recording that took a lot of the computer's processing power, such as a screen saver, a graphics program, a scanner, or another machine-intensive application. (You can also experience temporary effects like this for the same reasons when playing a song, but these are only temporary and don't affect the MP3 file itself.)

If you're having problems getting the recording process started, something may be accessing the CD-ROM drive. This is most commonly caused by the Windows CD Player starting automatically when you insert an audio CD in the CD-ROM drive. You can turn off auto-insert notification as described earlier in this chapter. If the CD Player is not running, see if there's something else running that is using the CD or audio on your computer, such as videoconferencing software, other music programs, games, and many multimedia CDs. One less likely possibility is that you may have had something using the CD or your computer's audio that crashed while doing so. Windows may then think the CD is still in use even though it isn't. If this looks like the problem, you'll need to reboot to clear it up.

PROBLEMS WITH RIPPING FROM CASSETTES

No matter what you do, you may find that MP3 files you make from cassette tapes sound bad even though the WAV file sounds okay. One possible solution is to encode the WAV files as MPEG Layer 2 rather than MPEG Layer 3. This creates a better-digitized file with some analog sound sources. The resulting MP2 files can be played with the MusicMatch Jukebox player, but you'll need to use a different encoder than the one in MusicMatch Jukebox to create the MP2 file. See Chapter 7, "Using Other Software," for a list of alternatives for MP2 and MP3 encoding.

You may also have problems getting a good-quality MP3 file from a tape because of the microscopic stretches and variations in the tape, which throw off the stereo channels enough to be noticeable. Try using an encoder that has dual-channel encoding options instead of the (more common) joint stereo.

DIGITAL MODE RECORDING PROBLEMS

The most common problem when trying digital recording is that it doesn't work: MusicMatch Jukebox will grind away for a moment (with the progress indicator at 0%) and then switch to analog mode. This probably indicates that your CD-ROM drive doesn't support digital recording at all. You may also see MusicMatch Jukebox record part of a track in digital mode, then switch to analog mode and start over, or you may get yellow boxes in the tracks' histograms, showing that the quality of the files is not as good as it could be due to error correction or other problems. This suggests that the CD-ROM drive is technically able to record in digital mode, but that there are too many errors for MusicMatch Jukebox to correct. You can try turning on error correction or tweaking some of the advanced recording options, but the solution will probably be to record in analog mode. Although this will take longer than digital recording, the difference in quality will be negligible. If you can record CDs most of the time in digital mode but sometimes you can't, it's usually a sign of a problem with the quality of the CD you're recording from rather than the CD-ROM drive.

Sometimes you can correct digital mode recording problems by reconfiguring the CD-ROM drive in MusicMatch Jukebox. You may encounter this if you didn't have an audio CD in the CD-ROM drive when you first ran the MusicMatch Jukebox recording process, or you're using a different CD-ROM drive to record than the one you usually use. To fix this, load an audio CD into the CD-ROM drive you want to use (if possible, one you know has worked for digital recording) and click Auto-Configure on the Record Advanced Options screen shown earlier in Figure 4.15. MusicMatch Jukebox will reconfigure itself to the optimal settings, after which you need to exit and then restart MusicMatch Jukebox.

If MusicMatch Jukebox was recording okay, but then doesn't, make sure you haven't installed other software that deleted some of the DLL files that MusicMatch Jukebox uses. The first solution to try is simply rebooting your computer—some files are replaced or rewritten when you reboot. Failing that, you may need to reinstall the MusicMatch Jukebox software.

———————◆———————

This chapter has shown you more about how digital music works and how to rip MP3 tracks from CDs, cassettes, vinyl, and radio. You also saw how to improve the quality of your MP3 files and how to solve a number of common problems that happen when ripping tracks. In the next chapter, you'll see how to play your MP3 files on your stereo and how to record them to cassettes, DAT tapes, and CDs.

Recording from Your Computer to Your Audio System

The preceding chapter taught you more about how digital music works and how to rip MP3 tracks from CDs, cassettes, vinyl, and radio. This chapter will reverse the process and show you how to play your MP3 files on your stereo and how to record MP3 files onto cassettes, DAT tapes, and CDs.

CONNECTING YOUR COMPUTER TO YOUR AUDIO SYSTEM

One of the biggest complaints about playing MP3 files on the computer is that most generic computer speakers suck. (That's a technical term for speaker quality). It was true for a long time, though: you couldn't have good speakers on a computer because, first, it just wasn't done, and second, even if you paid for a set of good speakers, the sound card wouldn't have enough oomph to drive them. Thankfully, this is changing: there is a growing selection of computer speaker sets (frequently known as "multimedia speakers") that will give you some substantial sound quality and there are sound cards that will let you get really good sound quality from your computer. (Some of the hardware options open to you are featured in Chapter 8, "Playing MP3 Files Away from Your Computer.")

Nevertheless, for the best audio, you'll probably want to feed the audio from the computer into your stereo amplifier (that's what it's there for) and play the sound through the good speakers that you have on your stereo. If nothing else, you won't have to buy a whole new set of speakers for your computer. You'll also have the full range of bass, treble, and filtering options your stereo has to enhance the sound of the tracks.

You saw in Chapter 4, "Creating Your Own MP3 Files," how to connect your computer to your stereo to rip files from cassettes and vinyl. The process for connecting your computer to your stereo for playback is even easier. As before, you'll need a set of stereo cables with a pair of RCA plugs to plug into the line-in jacks of the stereo amplifier and a 1/8" 3-conductor (stereo) mini-plug to plug into the line-out or speaker-out jack of your computer's sound card.

The type of inputs you have on your stereo will vary considerably depending on the make and model, whether you're using individual components or a modular setup, and how many gadgets you have hooked together. In general, though, you'll need to have line inputs free for your cassette deck, your stereo's CD player, and the sound card. If you have only one pair of auxiliary input jacks on your amplifier, or your amplifier's input jacks are all in use, you'll need to get a couple Y connectors to split the line so you can have input from the sound card and the amplifier's auxiliary input jacks. However, you should *never* send input from the sound card to the amplifier's phono input jacks, as these are enormously more sensitive than the standard line-in jacks. Normal sound-card output can permanently damage the phono inputs.

Once the cables are connected, you need to check your volumes and settings on the sound card. Many sound cards have some kind of amplifier built in to drive speakers; others have a soft control that is handled by the Windows Volume Control. If you have the sound card send too much signal to the amplifier, it can damage the amp, and the track will certainly sound distorted and fuzzy. Reduce the volume all

A WORD ABOUT SOUND CARDS

Sound cards are as standard as anything else in the computer industry (i.e., not very), but most sound cards these days have both a line-out jack and a speaker-out jack. The line-out jack bypasses any amplifier built into the sound card so you can connect the sound card to an external amplified source, such as amplified computer speakers or a stereo. The speaker-out jack lets you plug the sound card into a set of unamplified speakers and run them off the sound card's internal amplifier (which is usually only a few watts per channel). If your sound card has a line-out jack, use it. The output levels will most likely be exactly what you need for the stereo. If you have only a single output jack (probably labeled "Speakers"), use it, but be careful to keep your volume controls very low until you're sure you aren't going to overdrive your stereo amplifier.

the way on the Windows Volume Control. If your sound card has a volume control knob on the card itself, turn it down all the way to start with.

Now try a test to get the output levels set and to see what it all sounds like:

1. Turn on the stereo and set your amplifier's volume control down almost all the way. (If your initial settings are going to blast the amplifier, it's a good idea not to have the volume turned way up on the amp when you find out!)

2. Open MusicMatch Jukebox and start a few tracks playing. It probably doesn't matter what, but music is better than spoken words, as you'll hear the distortion easier.

3. If you don't hear anything coming through the stereo, either increase the volume control just a little using the Windows Volume Control or the sound card's volume control (you'll have to reach around the back of your computer to do the latter).

4. If you still don't hear anything coming through the stereo, turn the stereo's volume up slightly.

5. Repeat steps 3 and 4 as necessary. If everything is connected properly, you shouldn't have to do this more than once or twice to hear the music through the stereo. Make sure that the volume on the sound card is set so that the sound coming through the stereo is clear but not distorted. On the other hand, the sound should be loud enough so that you can set the volume about the same as you would for other devices on the stereo, like your cassette deck and CD player.

If you're not hearing anything yet, don't crank the levels too high on the sound card or the amplifier. Turn the volume controls down on the sound card and on the amplifier, then check each of the following items. Then run through the steps again.

+ The 1/8" mini-plug could be plugged into the wrong hole on the sound card. Make sure that the mini-plug is plugged into the line-out or speaker jack, as appropriate.

+ The cable isn't plugged into the right input jacks on the amplifier (or might even be plugged into the output jacks).

✦ The cable is plugged into the right input jacks on the amplifier, but the amplifier is set to the wrong auxiliary channel. (For example, you have an auxiliary switch on the input selector controls, or you have a "source/tape" switch that's set to the wrong setting.)

When you think everything is set up, queue up a playlist with a selection of different styles of tracks and see how they sound: you might want to make a few last adjustments to the volume control. Also experiment with the bass, treble, and filtering options on your amplifier to see what works best for playing MP3 files.

One final comment on the process of getting hooked up: you'll probably need to do a little tinkering with the cables and the volume controls before you get everything set up and working smoothly. Everybody does. Be careful with your volume levels and you won't damage the amplifier or scare yourself to death while you're doing so.

RECORDING MP3 FILES ON TAPE

Once you can play MP3 files through your stereo, you can record them on tape. Follow this procedure:

1. Turn on your stereo for recording. Insert a cassette tape in the deck and press Record but pause the tape so that all you need to do is press the Pause button to start recording.
2. Open MusicMatch Jukebox and queue up your playlist.
3. Click Play in MusicMatch Jukebox to start the playlist playing, then immediately release the Pause button on the cassette deck to start taping.
4. Check your record monitor levels to make sure the information is recording smoothly. It's a good idea to monitor the recording levels either by listening to the tracks through the stereo or by plugging headphones into the cassette's headphone jack.
5. When you are done with the playlist, click Stop on Music-Match Jukebox, then press the Stop button on the cassette deck.
6. Play the cassette tape back to check that the recording went smoothly.

This method will work fine, but if you're like most people, there's going to be a problem: your stereo probably isn't really close to your computer. This means that you either need two people to do record-

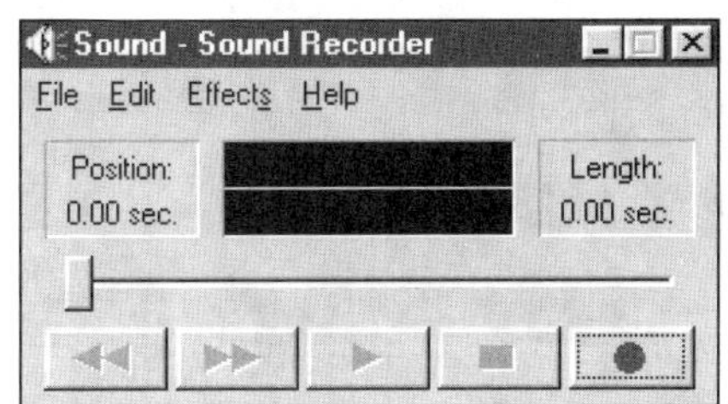

FIGURE 5.1:
The Windows Sound Recorder screen.

ing (one of you will start MusicMatch Jukebox and the other will start the cassette deck), you'll have to run very quickly from the computer to the stereo, or you'll have to start the cassette tape before the playlist. This last technique will work marginally well, but you may have more dead air recorded on the tape than you're comfortable with. Here's a better way:

1. Open the Windows Sound Recorder (shown in Figure 5.1).
2. Click the red record button to start recording. You don't need to have a microphone hooked up to the sound recorder; you'll just record silence.
3. After about 5 seconds, click the square Stop button to stop recording.
4. From the File menu in the Windows Sound Recorder, select Save. Save the file with a name of LEADER.WAV.

Now convert the WAV file to an MP3 file, as follows:

1. Click Options in the MusicMatch Jukebox Music Library and select Convert WAV files to MP3 from the menu. The File Format Conversion screen appears, as shown in Figure 5.2.
2. Make entries in the fields as follows:

FROM
Select WAV or MP3 from the drop-down list.

SELECT SOURCE DIRECTORY
Select the drive and directory to look for files of the type specified in the From field.

HIGHLIGHT FILES TO CONVERT
Select LEADER.WAV from the file list.

TO
Select the format from the drop-down list to convert the files to. For this file, MP3—128 kbps is just fine.

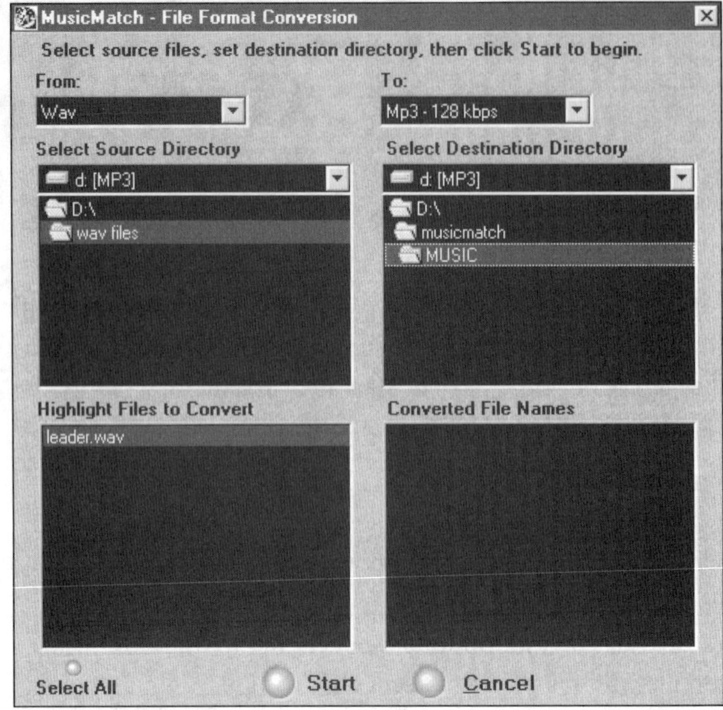

SELECT DESTINATION DIRECTORY

Select the drive and directory to put the converted files in.

3. When you are satisfied with your entries, click Start to start the conversion process. MusicMatch Jukebox will convert the LEADER.WAV file to an MP3 file (it won't take long).

4. When MusicMatch Jukebox is completed, click Cancel to close the File Format Conversion screen.

You've now got an MP3 file you can add to the playlist that will play 5 seconds of silence, after which MusicMatch Jukebox will play the next track in the playlist. You can even insert this file into the playlist between files to add a five-second pause between tracks. Figure 5.3 shows a playlist that uses the LEADER.MP3 file.

If you have a microphone attached to your computer, you can record an opening "timing" leader with your voice counting down from 5 to 1. You can use this as the first leader and use it to start the cassette tape recording after you hear "1."

CREATING AUDIO CDS FROM MP3 FILES

The final step in completing the cycle is to create your own audio CDs from the MP3 files you like. This will require some additional

FIGURE 5.3:
A sample playlist with leaders inserted between songs.

hardware and software; in particular, a CD-ROM burner and the software to run it.

UNDERSTANDING CD-ROM BURNERS

A CD-ROM burner is a CD-ROM drive that is also capable of writing ("burning") CDs. A few years ago, CD-ROM burners were very expensive ($1000 or more) but, like most computer technology, the street price has dropped substantially. At this point, you can buy CD-ROM burners for $200-$400.

There are two types of CD-ROM burners available these days: CD-R and CD-RW. CD-R burners burn a CD that can't be reused or reburned: once the information is on the CD, it's there forever. CD-RW burners look about the same, but they use a different CD blank that you can write data to, use like any other CD, and then erase the CD and write new information to it.

The advantages of CD-R over CD-RW are:

+ **CD-R blanks are much cheaper than CD-RW blanks.** CD-R blanks cost around $1 each these days (as little as 50 cents each if you buy in bulk or snag a good rebate deal), while CD-RW blanks cost around $5 (or a little less). You'd need to write and erase a CD-RW blank at least five times to make it cost-effective compared to CD-R blanks.

+ **CD-R burners are cheaper than CD-RW burners.** CD-R burners cost about $200 for a good low-end unit, while CD-RW burners start around $400.

+ **CD-RW CDs aren't universally compatible.** This sounds odd, but it's true: the CD you create in your CD-RW burner may not be readable by someone else's CD-ROM drive. This is because the CD-RW CDs are not as reflective as CD-R CDs, and the drive can't read the information on the CD. Newer CD-ROM drives (also known as "multiread CD-ROM drives") are able to handle the differences, but they're going to be a little more expensive, too.

✦ **It's easier to lend or give away a compilation CD on CD-R than on CD-RW.** If you've created a collection of your favorite tracks, lending or giving a copy to someone is much easier when you know that the CD blank only cost you a dollar at most. Besides which, giving a CD-RW away defeats the purpose: you won't be rewriting that CD again.

There is, however, an advantage to buying a CD-RW that you should know about: A CD-RW burner can read and write both CD-R and CD-RW blanks. If the initial price is not an issue, you should probably buy a CD-RW drive so you have the most flexibility. You can burn CD-Rs when you want to keep something forever and use CD-RWs when you just need a lot of external storage on a more temporary basis.

CD-ROM burners are usually pretty slow when writing (2x or 4x) and they're frequently no great shakes for reading CDs, either (6x or 8x). There are exceptions, such as the CD Rocket from Smart and Friendly (*http://www.smartandfriendly.com*), which, in its current incarnation, has an 8x write and a 20x read, but you can expect to pay a bit extra for this kind of speed, too. It's a good idea to have two CD-ROM drives: one that's a CD-ROM burner and one that's a fast CD-ROM drive just for playing or reading CDs (32x or 40x). Read-only CD-ROM drives are less than $100 and the time you don't spend waiting for CDs to read will pay for itself within the first couple of months. In addition, you'll be able to do CD-to-CD copies if you need to.

What about DVD? *DVD* (an acronym for *digital versatile disc*) format may supplant CD-R and CD-RW entirely. DVD is still relatively new in the marketplace, with the concomitant flurry of standard and proprietary formats. Depending on the type of DVD drive, you can store from 2.6GB to 5.2GB per side (DVD discs can be recorded on both sides), or 4 to 8 times as much as a standard CD. While it's certain that DVD drives or something like them will start squeezing CD-R and CD-RW drives out of the market, it's going to be a year or two before there is something resembling a DVD standard and DVD drives become affordable. The cost per DVD disc is still extremely high by comparison to CD-R and CD-RW blanks: DVD blanks cost perhaps 20 times as much as a CD-R blank and 4 or 5 times as much as a CD-RW blank. The bottom line is, if you're buying a burner now, don't buy DVD yet. Wait at least a year and see what happens.

SCSI VERSUS IDE

When you're shopping for a CD-ROM burner, you'll need to know if you want an IDE or a SCSI drive. IDE (an acronym for *Integrated Device Electronics*) and its big brother, EIDE (*Enhanced IDE*) are an inexpensive and popular interface for PC hardware and devices. SCSI (an acronym for *Small Computer System Interface* and pronounced "scuzzy") is more expensive and not as common on Windows computers (though standard on Macintosh computers). If you don't already have a SCSI device on your system, you'll also need to get a SCSI adapter card (another $50-100) to use a SCSI CD-ROM burner.

SCSI is still the preferred format for CD-ROM burners, but you can find inexpensive CD-ROM drives that use IDE. The possible problem with this is that IDE CD-ROM burners can't handle data as quickly as SCSI CD-ROM burners, meaning that IDE burners are more likely to have a *buffer underrun* when you're recording a CD. This means that the *data buffer* (the area on the hard disk where information is stored, typically C:\Windows\Temp) runs out of data to record on the CD and can't get more in time, so the CD-ROM burner aborts the recording then and there, and you're out one CD blank. (If you have an IDE CD-ROM burner, you can partially offset this problem by hooking the CD-ROM burner up to a different IDE channel than the hard disk you're using as the data source and also making sure that DMA is not enabled on the IDE hard drive that is the buffer drive.) The ability of SCSI CD-ROM burners to handle more data than IDE CD-ROM burners also makes a difference if you're duplicating audio CDs. IDE CD-ROM burners can inject a lot of noise into the final CD.

Unless you're willing to take a chance, you'll probably be happier with a SCSI CD-ROM burner than an IDE CD-ROM burner. Yes, it'll cost you a little more for the burner itself and very possibly more for the adapter card, but the results will usually be substantially better and smoother.

DESIGNING A CD

Tracks appear on the CD list in the order that you add them. If you converted a bunch of MP3 files to WAVs and then just selected the directory and added it, you'd get files in name order or whatever order they appeared on the Song Selection screen. But building a good CD takes more than that. You'll want to alternate material throughout the CD. You don't want three fast songs followed by three slow songs; instead, have a strong song that really grabs the attention as the first cut, followed by a medium slow song, followed by a medium fast song, followed by another fast song, and so on.

Look at some of your favorite CDs and note how they're structured. This may take some practice to get it just the way you like, but remember that there are people in the recording industry who do nothing but this and get paid a lot of money to do it well. But remember that the biggest factor in deciding "What sounds good for this collection of tracks?" is what sounds good to you.

BURNING A CD

The general process for burning a CD is the reverse of the process you went through to rip tracks from a CD: you create WAV files from the selected MP3 files, then output the WAV files to a CD in CD-DA format using CD-ROM mastering software. Most CD-ROM burners come bundled with CD mastering software these days. The most popular CD-ROM burning package is Easy CD Creator Deluxe from Adaptec (*http://www.adaptec.com*).

The first step in preparing to record MP3 files to a CD-ROM is to create WAV files, as follows:

1. Click Options in the MusicMatch Jukebox Music Library and select Convert MP3 files to WAV from the menu. The File Format Conversion screen appears. Figure 5.4 shows this screen with sample files selected for conversion.

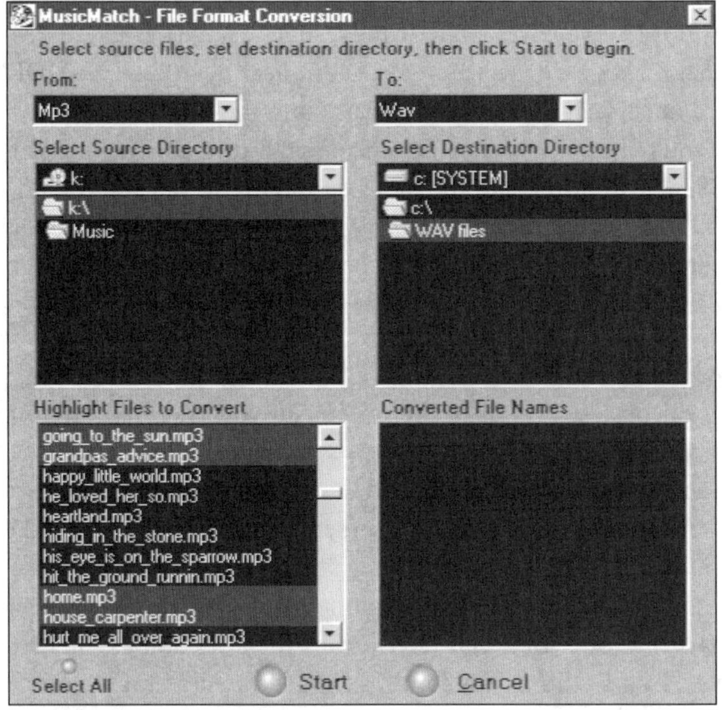

FIGURE 5.4: The File Format Conversion screen.

2. Select the files you want to convert to WAV files. (This is basically the reverse of the conversion from WAV to MP3 files you did in Chapter 4, "Creating Your Own MP3 Files.") Remember that each file you convert to a WAV file will have about 11 megabytes for each minute of sound. To put it another way, if you selected a dozen tracks to convert, you'd be creating about half a *gigabyte* of files! Make sure you have enough room on your hard disk for the files. In fact, if you're creating CDs on a regular basis, you may want to dedicate a one- or two-gigabyte volume of the hard disk for working area for CD images as you're building them.

3. When you are satisfied with your entries, click Start to start the conversion process. MusicMatch Jukebox will convert the MP3 files to WAV files. This will take a little while.

4. When MusicMatch Jukebox is completed, click Cancel to close the File Format Conversion screen.

This completes the first part of the conversion process. As when you were ripping tracks from a CD, you'll get the best results if you don't run other applications while converting tracks to WAV files. Converting, like ripping, is a CPU- and memory-intensive process. If you're in the middle of ripping a bunch of tracks, then start another program, log on to the net, or scan a picture, it's the computer equivalent of driving uphill in high gear. Similarly, don't run other applications that are writing to the hard disk. The computer's CPU may not have enough power to handle everything, and the resulting WAV file may suffer.

Once you've created the WAV files, it's a good idea to listen to each of them to make sure that the conversion process hasn't injected distortion or noise in the form of tiny crackles or a slight hiss. You may be able to overcome this by reconverting the file, but if necessary, you may want to use an editor as described in Chapter 6, "Editing and Enhancing MP3 Files."

When you are satisfied with the WAV files, you're ready to burn them onto a CD, as follows:

1. Start Easy CD Creator Deluxe. The Easy CD Creator Deluxe main screen appears and displays the Easy CD Creator Wizard, as shown in Figure 5.5. The Easy CD Creator Wizard is a very convenient tool that steps you through the CD creation process.

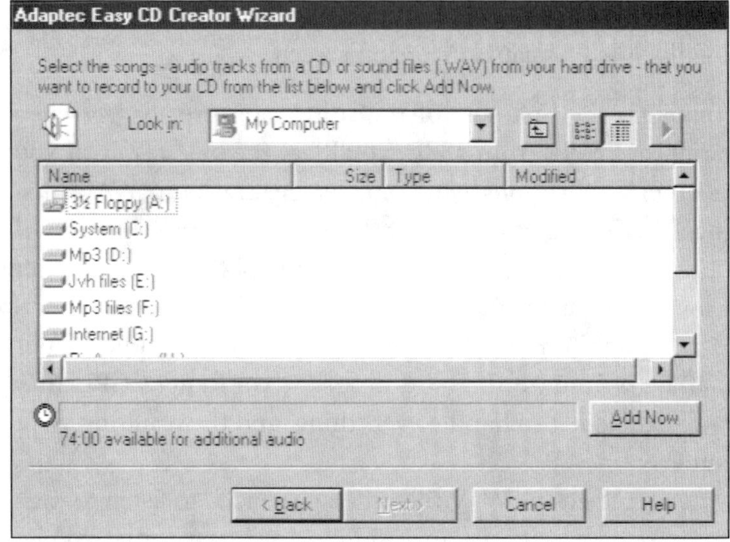

2. Click Audio CD on the wizard and click Next. The Wizard Song Selection screen appears, as shown in Figure 5.6.

3. Navigate to the drive and directory where your WAV files are saved, as shown in Figure 5.7.

4. Start adding files by highlighting them in the window and clicking Add Now. As you do so, the bar showing the available room on the CD starts filling up. Each track is a different color, giving you a very clear idea of how much room you have to work with. If you want to hear what a track sounds like, you can double-click it to get a simple WAV player, shown in Figure 5.8.

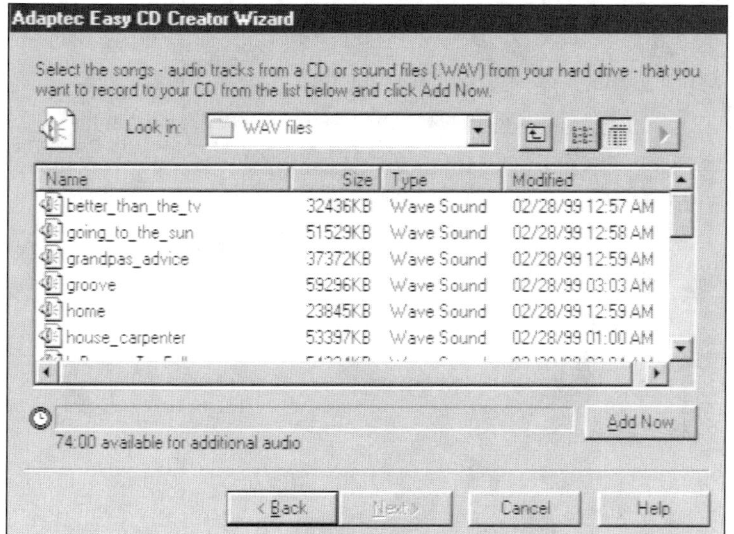

FIGURE 5.7:
The Wizard Song Selection screen showing the WAV file directory.

FIGURE 5.8:
The Easy CD Creator WAV player.

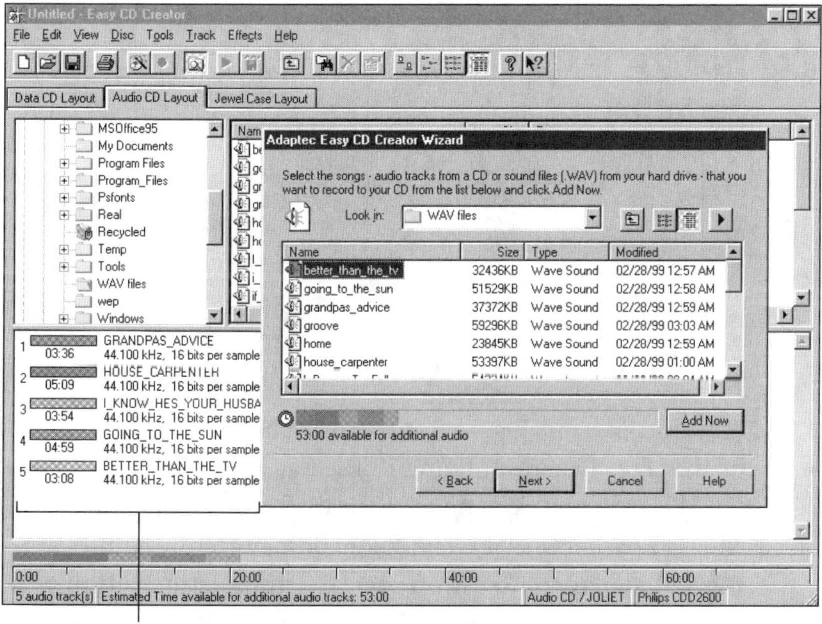

FIGURE 5.9:
Adding tracks to a CD.

5. As you add tracks to the CD list using the Wizard Song Selection screen, the tracks appear on the main Easy CD Creator screen, as shown in Figure 5.9. The track name appears in the display.

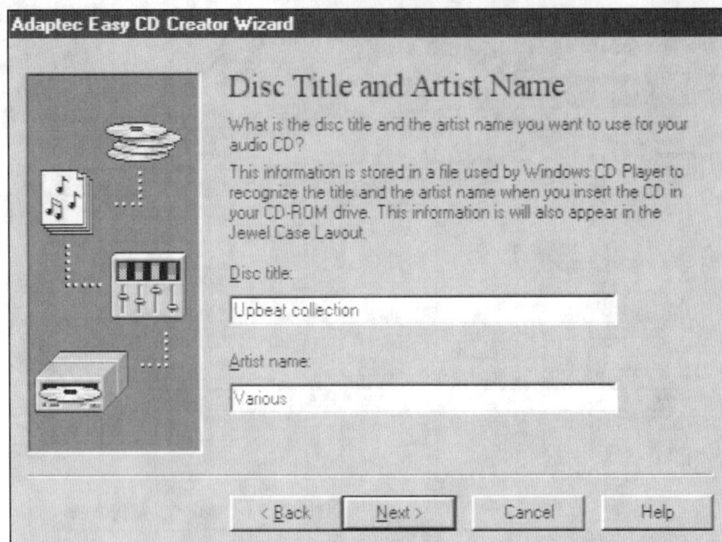

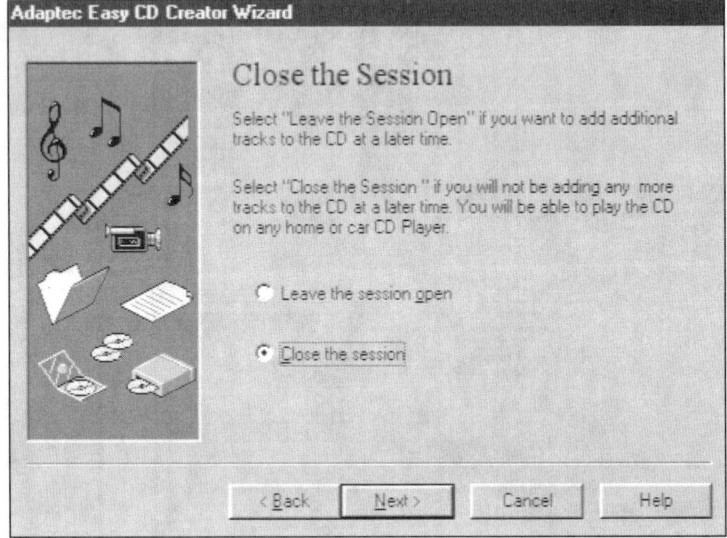

6. As you can see in Figure 5.9, there is a bar at the bottom of the screen corresponding to the bar at the bottom of the Wizard Song Selection screen that shows how much time is used on the CD. The color coding nicely identifies the individual tracks. More detailed track information appears in the screen itself. When you are satisfied with your entries, click Next. The Wizard Disc Title screen appears (shown in Figure 5.10).

7. Enter the title for the CD and the artist name. (Sample entries appear in Figure 5.10.) When you are satisfied with your entries, click Next. The Wizard Close Session screen (shown in Figure 5.11) appears.

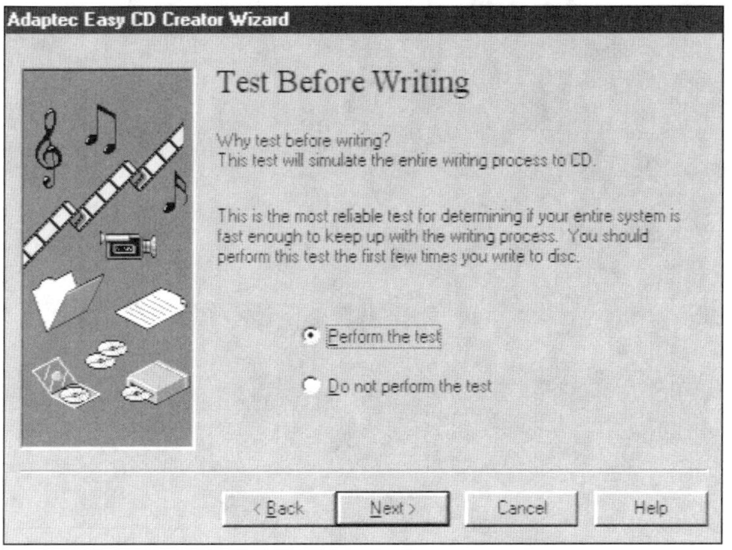

FIGURE 5.12:
The Wizard Test Before Writing screen.

8. Select whether you want to leave the session open or not. If you leave the session open, you can add more tracks to the CD later. This option is very convenient if you don't have all the tracks available and want to get many of the tracks recorded now. On the other hand, leaving a session open is a little tricky if you're not used to burning CDs. You also won't be able to play the CD in a CD player until it's closed, at which time you can't add more tracks to the CD. Most of the time, you'll probably want to close the session as part of the recording process. When you are satisfied with your entries, click Next. The Wizard Test Before Writing screen appears, as shown in Figure 5.12.

9. The first few times you create a CD, you should perform the test before writing the CD. This will ensure that you can write to the CD correctly. When you are satisfied with your entries, click Next. The Wizard Ready to Create CD screen appears (as shown in Figure 5.13).

10. Select Create CD now, then click Finish to start the CD-burning process. (If you prefer, you can select Create CD later to save the track entries and options you've specified. You can then use this information to create a CD when it's more convenient. You're able to edit this information further before creating the CD if you wish.) The CD Creation screen appears (shown in Figure 5.14 with the creation details displayed).

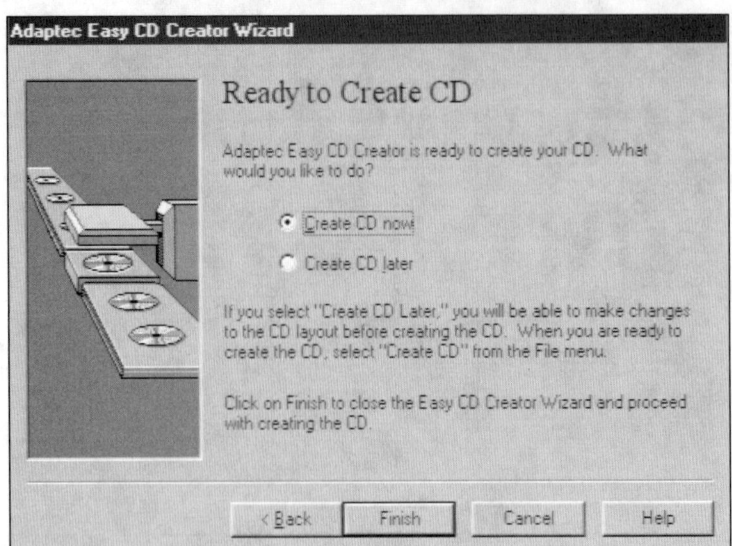

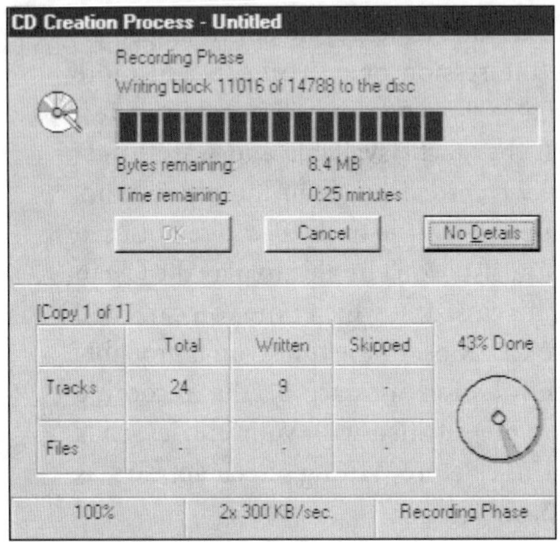

	Total	Written	Skipped	43% Done
Tracks	24	9	-	
Files	-	-	-	

11. As the program adds each track to the CD, it displays the progress on the top part of the CD Creation screen. The details (shown in Figure 5.14) tell you how many tracks have been written and how far along the CD is in the recording process. The CD-burning process for a full audio CD will take anywhere from half an hour to upwards of an hour, depending on the speed you're burning at. When the process is complete, Easy CD Creator Deluxe will display a completion screen like the one shown in Figure 5.15.

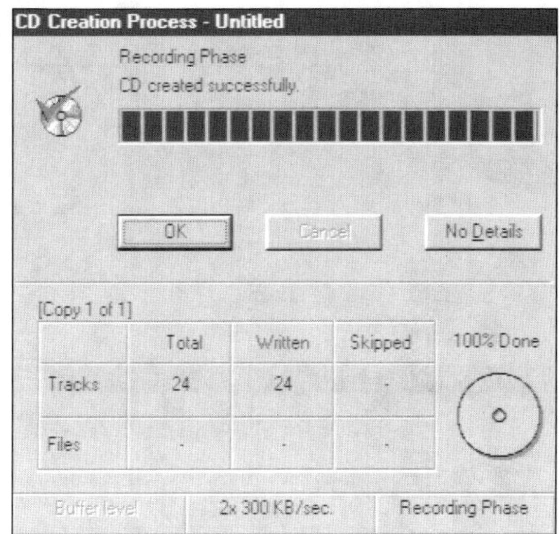

FIGURE 5.15: The CD Recording Completion screen (with details displayed).

12. Congratulations! The CD is now complete. Remove it from the CD-ROM burner and label it. Most people will just use an indelible marker, but there are more attractive alternatives. For example, Easy CD Creator Deluxe lets you print labels for CDs (there are CD label blanks included with the commercial version of the software) as well as CD jewel-case inserts. If you're making a fair number of CDs, you may want to use a product called the Neato CD Labeller (*http://www.neato.com*), a very good product that also lets you print labels on your printer. The Neato CD Labeller comes with labeling software (for both PC and Macintosh) and a collection of templates for labels. It also has a disk holder that makes sure that the CD labels are centered.

OTHER CD-ROM MASTERING SOFTWARE

Easy CD Creator Deluxe is a smashingly good program for mastering CDs, but it's not the only one. The following other programs are worth looking at.

WinOnCD from CeQuadrat (*http://www.cequadrat.com*) is a complete CD-ROM mastering package selling for $99. You can use WinOnCD to create CDs as well as to edit audio files. It's a very good package to consider for creating CDs that are compilations of different artists. The Power Edition lets you use MP3 directly as input for audio CDs without having to convert them to WAV files first. Figure 5.16 shows you the main WinOnCD screen.

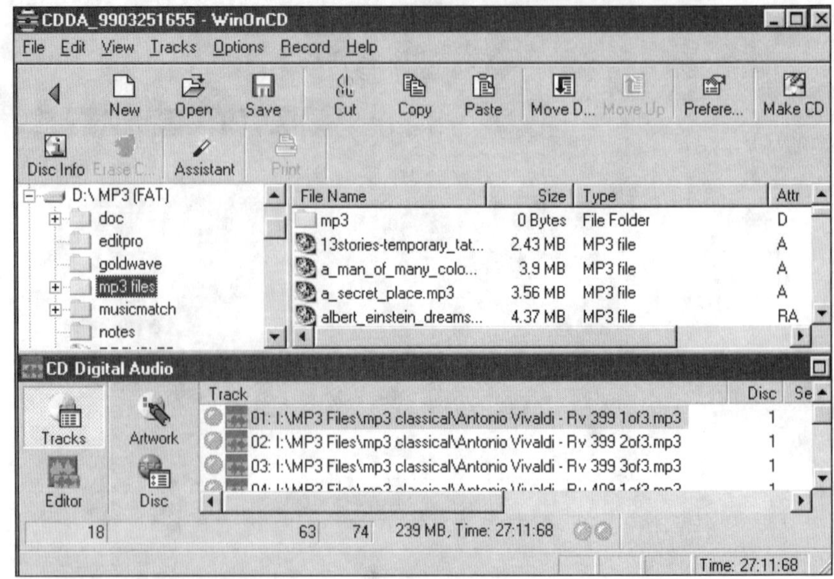

CDRWIN from Golden Hawk (*http://www.goldenhawk.com*) is a snappy, easy-to-understand CD-ROM mastering program. It's available in a demo mode from their web site. You can use it to record in the demo mode, but you can only record at 1x speed. Registering lets you record at the maximum rate your CD-ROM burner can handle. CDRWIN costs $59 to register. As you can see from Figure 5.17, the main CDRWIN screen is attractive, economical, and easy to understand.

Click any of the icons to start a feature. To record a disc, click the Record Disc icon in the upper left. The CDRWIN Record Disc screen appears (as shown in Figure 5.18).

As you can see, the screen is fairly straightforward and uncomplicated. CDRWIN does not have wizards that step you through the process but is a good program for burning and copying CDs.

HyCD Play&Record from Creative Digital Research (*http://www. hycd.com*) is an all-in-one shareware package that costs $59.95 to register. HyCD Play&Record lets you create audio CDs directly from MP3 files without having to go through the intermediate step of creating WAV files—it takes care of that for you. One of the outstanding

NOTE

HyCD Play&Record also plays files and can do file editing and MP3 encoding as well as CD-ROM burning. It's covered in more detail in Chapter 7, "Using Other Software."

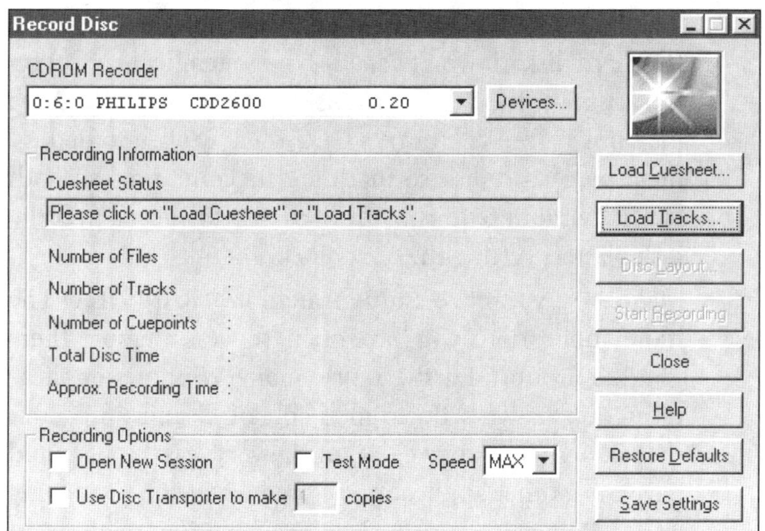

FIGURE 5.18:
The CDRWIN Record Disc screen.

features of HyCD Play&Record is that you can use it directly from the Windows Explorer: when you right-click on an MP3 file, you can do a HyCD Copy and then right-click again to do a HyCD Paste to your CD-ROM burner. All you then need to do is arrange the tracks in the order you wish, set any options, and voila! Everything's taken care of for you on the fly.

TROUBLESHOOTING

There are things that can go wrong with the CD-ROM burning process, many of which are similar to the problems you can have when creating MP3 files. Here are some tips for making sure that the CDs you create will be of the highest quality:

+ **Don't run other applications while burning a CD.** Just like ripping a track, burning a CD is a CPU- and memory-intensive process. In particular, burning a CD requires a smooth and uninterrupted flow of data from the hard disk to the CD-ROM burner. If you're in the middle of burning a CD and then start another program, log on to the net, or do anything that causes the hard drive to have to shift its attention from the CD-ROM burning process, there may not be enough data coming in to the CD-ROM burner, and you'll have a buffer underrun, resulting in an aborted session and a CD blank that's now only good as a coaster. (One advantage of having IDE or EIDE drives on your computer for general storage and a SCSI CD-ROM burner and a SCSI hard drive dedicated for a workspace for creating CDs is that if you do something that uses the IDE hard disks, it won't usually have a significant effect on the action of the SCSI hard disk.) As a related preventive measure, before you burn a CD, you may want to defragment your hard disk so that the data comes in a smooth stream without requiring the hard disk to seek all over the disk platters getting the next block.

✦ **Make sure you have enough memory (RAM) free.** The more applications you have open, the less memory there is to go around. Furthermore, many Windows applications don't always do a good job of cleaning up after themselves when they close. At the very least, you should have most other applications closed when you're burning a CD so the maximum RAM is available. You might want to consider rebooting your computer before burning a CD so that it's running as cleanly as possible.

This chapter has shown you how to play your MP3 files on your stereo and how to record MP3 files to cassettes, DAT tapes, and CDs. It has also introduced you to several kinds of CD-ROM mastering software and shown you how to solve some of the most common problems related to burning CDs. In the next chapter, you'll see how to edit and enhance your files in a variety of ways to get the best possible sound quality.

Editing and Enhancing MP3 Files

I n the preceding chapter, you saw how to play your MP3 files through your sound system and how to record your own audio CDs. In this chapter, you'll see how to edit and enhance your files in a variety of ways to get the best possible sound quality.

There are several stages where you can improve the quality of the sounds you turn into MP3 files or output to cassettes or CDs:

+ By filtering or using Dolby on tapes or vinyl.
+ When the audio or MP3 files are turned into WAV files in the transition stage.
+ When the MP3 files have been created.

This chapter will show you how to edit your audio at each of these stages.

BASIC AUDIO CONCEPTS

Before you begin working on files, there are some audio concepts that you should know about.

The *signal* is the song, music, or other sound recorded on the track. *Noise* is anything that obscures the signal: pops, clicks, static, hiss, rumble (low-frequency noise sometimes caused by turntables), and hum (usually a 50 Hz or 60 Hz hum or related harmonic caused by an improperly shielded signal path, a power supply, or a motor leaking current into the audio section of the amplifier). Noise can also be distortion incidental to the digital/analog and analog/digital conversion process.

Attenuation is the reduction of the level of a signal, either total or partial (such as attenuation of all frequencies above 12 kHz). Attenuation may also have preset equalization levels; for example, you might set the attenuation for a general noise reduction control and have the program attenuate the high-end frequencies, something like setting the equalization levels for 10 kHz and above down a couple of notches. Similarly, you might attenuate rumble by attenuating the lowest parts of the signal, so that you suppress the low frequency noise. You can frequently set an attenuation *threshold* as well, so that sound above a certain level is suppressed.

The *decibel* is a unit of sound. Decibels are logarithmic rather than additive. Someone whispering quietly is about 30–35 dB; a loud whisper is 35–40 dB. Normal conversation will range from 65–70 dB. A symphony orchestra is around 65–110 dB, except for the climaxes, which probably go to 115 dB. Foghorns and rock concerts are 115–130 dB. (Anything above 130 dB will cause immediate pain.) A jet plane generates 135–175 dB of noise, so don't stand next to the engines. As you might expect, the farther away you are from the noise, the more the dB drops off.

As you've seen, when you're referring to whole songs (whether MP3 files, WAV files, or original cuts from cassettes, vinyl, or CDs), they're frequently referred to as *tracks*. This is decades-old industry jargon from radio DJs and the music business in general. However, when you're editing music, a *track* is actually an individual track of information, such as the bass guitar, vocals, or rhythm. Multiple tracks are combined in a *mix* to create the finished song that you hear on a CD or an album. The more tracks of information you have to work with, the more detailed you can be about the quality and level of the sound of each element as it appears in the finished product. WAV file editing software typically offers a minimum of 8 tracks of information per stereo channel, but it's not uncommon to see up to 32 tracks per stereo channel in some of the higher-end editing software. You can use a *mixer* to create several different versions of the same song depending on the volumes, tempos, and effects you choose in the mix. The individual tracks are combined into a mix that usually has only two tracks (stereo). Making different versions of a song using the same tracks is known as a *remix*.

FILTERING YOUR TAPES AND VINYL

The first (and usually the best) place to edit the sound quality is at the source. Tracks ripped from CDs will sound pretty clean, but tracks ripped from tapes or vinyl can have all sorts of distortion and noise.

Furthermore, if you're ripping from vinyl, you may have extra noise from scratches or wear on the records.

If you're ripping from tapes, you should use Dolby to filter the tape. If you are using a preamp with the tape or the turntable, you may also have filtering options that you can use to clean up some of the noise as well. Even so, you may not be able to clean up every pop or hiss on the tape.

There are a number of hardware options for editing and enhancing the sound from your cassettes and vinyl, including preamps, equalizing units, filters, and noise reduction units.

EDITING WAV FILES

Once a file has been ripped from cassette or vinyl into a WAV file, you have a wide range of software tools for filtering, editing, and enhancing the sound before you encode it into an MP3 file. The programs listed in this section range from simple filtering programs to complete WAV-editing suites. Many of them do complex audio manipulation as well as WAV editing. Feel free to try them out, but don't feel like you have to go for the biggest and most powerful; a simple noise-filtering program might be all you need to create the sound quality you're after. You probably won't need to edit WAV files created directly from CDs to improve the sound quality, but it's possible that you may want to add some audio effects.

SPIN DOCTOR

One of the first programs you should look at is Adaptec's Spin Doctor, which is part of Easy CD Creator Deluxe (featured in Chapter 5, "Recording from Your Computer to Your Audio System.") Spin Doctor's primary focus is taking files from a variety of sources—tapes, vinyl, radio, CD-ROM drives, WAV files—and then outputting them directly to audio CDs. You can also save the files in WAV file format, making Spin Doctor a good tool for editing WAV files prior to ripping them into MP3 format. Follow this procedure to do basic file cleaning and filtering using Spin Doctor:

1. When you start Spin Doctor, you see a simple, easy-to-use screen (shown in Figure 6.1).
2. Click the "1" to select the source for the music. When you've selected where you want the files to come from, click the "2" to select the destination of the music. You can set filtering options by selecting Properties from the Options menu. The filtering options allow you to preview

the sound by playing a selected track and then adjusting the slider controls shown in Figure 6.2.

Besides the cleaning options shown in Figure 6.2, Spin Doctor also has *morphing* options, which let you add effects like reverb to a file. There is also track splitting, an exceptionally handy feature: whenever silence is detected (like between cuts on a record or cassette), the track splitter automatically breaks the input into separate tracks for you.

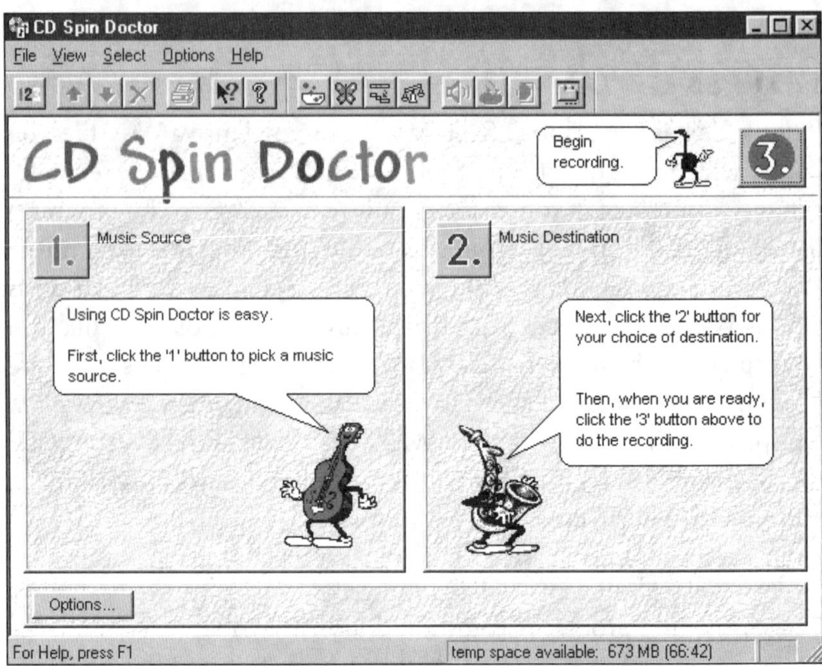

FIGURE 6.1: The Adaptec Spin Doctor main screen.

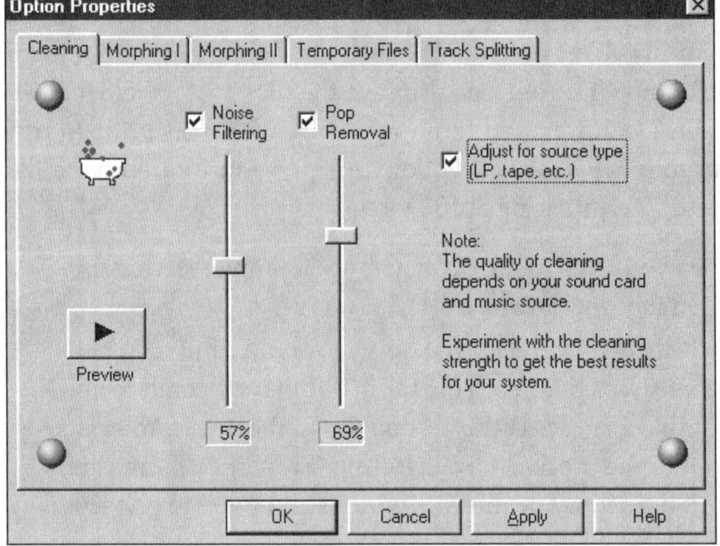

FIGURE 6.2: The Cleaning folder on the Option Properties screen.

It's also worth noting that you can select WAV files as the source, add cleaning and morphing options, and then output WAV files again. You could also output directly to CD from WAV files or even from cassette or vinyl, although it's probably a good idea to go from cassette or vinyl to WAV files first to give you a chance to experiment with the quality of the sound and to prevent problems with the tape jamming or the record getting bumped.

3. When you are satisfied with your entries, click OK. You'll need to turn on Cleaning by selecting Clean Tracks from the Options menu. Figure 6.3 shows the Spin Doctor screen right before filtering a group of WAV files. Note the small "sink" icon at the bottom of the screen, showing that the cleaning option is turned on.

4. Click the Record to disk icon to start the conversion. Spin Doctor displays a conversion screen with some fun animation, as shown in Figure 6.4. (You can stop the animation if you want by clicking Freeze the animation.)

5. When the conversion is completed, you can play the files by double-clicking them in the destination window. (You can do a before-and-after comparison to hear the changes in the file.) You can then rip them into MP3 files, output them to tape or CD directly from Spin Doctor, or play them, again using Spin Doctor if you like.

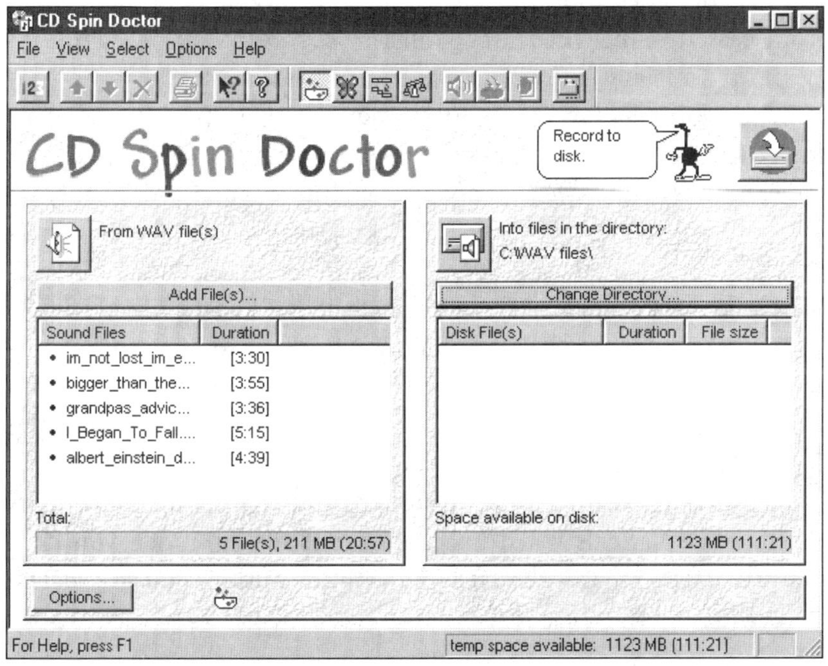

FIGURE 6.3:
The Adaptec Spin Doctor main screen ready to filter a group of WAV files.

FIGURE 6.4: Converting files in Spin Doctor.

Spin Doctor is a really delightful product that is easy to use for someone who wants to do basic filtering and file manipulation. It's available as part of the Easy CD Creator Deluxe package, available for $99 from Adaptec (*http://www.adaptec.com*).

RAY GUN

Ray Gun is a snappy little shareware product from Arboretum Systems (*http://www.arboretum.com*) that runs on Windows and Macintosh. It's designed to improve the sound quality of WAV files ripped from cassettes and vinyl. Ray Gun lets you edit your WAV files to clean up noise and pops and to set your recording levels.

When you start Ray Gun, you see the Ray Gun main screen, shown in Figure 6.5.

Using Ray Gun is very simple. You tell it to open a WAV file, set your options, and play the file by clicking Play to see what it sounds like. (Figure 6.6 shows the Ray Gun main screen playing a file with the Noise Reduction and Pop filters selected.)

When you are satisfied with the way the track sounds, click Apply to save the processed file as a WAV file. If you want to digitize audio from vinyl or cassettes, click Record. The Recording screen (shown in Figure 6.7) appears.

You can specify the format you'd like for the sampling rate and the number of channels you'd like the output file in. When you click Start, Ray Gun records the WAV file with the options you've selected. It's that simple!

TIP

As with any program that edits WAV files, be sure that you have enough disk space.

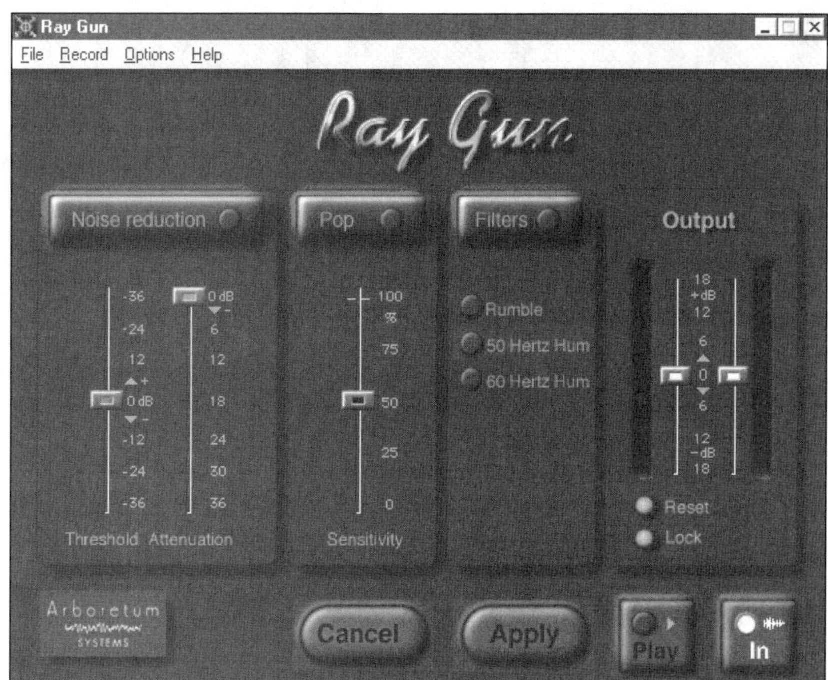

FIGURE 6.5:
The Ray Gun main screen.

FIGURE 6.6:
The Ray Gun main screen when playing a WAV file.

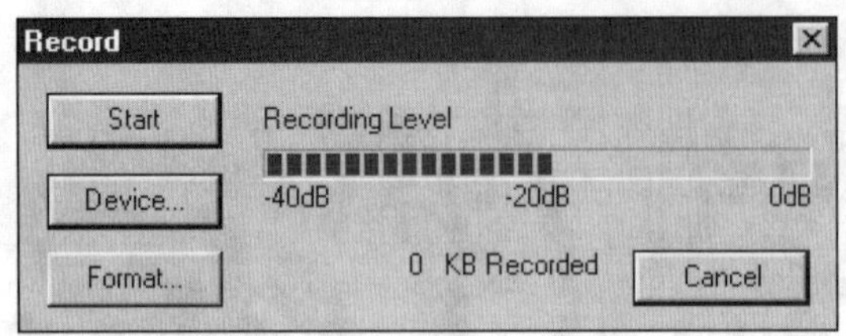

You can use Ray Gun to pull sounds directly from other sources in your computer, like your sound card. Ray Gun can also be used as a plug-in product for other programs that support the Windows DirectX format, such as Cool Edit 96, Sound Forge, WaveLab, and Cakewalk.

Ray Gun is a good basic product for editing WAV files. It's easy to use and easy to understand. Ray Gun costs $99, for which you get all Windows and Macintosh versions.

WaveLab

WaveLab from Steinberg Soft und Hardware GmbH (*http://www. steinberg.net*) is a solid program designed to edit WAV and other files and create audio CDs from them. As such, it's perfectly suited for many MP3 enthusiasts. Figure 6.8 shows the WaveLab main screen with a sample WAV file loaded.

As you can see in Figure 6.8, each channel is displayed separately. There are two displays: the lower shows the WAV file information blocked out in 2-second units (the lower display represents 10 seconds of the WAV file) while the upper display shows the WAV file information in 20-second units.

To add an effect such as normalizing, fade-in, or fade-out, you start by highlighting the section of the wave file you want to edit. (You can play the highlighted section using the buttons on the Transport menu to make sure you've highlighted the desired segment of the WAV file.) You then select the option you'd like to apply. Figure 6.9 shows a fade-in about to be applied to the first 6 seconds of the WAV file.

WaveLab has a wide variety of editing features, including a 100-voice chorus and a 16-voice harmonizer. You can cut, copy, and paste, loop, filter, normalize, shift the pitch, add reverb, delay, and do many other edits and enhancements. In addition, there are a large number of plug-ins for adding features. Figure 6.10 shows the standard Wave-Lab equalizer with some adjustments to the default settings.

WaveLab also comes with CD-ROM premastering software so you can create WAV files from your MP3 files, edit them, and then create an audio CD with them.

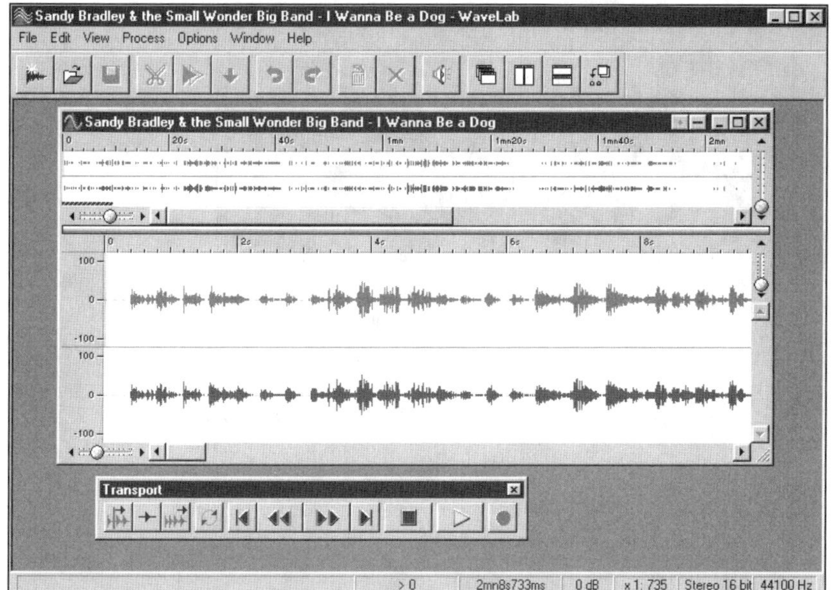

FIGURE 6.8:
The WaveLab main screen.

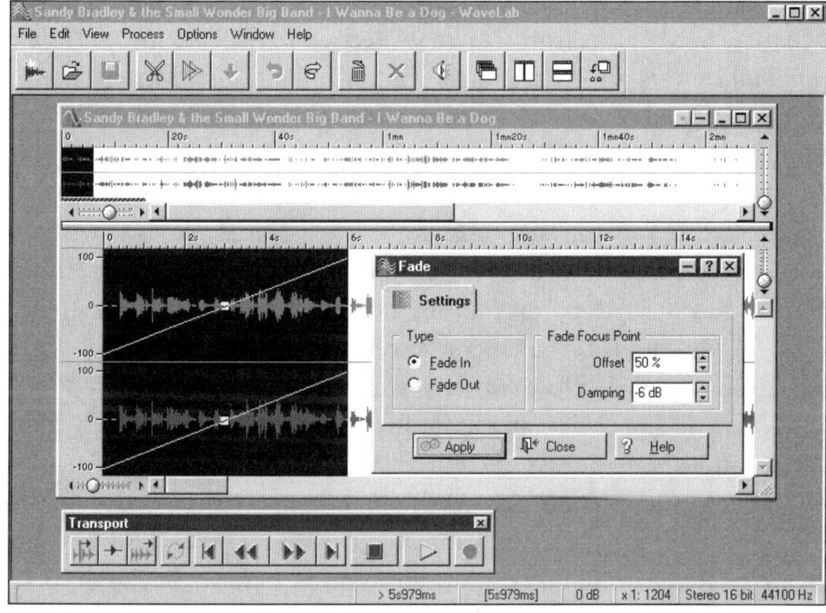

FIGURE 6.9:
Applying a fade-in to the WAV file in WaveLab.

WaveLab is a great program for basic WAV file editing. It does everything you're likely to want. There are plug-ins to enhance the feature set as well. A "lite" version of WaveLab ships with Mixman Studio Pro so you can do editing of your WAV files before you mix them. (Mixman Studio Pro is described later in this chapter.) The professional (retail) version of WaveLab costs $499.

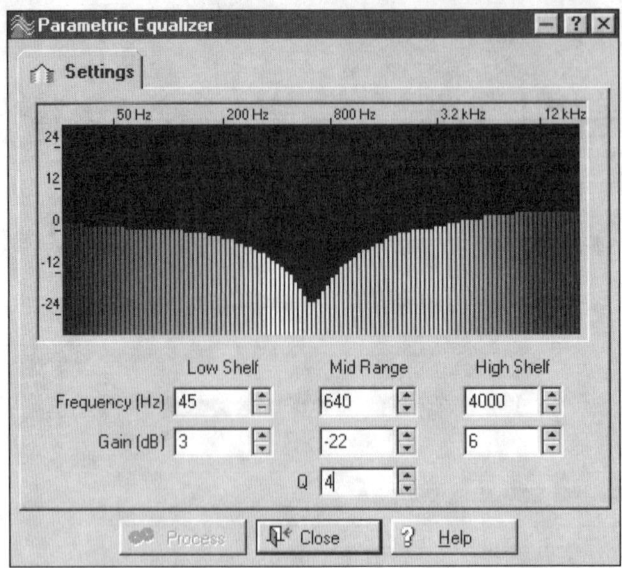

MIXMAN STUDIO PRO

Mixman Studio Pro from Mixman Technologies, Inc., (*http://www. mixman.com*) is a software mixer for your audio files. Mixers let you blend WAV and other audio files into a single piece of music. Mixman Studio Pro is set up along the lines of a classic recording studio: you are creating a *mix*, a collection of music and sounds on up to 16 different tracks. You can add, change, or delete tracks as you wish to achieve the perfect blend. For example, you can use Mixman Studio Pro to add a rhythm track to an existing WAV file for additional oomph. You could also enhance a voice-only recording by adding quiet background music before converting the resulting WAV file to MP3.

When you start Mixman Studio Pro, the Mixman Studio Pro main screen appears, as shown in Figure 6.11.

To enter tracks in a mix, start the Remixing Studio by clicking the dual turntable image in the upper left of the Mixman Studio Pro main screen. The Remixing Studio appears (shown in Figure 6.12 with a sample mix file loaded).

You add track information by clicking on the spokes of the turntables and opening a WAV file or one of the many track files included with Mixman Studio Pro for such things as bass beats, drums, guitar, background vocals, and so on. You can experiment playing the mix at any time, including various tracks to see what the overall sound is like. You can then save the mix and edit it more closely in the Editing Studio screen, shown in Figure 6.13.

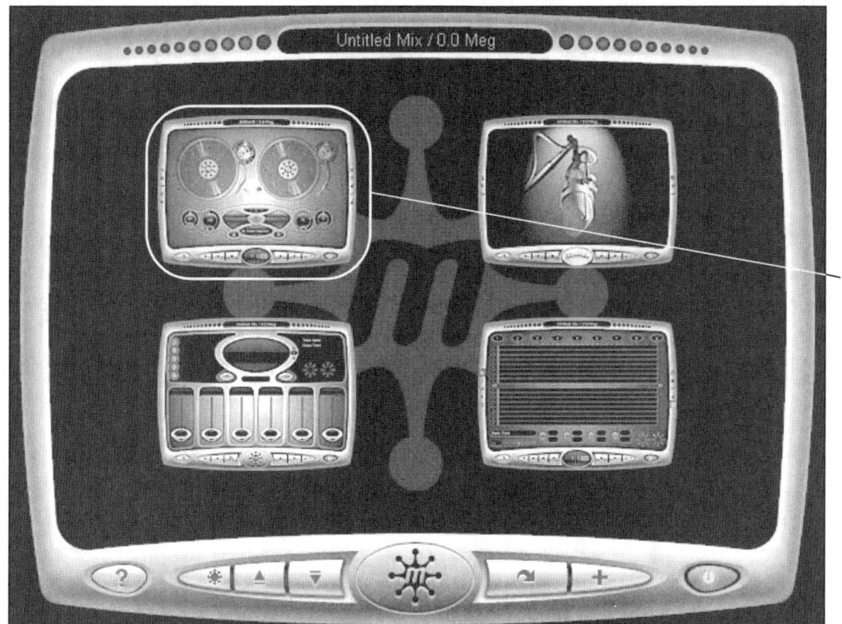

FIGURE 6.11:
The Mixman Studio Pro main screen.

Remixing Studio icon

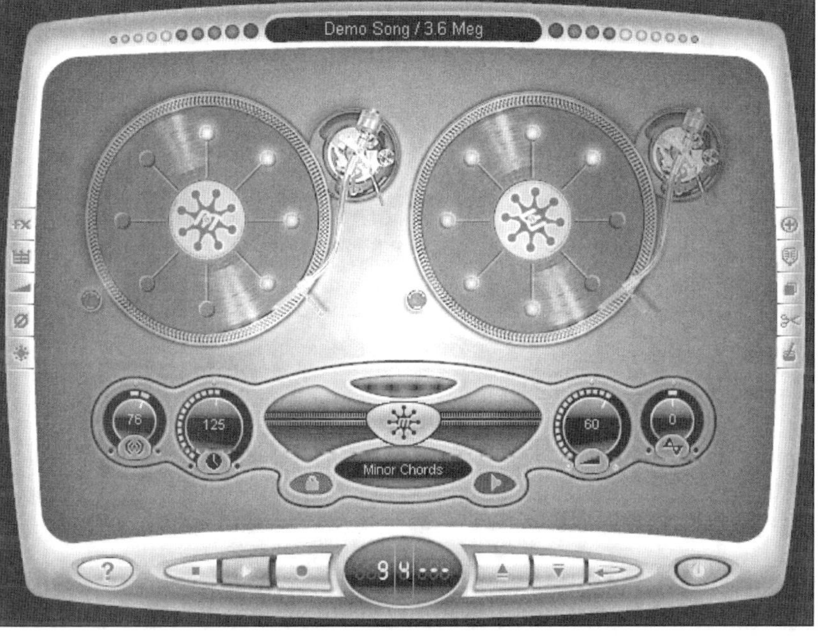

FIGURE 6.12:
The Mixman Studio Pro Remixing Studio screen.

In the Editing Studio, you can adjust the levels for each of the tracks, change the tempo and volume, and fine-tune the blend of component tracks. You can also add special effects to a specific track using the FX Studio screen, shown in Figure 6.14.

When you are satisfied with the way the mix sounds, you can record it to a WAV file and then convert it to an MP3 file using your favorite encoder.

Mixman Studio Pro provides a lot of value. It lets you customize your WAV files by adding and blending WAV files, sound effects, and other information. You can also use the Recording Studio in Mixman Studio Pro to add voice and other recordings. Mixman Studio Pro costs $89.95. There is also a Mixman Studio for $49.95 that has only the Recording Studio and the Remixing Studio, but does not have the FX Studio or the Editing Studio.

SuperSonic

SuperSonic from Morton Software (*http://www.gosupersonic.com*) is not just a WAV editor; it's a multimedia audio rack. SuperSonic has basic WAV editing features, but its real strengths lie in its ability to combine and play inputs from a wide variety of audio sources. The SuperSonic main screen appears in Figure 6.15.

As you can see in Figure 6.15, the default main screen shows the SuperSonic mixer and the first two screens (in this figure, the wave analyzer and spectrum analyzer), but you can show any combination of features you like. SuperSonic has the following components:

- ✦ mixer
- ✦ wave analyzer
- ✦ spectrum analyzer
- ✦ peak analyzer
- ✦ CD player
- ✦ MIDI player
- ✦ MOD player
- ✦ WAV player
- ✦ Favorites
- ✦ WAV editor
- ✦ DJ
- ✦ tuner

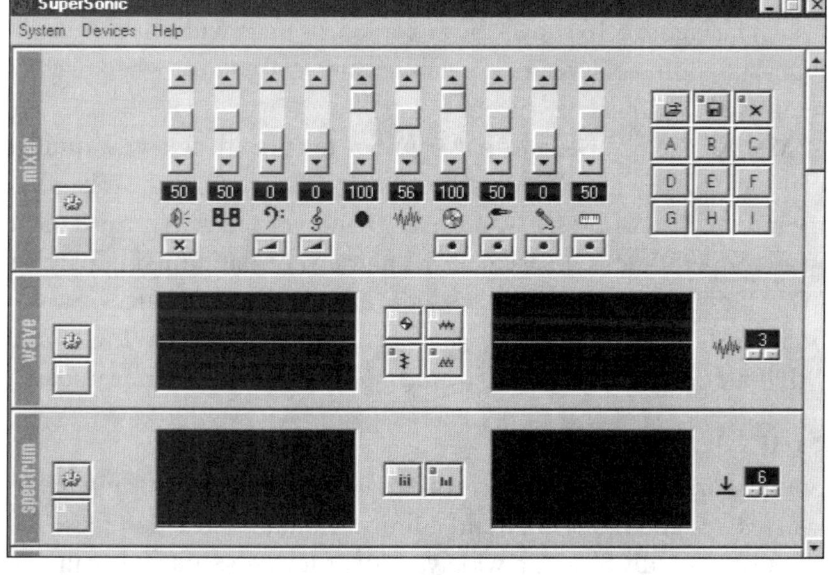

FIGURE 6.15:
The SuperSonic main screen.

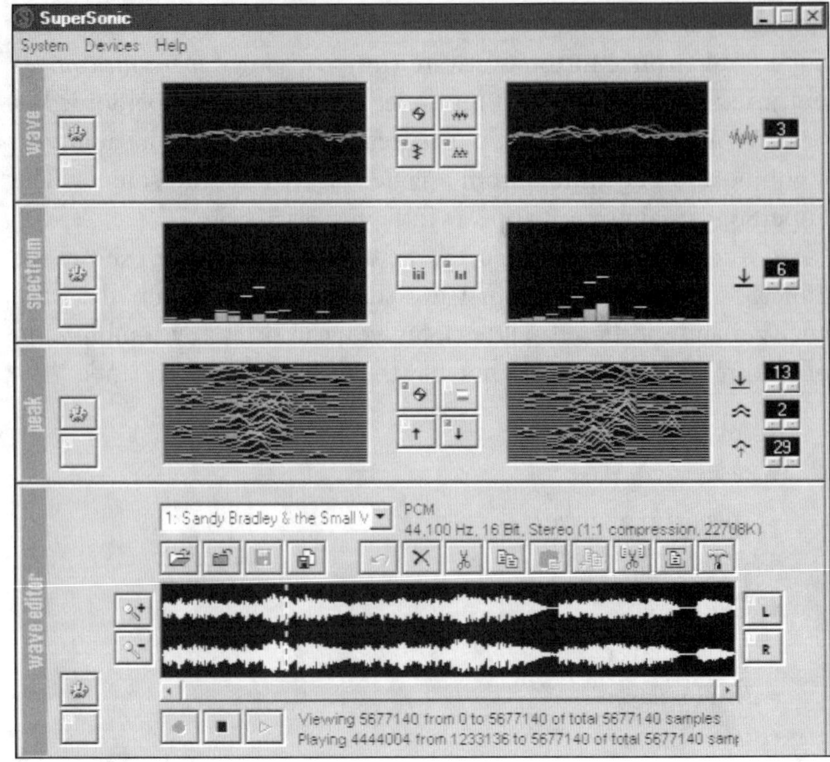

You're already familiar with most of these features. The DJ component lets you set up playlists. The tuner is for computers that have a radio tuner card installed.

The simplicity of the screen and component design is one of SuperSonic's charms. In fact, there is a fair amount of depth to the features available. Figure 6.16 shows the SuperSonic screen with the wave analyzer, spectrum analyzer, peak analyzer, and WAV editor when playing a sample WAV file.

Most of the components have options for presetting levels, tuning, playback, playlists, and so on. As you saw in Figure 6.15, the mixer has a whole keypad of presets you can configure for quick and convenient work. SuperSonic is a very handy program for basic mixing of your WAV files as well as playing tracks from a variety of sources. SuperSonic costs $39.95 to register, which gets you a CD of WAV, MOD, and MIDI files, and a collection of sound effects, as well as lifetime updates.

SOUND FORGE XP

Sound Forge XP from Sonic Foundry, Inc., (*http://www.soundforge.com*) is designed as a high-end editor for audio and video files. You can use it to edit files in a wide variety of formats: not only can you edit your WAV files, you can also use it to synchronize your audio

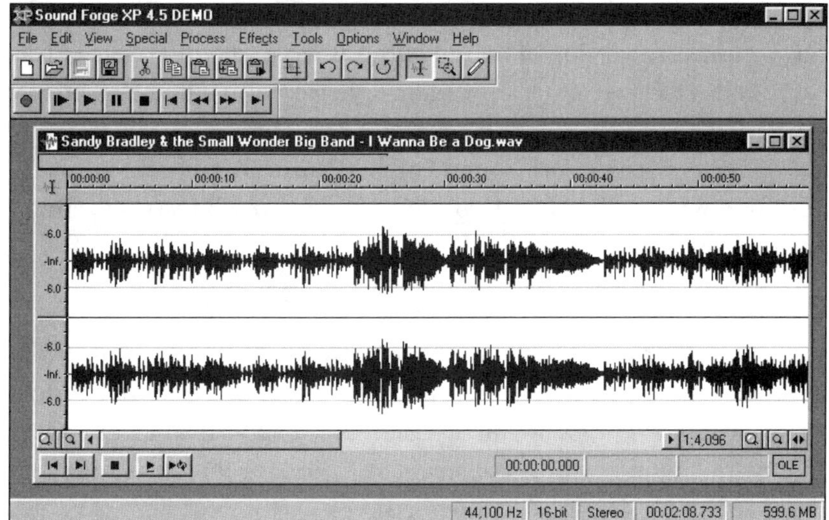

FIGURE 6.17:
The Sound Forge XP main screen.

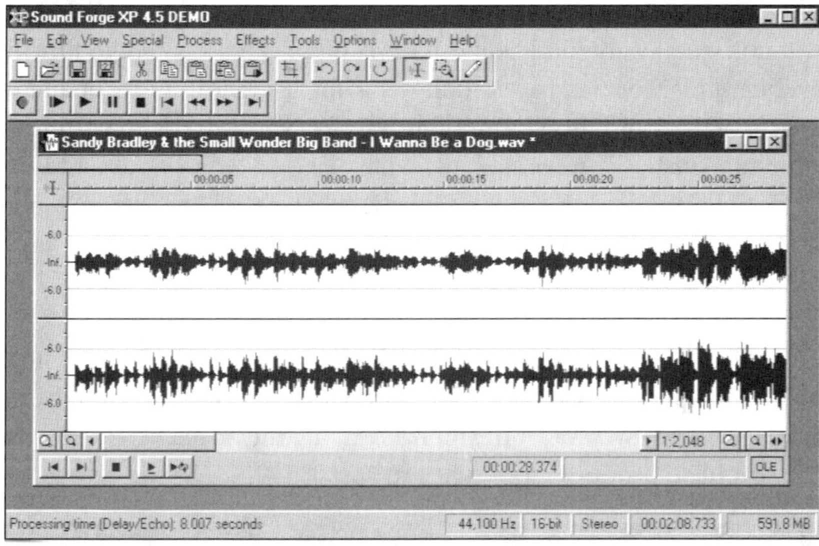

FIGURE 6.18:
Adding an effect in Sound Forge XP.

with AVI and other video files as well! Figure 6.17 shows the Sound Forge XP main screen with a sample WAV file loaded.

As with other WAV editors, both channels of information are displayed in the main screen when you load a WAV file. You can select a section of one or both channels and apply effects. Figure 6.18 shows a sample file after an echo has been added to the top channel. Note the difference in the waveforms between the upper and lower track displays.

Sound Forge XP has a fair range of effects available. Once you have registered the product, you can also download additional effects (the ExpressFX suite) from their web site; for example, you can expand your reverb settings to include a variety of preset room sizes and conditions.

If you're after something more comprehensive, you may want to try the professional version of Sound Forge. It has a very full range of features and effects. The full professional version also supports DirectX plug-ins, giving you the range of third-party DirectX products.

Demo versions of both Sound Forge XP and Sound Forge are available for download from the web site. Sound Forge XP costs $49; Sound Forge costs $499.

COOL EDIT 96

Cool Edit 96 from Syntrillium (*http://www.syntrillium.com*) is a very approachable WAV file editor. It's one of the most popular WAV editors available today. The Cool Edit 96 main screen appears in Figure 6.19.

One of the interesting features that Cool Edit 96 has is the spectrum analyzer (shown in Figure 6.20).

Cool Edit Pro is the upscale version of Cool Edit 96. It's arguably the most feature-rich program for WAV editing and mixing available. It will do virtually anything you can think of when editing audio files in every popular format. In addition to having a larger number of audio effects than Cool Edit 96, Cool Edit Pro lets you work with 64 tracks simultaneously. Figure 6.21 shows a file being edited in Cool Edit Pro.

Cool Edit Pro supports the DirectX plug-ins, so you can mix and match programs. For example, if you like Ray Gun (which uses DirectX also), you can use Ray Gun to do filtering from within Cool Edit Pro. This gives you the best of both worlds!

Cool Edit 96 costs $50. You can download the shareware version and then register it. Cool Edit Pro is available in a demo version from the Syntrillium web site, but you have to buy the boxed version to get the complete product. Cool Edit Pro costs $399.

FIGURE 6.19:
The Cool Edit 96 main screen.

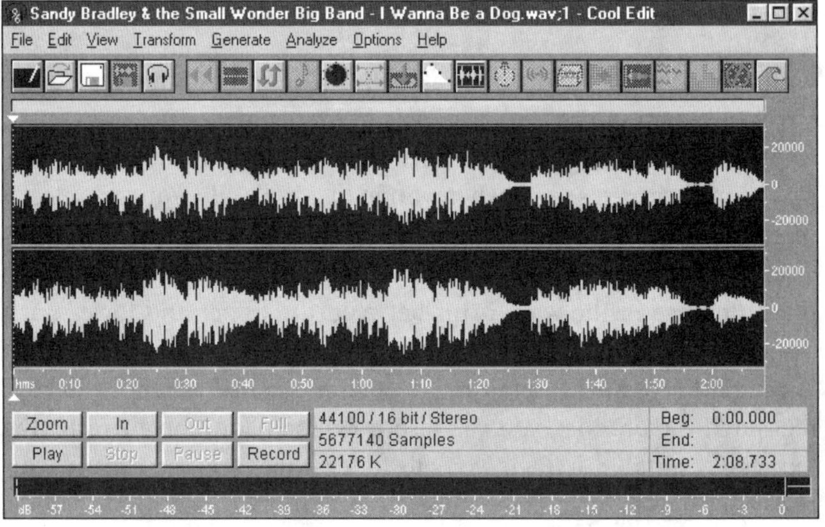

FIGURE 6.20:
The Cool Edit 96 Spectrum Analyzer screen.

FIGURE 6.21:
WAV file being edited in Cool Edit Pro.

OTHER PROGRAMS

In addition to the programs listed in this section, there are many other WAV editors and mixers available. Check the MP3 web sites for information on WAV editors and mixers. Many MP3 sites also have lists of straight audio links—be sure to look for some of those as well.

Almost all the programs mentioned here are available in shareware or demo versions from the companies' web sites. If you're interested in a few of these programs, be sure to try them all out. As with MP3 players and utilities, there's no reason why you can't have several WAV-editing programs on your computer.

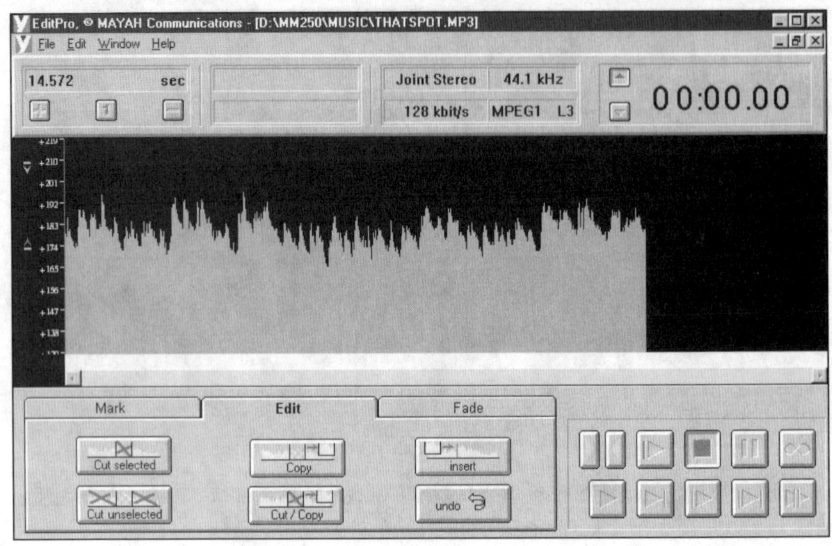

EDITING MP3 FILES

There are only a few programs for editing MP3 files. MP3 files are a compressed format (as opposed to WAV files), making them hard to edit well. You will be able to do a better job editing the WAV files before they are encoded as MP3 files, as well as having editing programs that offer a much wider range of features and effects.

EDITPRO

EditPro from MAYAH Communications (*http://www.mayah.com*) is a basic MP3 file editor. You can use this to do basic edits, including cutting, copying, and pasting file sections, and adding fade-ins and fadeouts. Figure 6.22 shows EditPro with a sample file loaded for editing.

As you can see from Figure 6.22, the editing capabilities are substantially limited compared to the features available in WAV editors such as Cool Edit 96 and Sound Forge. However, you can apply fades as well as trim and paste sounds. EditPro costs €520. There is also a smaller version called RealEdit, which will do single-window MP3 editing, for €60.

OTHER UTILITIES

In addition to the programs already mentioned in this chapter, there are a couple of utility programs that you should know about.

MP3 TO EXE

MP3 to EXE from Oliver Buschjost (*http://software.webset.de/buschjost/ mp3eng.htm*) is a very handy utility for sharing MP3 files with friends to show them what all of this is about without requiring them to

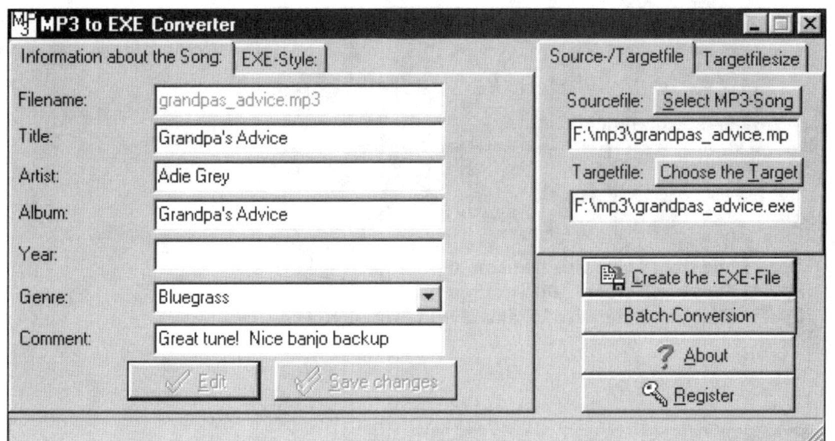

FIGURE 6.23:
The MP3 to EXE
Converter screen.

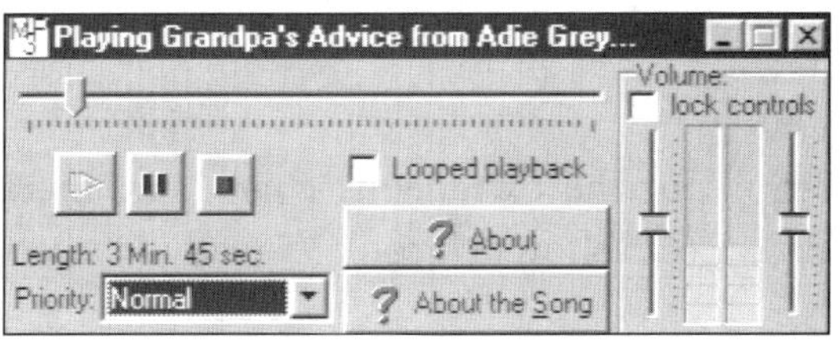

FIGURE 6.24:
The MP3 to EXE
Player screen.

download MusicMatch Jukebox or another player and install it on their system. When you run MP3 to EXE, it attaches a simple MP3 player to the MP3 file you've selected and then stores the whole thing as an EXE file. You can then e-mail this file to a friend and say "Double-click this file and listen!" Figure 6.23 shows the MP3 to EXE Converter screen with information for a sample MP3 file.

When you are satisfied with your entries, click Create the EXE File. When you click the resulting EXE file, you see the MP3 to EXE Player screen, as shown in Figure 6.24.

You're allowed to create as many self-playing MP3 files as you like with the program, but you're on your honor to register MP3 to EXE for $15 before you distribute any of them. It's clearly worth it.

UNCOOK 95

Uncook 95 is freeware by John Tesoriero (*http://www.free-music.com/ uncook95.htm*). It's a very handy utility for solving a common problem when downloading files from newsgroups. Some newsgroup servers send binary information (such as MP3 and WAV files) with extra linefeeds added to the file. When the newsreader decodes this information and turns it back into an MP3 file, the extra linefeeds embedded in the file cause the resulting file to sound choppy and squeaky. (There are example files at the *free-music.com* web site so you know what you're listening for.) Uncook 95 goes through the files and

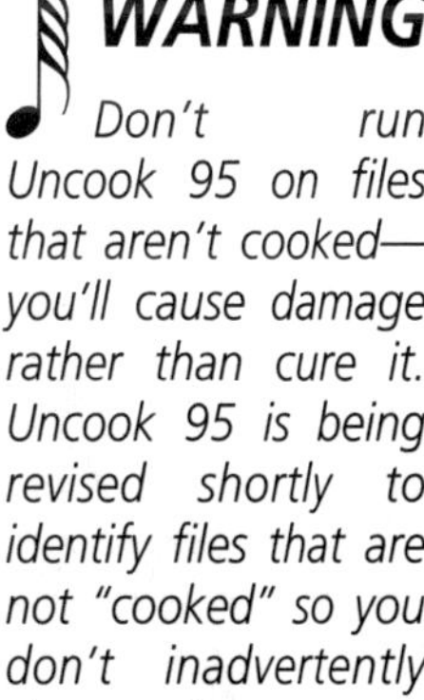

Don't run Uncook 95 on files that aren't cooked—you'll cause damage rather than cure it. Uncook 95 is being revised shortly to identify files that are not "cooked" so you don't inadvertently damage them.

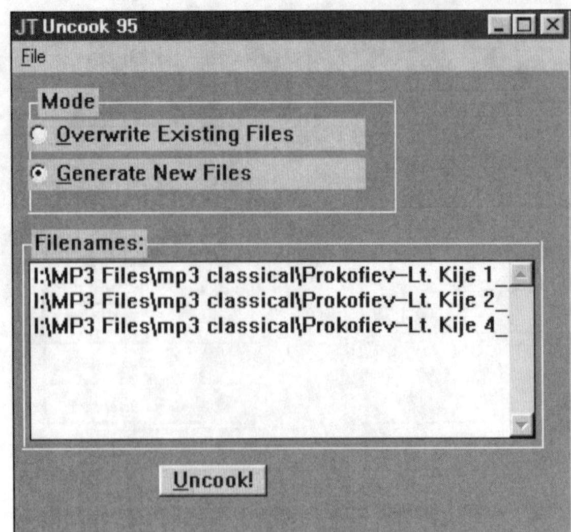

FIGURE 6.25:
The Uncook 95 main screen.

strips out the extraneous characters, thereby "uncooking" the file. Figure 6.25 shows Uncook 95 ready to uncook a selection of files.

This chapter has shown you how to edit and enhance your files in a variety of ways to produce the best possible sound quality. In the next chapter, you'll learn about other popular programs, including players, rippers, encoders, and other utilities to make working with MP3 files easier and more fun. You'll also be introduced to software for the Macintosh so you can still play and rip MP3 files if you're using a Mac.

Using Other Software

I n the last chapter, you saw how to use various programs to edit and enhance your MP3 files. In this chapter, you're going to see some of the other popular software options out there, including players, rippers, encoders, and other utilities to make working with MP3 files easier and more fun. You'll also be introduced to software for the Macintosh so you can still play and rip MP3 files if you're using a Mac.

STAND-ALONE MP3 PLAYERS

The largest category of MP3 software is players for MP3 files. There are over 100 MP3 players of all kinds just for Windows. Almost all of these work under Windows 95 and Windows 98. A large percentage of these work under Windows NT as well. One of the best things about these players is that you can use them as part of MusicMatch Jukebox if you like: as you read in Chapter 1, "Getting Started," you can use the Winamp player and many other MP3 players to supplant the standard MusicMatch Jukebox player.

WINAMP

Nullsoft's Winamp is the most popular stand-alone MP3 player, and one of the most popular MP3 products overall. Winamp is a player that works under Windows 95, Windows 98, and Windows NT. You can play files in many formats with it, including MP3, CD-DA, MP2, WAV, MIDI, and a host of other formats as well. Figure 7.1 shows the Winamp main screen.

As with most MP3 players, Winamp has a player window and a playlist window. Unlike many other MP3 players, the features in Winamp are very modular; if you want, you can stack them on your screen in any order, as shown in Figure 7.2.

FIGURE 7.1:
The Winamp
main screen

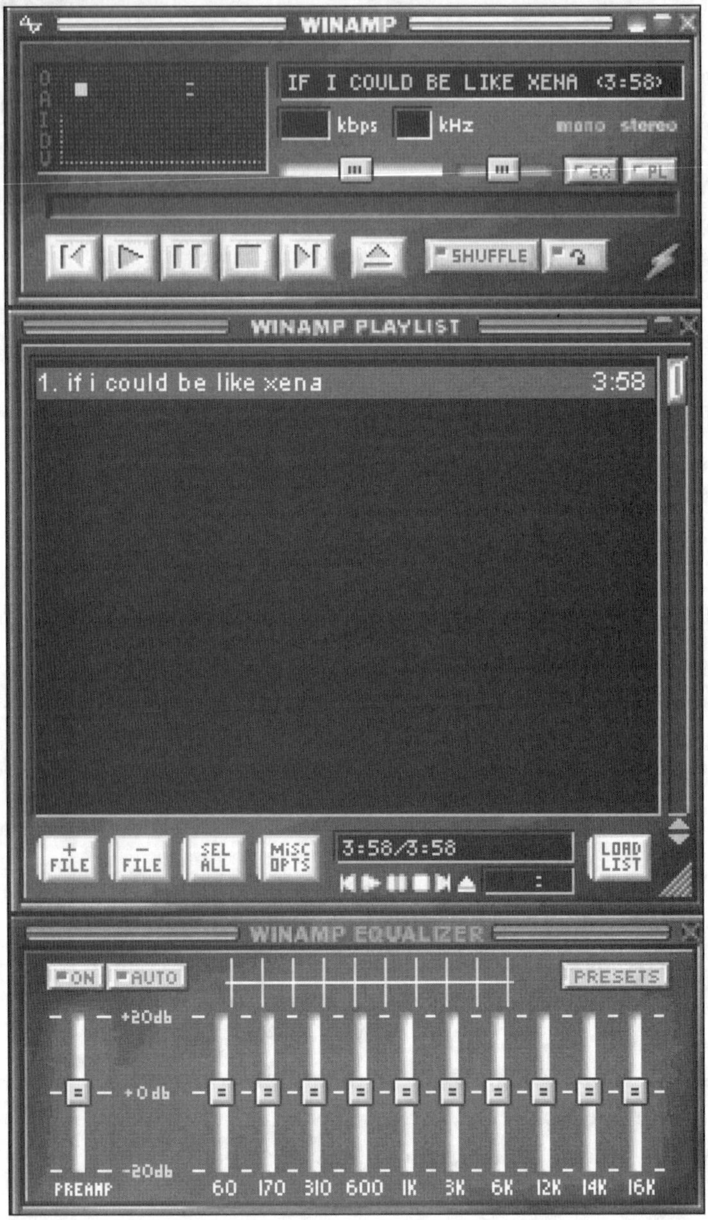

FIGURE 7.2:
The Winamp main
screen stacked
vertically.

You can move the modules around as you wish. Whenever you line up edges of two modules, they "stick" so that you can grab the title bar of the Winamp player window and move everything around as a unit.

The Winamp player window is substantially different from the one in MusicMatch Jukebox. Take a look at the player window shown in Figure 7.3.

As you can see, the command buttons are reasonably self-explanatory, using the same "cassette deck" look and feel that MusicMatch Jukebox does (as do most other MP3 players, for that matter). The volume control and the balance feature are accessed with the two small slider controls in the center of the window. The Winamp menu is accessed by clicking on the small character in the upper left corner of the window. Clicking the lightning bolt icon in the lower right of the window displays the Winamp help screens shown in Figure 7.4

FIGURE 7.3:
The Winamp player window.

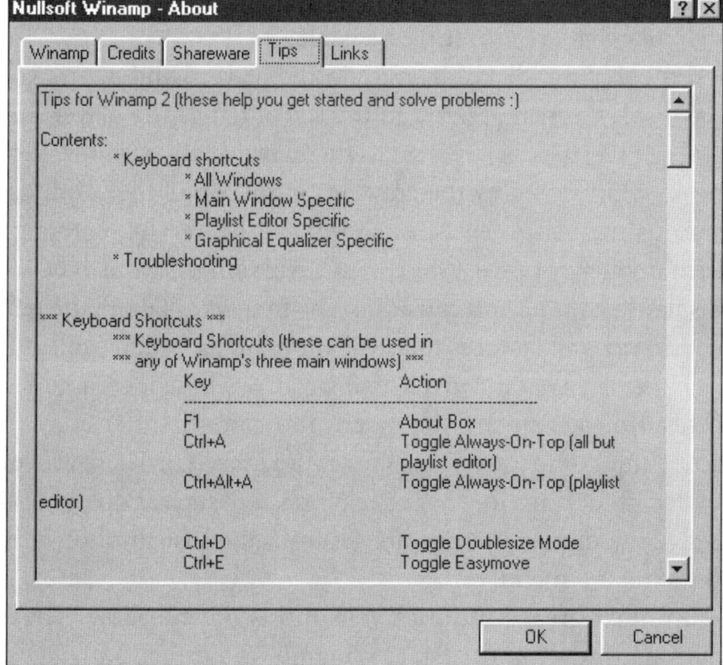

FIGURE 7.4:
The Winamp help screen.

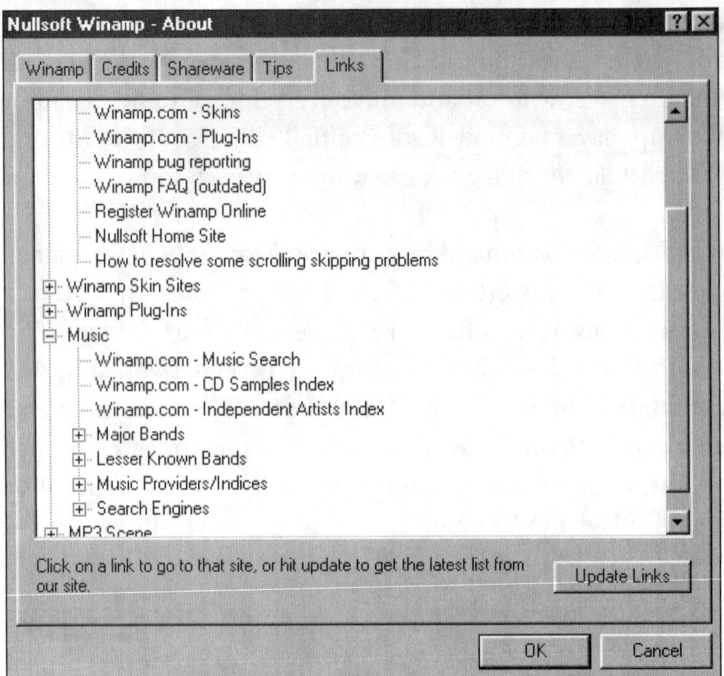

(which are only tips in the current version; full online documentation is slated for a future release).

One really helpful feature in the help screens is a collection of hot links to web sites. Even better, this list is not hard-coded in the file; when you first load Winamp, you click Update Links and get the latest collection of links that you can access. Figure 7.5 shows some of the links that are currently available.

Probably the slickest feature in the player window in Figure 7.3 is the display, which appears to the upper left of the player window. As you can see, the display is set to frequency analyzer mode, showing the peaks, represented by the gray bars at the top of the columns, and the various frequency levels, as shown by the varying colors of bars in each frequency range. (Stereo buffs will recognize this type of analyzer display instantly.) You can adjust the frequency falloff, the refresh rate, and so on—all features that will appeal to any audiophile.

However, what if you'd like to see an oscilloscope trace of the music instead of a frequency analyzer? You can set the display to show a scope trace of the music, as shown in Figure 7.6. There are several sets of display options for the scope mode, too, such as dot, line, and solid. All of the display options are set from the Visualization submenu of the Winamp menu.

Another great feature in Winamp is the equalizer. The equalizer appears when you first start Winamp. You can also toggle the equal-

FIGURE 7.6:
The Winamp player window showing a scope trace.

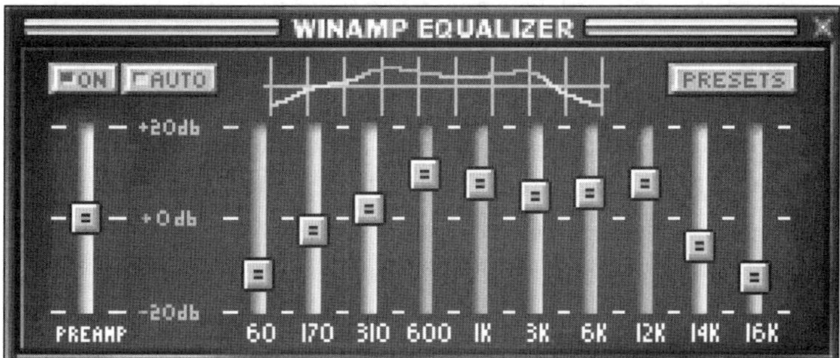

FIGURE 7.7:
The equalizer window.

izer screen by clicking EQ on the player window. The equalizer window appears in Figure 7.7.

The equalizer lets you filter specific frequency ranges for MP3 files, just like the equalizer on your stereo. You can change the settings by moving the slider bars for the frequency range. As you do so, the colors for the adjustment will go from dark green (the lowest setting) to bright red (the highest setting). In addition, the wave form above the sliders will change to reflect the settings. You can create preset equalization settings for specific types of music and load them depending on what you're playing and how you want it to sound.

You can also set the preamp using the preamp slider. The preamp sets the level of the music before it is amplified, just like the preamp on a stereo. The preamp is particularly helpful if you have an MP3 file that was recorded at too low or too high a level. By setting the preamp level appropriately, you can partially counteract bad level settings on a recorded file. Using the preamp is the same as raising all the equalization levels by the same amount. As with the sliders on the equalizer, the preamp slider will change from dark green to bright red depending on the setting, and the horizontal bar will move up and down on the display as appropriate.

The playlist window has an extensive array of features, such as move forward or backward 5 seconds, jump to a specific file in the playlist, and jump to time, which lets you jump to a specific time in the selected

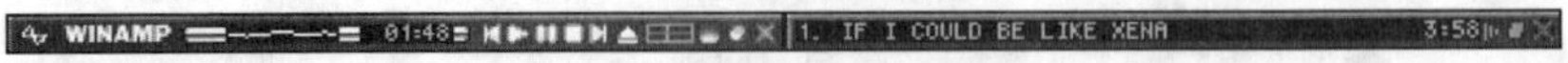
WINAMP
01:48
1. IF I COULD BE LIKE XENA
3:58

FIGURE 7.8: The Winamp player and playlist windows in window-shade mode.

track. There are many different display options for the various Winamp modules, one of which is that you can switch to "window-shade" mode, which displays just a single line of information. Figure 7.8 shows the player and the playlist windows in window-shade mode.

You can see all of the basic controls for the player (appearing as very small cassette buttons), a very small time display, and even a minimalist display window (set in Figure 7.8 to oscilloscope mode). The playlist window also shows the track being played. One other particularly nice feature worth noting is the Double Size selection on the Options menu, which doubles the size of the Winamp screens, making them easier to see and work with, particularly if you've got a small monitor.

Winamp works with an extensive array of plug-ins produced by Nullsoft and by many third-party providers. Plug-ins expand the capabilities of Winamp beyond the basic features. Some of the more popular plug-ins include Aquamarine 3 by Pablo Rewak, which displays a spectrum analyzer in 3D mode, StyxVis, a full-spectrum analyzer by Matthew Versluys, and Prince's 3D OpenGL Plugins by CJ Cliffe, a truly spectacular audio light display. An example of the StyxVis analyzer plug-in in operation appears in Figure 7.9.

The Winamp web site has over 100 plug-ins for you to choose from. Many of the major MP3 web sites also have a selection of plug-ins you can download. The selection of plug-ins includes enhancements to the analysis display options, input and output audio effects, screen savers, and light displays. There are even plug-ins that let you use a standard remote control to control the playback on Winamp—pretty cool, no?

NOTE

Creating a skin will take some extra effort on your part but it can be a lot of fun. The Winamp web site (http://www.winamp.com) *has instructions on how to create skins if you're feeling adventurous.*

What is undoubtedly Winamp's most popular feature, however, is the ability to use skins. *Skins* are a way for users to alter the way the program looks. You can design a new look for Winamp—high-tech, burnished aluminum, carved wood, icicles, the dashboard of a '57 Chevy—and display the features in whatever order you like. Figure 7.10 shows the Cold Fusion skin by Richie Jackson and Figure 7.11 shows the X-Stream Amp skin by Aaron Lehman. Note that these show the same information as was shown in Figures 7.1 and 7.3, but the skin has changed the look of the player.

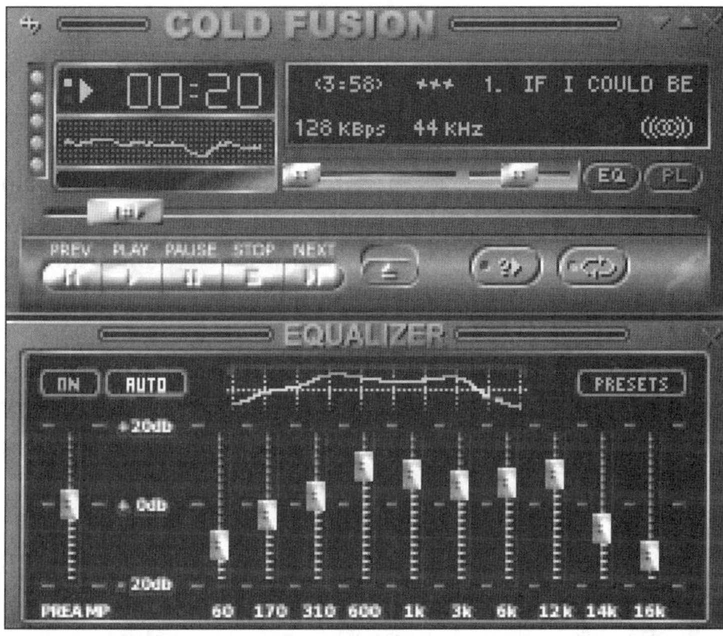

FIGURE 7.9:
The StyxVis
analyzer plug-in.

FIGURE 7.10:
The Cold Fusion
skin.

There are over 2500 skins available on the Winamp web site, sorted into categories such as General, Game, Car, Drink, Human, Movie/TV, and Ugly. (Be sure to look at Enrique's BroccoliAmp skin in the latter category.)

FIGURE 7.11: The X-Stream Amp skin.

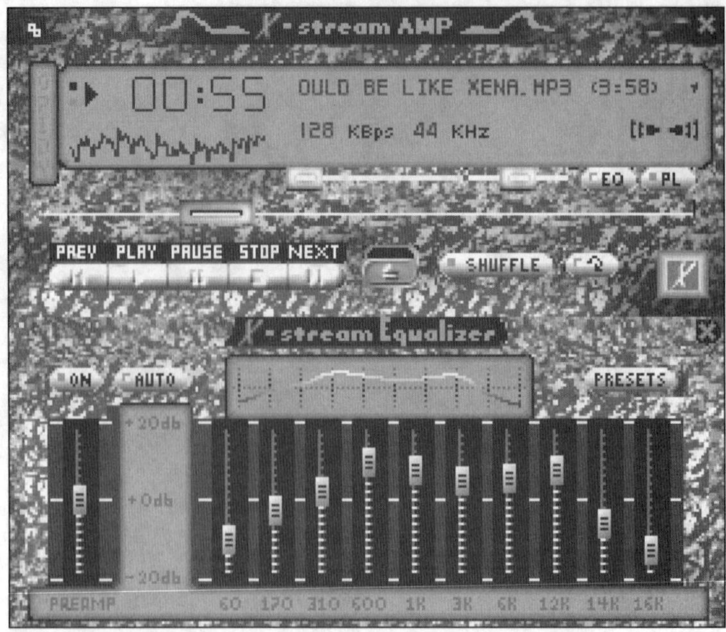

Like MusicMatch Jukebox, Winamp is shareware. You can download it and use it for 14 days for free, but if you want to continue using the software after the 14-day free-trial period, you must pay a $10 registration fee for personal use, or $25 for commercial use for each computer on which you're using the software. You can register by credit card at the Nullsoft web site (*http://winamp.com*) or may send cash, US bank check, or international money order, along with your e-mail address, to Nullsoft, Inc., 60 Palisades Drive North, Sedona, AZ 86336. Registration will not get you any additional features at this time, but you'll feel good for having done so.

SONIQUE

Another very popular stand-alone MP3 player is Sonique from Night 55, Inc. Sonique is an extremely attractive freeware MP3 player that plays MP3, CD-DA, MP2, WAV, and many other audio formats. Figure 7.12 shows the Sonique main screen.

As you can see, the screen is unusual and attractive. (Sonique would be worth looking at for the interface alone.) There are many usable features in an economic and easy-to-use format.

As with virtually all other Windows MP3 players, you can drag and drop files onto the player to play them, but you've seen in Chapter 2, "Creating and Using Playlists," how handy playlists are. To access the Sonique Playlist Editor, click the jump up once button (⬆) in the upper window. The Navigation Console appears, as shown in Figure 7.13.

FIGURE 7.12:
The Sonique
main screen.

FIGURE 7.13:
The Sonique Navigation
Console screen.

You can select any of the options displayed by clicking on them. When you click on Playlist Editor, the Playlist Editor screen (shown in Figure 7.14) appears.

The controls in the main part of the screen let you add and remove tracks to the playlist in standard fashion. Figure 7.15 shows a number of tracks loaded into the Playlist Editor.

To see information about the track that's playing, right-click in the window of the Navigation Console screen to display the options shown earlier in Figure 7.13, then click Enlarged Mode. Figure 7.16 shows a song playing.

The Enlarged Mode screen is a wonderful example of the way Sonique uses color. The track name appears at the bottom of the window. As the track plays, the color in the playlist and track progress displays changes from cool to hot colors. Sonique also displays information about the track being played—file format, sampling rate, and so on—on the right side of the window.

Like Winamp, Sonique has a frequency display and an oscilloscope. You can select displays by clicking the previous and next buttons in the display window. You can also display a simple track display that shows the number of tracks in the playlist and which track is playing. The display in Figure 7.16 is displaying the VU Sweep.

FIGURE 7.16:
The Sonique Enlarged Mode screen.

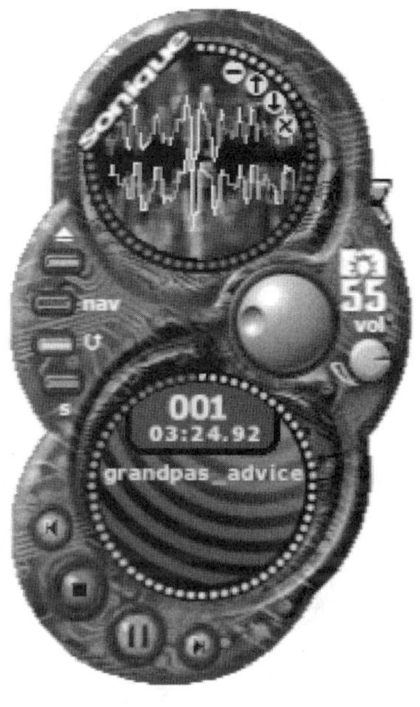

FIGURE 7.17:
The Sonique main screen with a track playing.

You can change the screen to look like the main screen by clicking the jump down once button (⊕) in the upper window. The main screen appears, as shown in Figure 7.17.

Take a look at the screen. The selected audio display appears in the upper window. (Figure 7.17 shows the track playing with the waveform display showing). You can change the type of display by moving the mouse pointer over the upper window. The display control will appear and you can select the type of display you like. The ring around the lower window shows the time played and time remaining on the track (as the track plays, the beads in the ring light up going from green to red). The volume and pitch controls are on the right.

You can change Sonique to a window-shade style display if you like by clicking the jump down once button ( ) in the upper window of the main screen. The Sonique screen changes to a window shade, as shown Figure 7.18.

The Sonique window-shade screen shows the minimum information necessary: the track number in the playlist and the elapsed time. The bars above and below the time and track display show the playlist progress and the track progress. The bars on either side next to the knobs actually flicker as if they were a display, but it's not going to do you much good for knowing what's happening.

When you move the mouse pointer over the bar, you also see the window-shade drop-down (also shown in Figure 7.18), which has the cassette buttons, the screen controls, and the track name. You can click the jump up once button ( ) to return to the main screen or the jump up twice button ( ) to return to the Navigation Console screen.

Sonique has an equalizer, accessible by clicking the audio enhancement control bar at the bottom of the Navigation Console screen. The equalizer controls drop down. You can see the controls in more detail, together with a visual display of the frequency levels, by clicking Audio Controls in the Navigation Console screen. An example of this is shown in Figure 7.19.

You can adjust the controls like any other equalizer by sliding the controls up and down. If you have the spline tension box checked, Sonique will move the surrounding controls to a lesser degree so that you get a smoother frequency line. As you adjust the controls, the display in the main part of the window will change accordingly. When you are satisfied with your settings, click the gray bar and it will pull up into the body of the screen.

In addition to the dazzling colors and screens in Sonique, most of the controls are animated. When you click something, you don't just get a new screen; the screen elements move on and off the screen. Buttons light up and change color when you press them. It isn't more useful, but it's very attractive and it's a welcome change to most interfaces. (You can, if you're feeling irritable, turn the animation off easily through the Setup Options window.)

TIP

If you don't like clicking buttons to switch between screen types, you can simply double-click on the gray border of any Sonique screen to switch to another display mode.

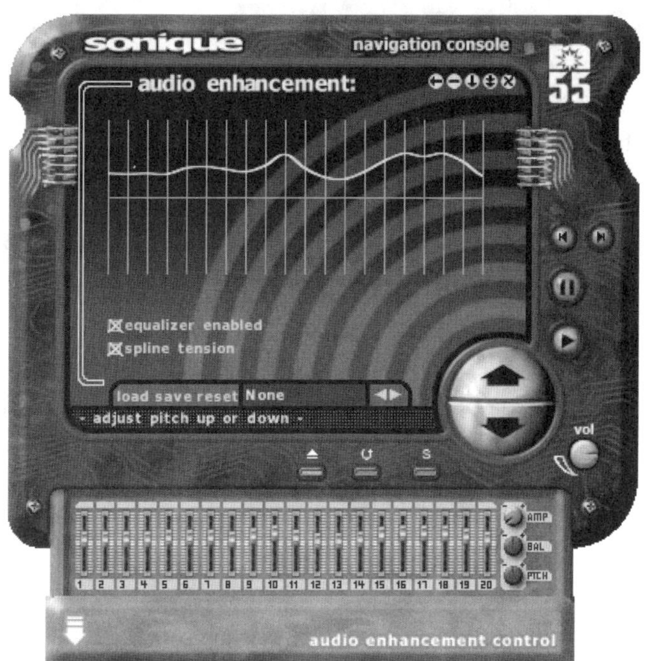

FIGURE 7.19:
The Sonique Audio Controls window.

FIGURE 7.20:
The Sonique Online Tools window.

Sonique also has a screen of hot links for accessing the latest news, music, and CD information (shown in Figure 7.20) that appears when you click Online Tools in the Navigation Console screen.

Sonique is just starting to support plug-ins, so there isn't the range of enhancements yet that are available for Winamp, but be sure to check the Sonique web site at *http://www.sonique.com* to see what's available. Sonique also doesn't support skins, but the user interface is a lot of fun as is. There's no documentation to speak of, which can be a problem when trying to figure out what to do, but the features are simple enough to make it relatively easy to figure out the program in an hour or so. Best of all, Sonique is freeware: if you like it after 14 days... keep it!

Unreal Player Max

Another good stand-alone player is Unreal Player Max from 303Tek (*http://www.303tek.com*). Unreal Player Max is a solid product with a clean, uncomplicated interface that supports over two dozen formats, including a wide variety of audio formats and many zipped formats as well. The main screen for Unreal Player Max is shown in Figure 7.21.

As you can see from Figure 7.21, the main screen for Unreal Player Max is laid out like a typical cassette deck. Basic player controls are handled by the standard cassette buttons. To open a single track, click Open and select a track. Figure 7.22 shows a track playing in Unreal Player Max.

The levels for the tracks appear on the right side of the display window. Volume and balance controls appear on the far right of the Unreal Player Max main screen.

To open the playlist editor, click Edit. Figure 7.23 shows the playlist editor with several tracks loaded.

FIGURE 7.21: The Unreal Player Max main screen.

FIGURE 7.22: The Unreal Player Max main screen with a track playing.

You can move the tracks around, shuffle them, save and load playlists, and other standard features for playlist editors. Unreal Player Max also lets you add a URL to your playlist for a streaming MP3 file; that is, an MP3 file that is downloaded as it's played.

Unreal Player Max supports plug-ins. The ones included with the program are a few background plug-ins that provide a different background to the main window and a full-screen plug-in. Unreal Player Max also supports many of the Winamp plug-ins as well. Figure 7.24 shows the Unreal Player Max screen with the starfield plug-in.

One of the interesting things about Unreal Player Max is the "DJ" feature, accessed by clicking DJ. The DJ panel (shown in Figure 7.25) lets you set a variety of playback options, including reverb, delay, and other features. Unreal Player Max may be the only MP3 player that has a karaoke option.

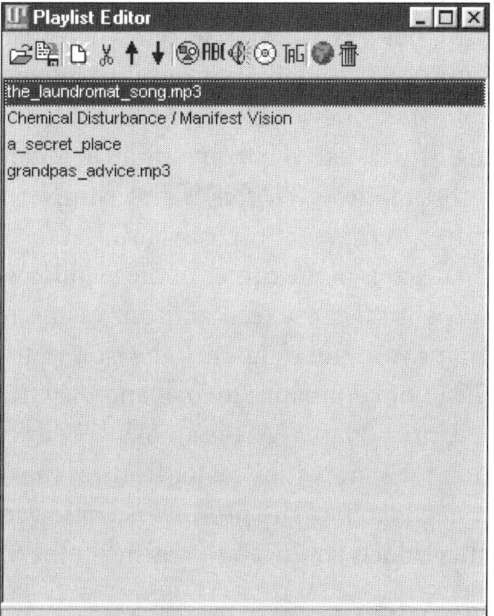

FIGURE 7.23:
The Unreal Player Max Playlist Editor screen.

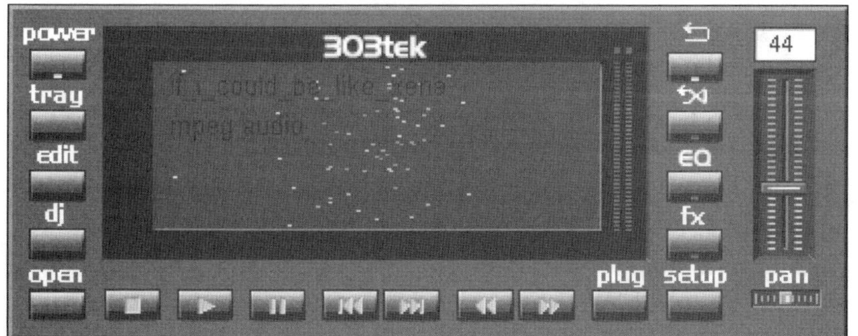

FIGURE 7.24:
The Unreal Player Max main screen with the starfield plug-in.

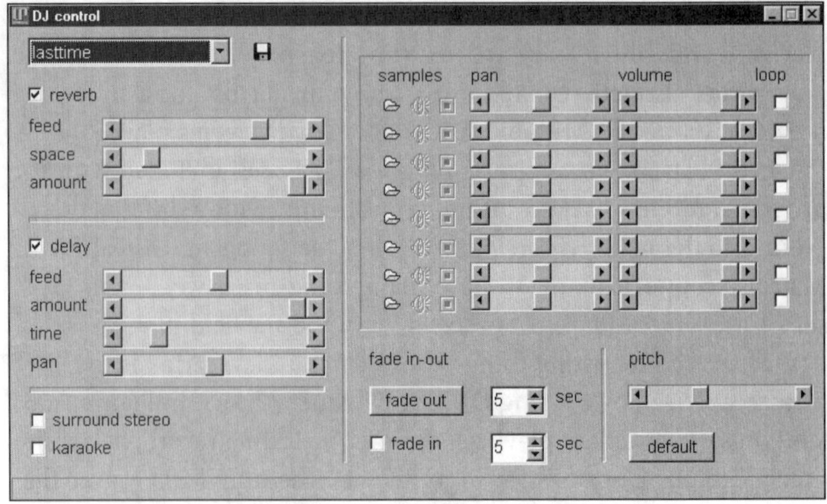

Other things worth knowing about the program: right-clicking on the Unreal Player Max screen will display a floating menu of options. Setup and configuration options are available when you click Setup. Some help is available online rather than as part of the program: pressing F1 will take you to an online manual on the *http://www.303tek.com* web site; however, this is not complete. One nice feature of Unreal Player Max is that you can shrink it to an icon on the system tray (the small icons in the corner of the Windows taskbar) by clicking Tray. This keeps it off the screen and out of the regular list of minimized programs. You can right-click the icon in the system tray and get a simple menu of commands to load and play tracks.

Unreal Player Max is an okay product, but the lack of documentation for some of the better features makes it a little harder to use than it needs to be. The product is shareware: you can use it for 30 days, after which you need to register it for $19.95.

OTHER WINDOWS PLAYERS

There are many other stand-alone players for Windows worth considering. Jet-Audio from COWON Systems, Inc., (*http://www.cowon.com*) has one of the most delightfully ostentatious interfaces of any player, as you can see from Figure 7.26.

The player interface has a burnished brass look to it and the modules stack up on top of each other. There's even a remote control (shown in Figure 7.27) that will let you trigger the various modules. Jet-Audio definitely offers everything to the person who loves bells, whistles, and flashing lights on a player that can probably play anything. Jet-Audio is shareware that costs $49.95 to register.

FIGURE 7.26:
The Jet-Audio main screen.

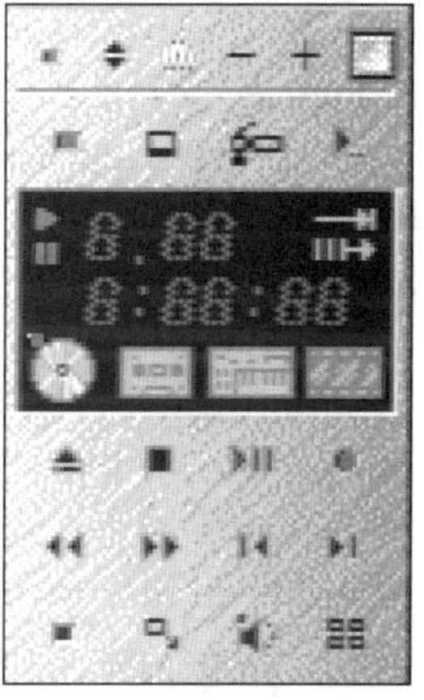

FIGURE 7.27:
The Jet-Audio remote control.

K-Jöfol from aEGiS cORP (*http://www.kjofol.org*) has an interface reminiscent of Sonique. The K-Jöfol main screen is shown in Figure 7.28.

In addition, you can expect many other MP3 programs to include basic playing features. Check the web sites listed in Appendix A, "Resources," for information on the current MP3 players.

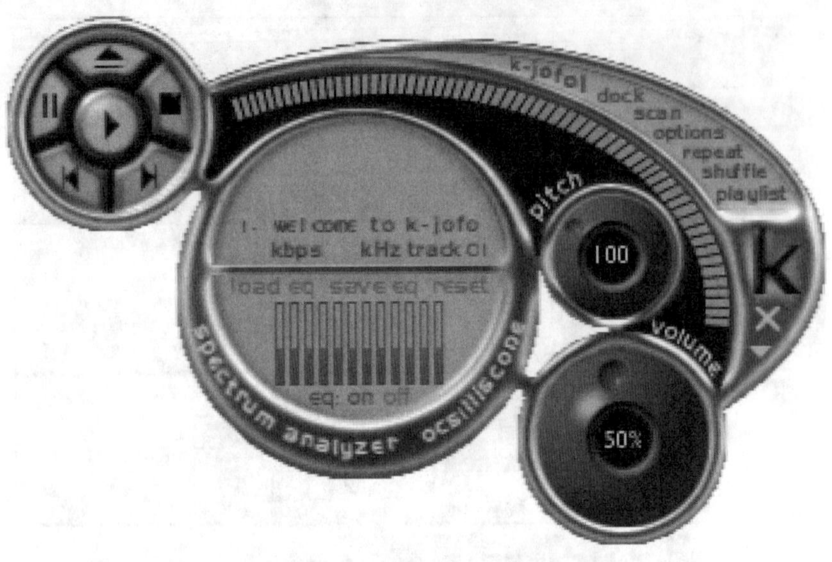

FIGURE 7.28: The K-Jöfol main screen.

FIGURE 7.29: The MacAMP main screen.

MACINTOSH PLAYERS

There are relatively few Macintosh MP3 players. The two most notable are MacAMP and SoundApp.

MacAMP, from @Soft (*http://www.macamp.com*), is a very popular MP3 player for the Macintosh. The MacAMP main screen appears in Figure 7.29.

MacAMP supports skins, plug-ins, and has a number of playback options. Previous versions of MacAMP have been freeware, but this may change in the near future to shareware. Check the MacAMP web site for the latest information on registration.

SoundApp by Norman Franke (*http://www-cs-students.stanford. edu/~franke/SoundApp*) is a freeware MP3 player for PowerPC-based Macs and a converter from MP3 into AIFF format on 68K Macs. It supports an extensive list of other file formats as well. The SoundApp main screen appears in Figure 7.30.

RIPPERS AND ENCODERS

As you read in Chapter 1, "Getting Started," rippers convert CD tracks into WAV files. Rippers will frequently have some filtering and editing capabilities that you don't have with MusicMatch Jukebox. Rippers are frequently bundled with encoders, which complete the process by converting WAV files into MP3 files.

Not all rippers are the same. Many offer different filtering and normalizing features as well as a variety of interface options. (*Normalizing*

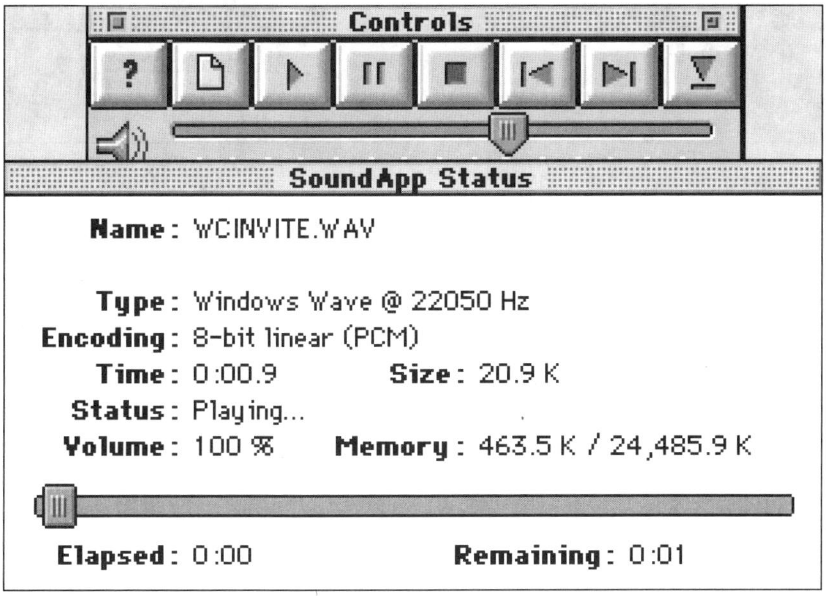

FIGURE 7.30:
The SoundApp
main screen

is the process of setting the various frequency ranges so that the tracks sound more... normal. Normalizing is very useful if you're recording from different CDs that have been recorded under different conditions or at different volume levels.)

All encoders are not the same, either; they're optimized for different features. Some encoders produce a higher-quality sound but are slow and produce large MP3 files. Other encoders are fast but don't produce the highest-quality audio. Still others may produce very compact MP3 files of reasonable quality, but they may not be fast. The ripping and encoding software in MusicMatch Jukebox produces good-quality files, but it's optimized for speed and convenience. If you're willing to use separate components and take longer with your file ripping and encoding process, you can get better-sounding MP3 files. It's very much like using an all-in-one sound system or buying individual audio components to squeeze the best possible sound out of your system. This section will introduce you to some of the other rippers and encoders you can use.

Audiograbber

Audiograbber is a very good ripper by Jackie Franck (*http://www. audiograbber.com-us.net*). It lets you create WAV files from CDs, edit them to remove silence from the end of the WAV file, set start and stop points for recording a clip, and even shut down the computer when you're done. Figure 7.31 shows the Audiograbber main screen with a sample CD displayed.

> **NOTE**
>
> *The unregistered version of Audiograbber will only rip half the tracks on the CD, denoted by the checkboxes to the left of the track in the main screen.*

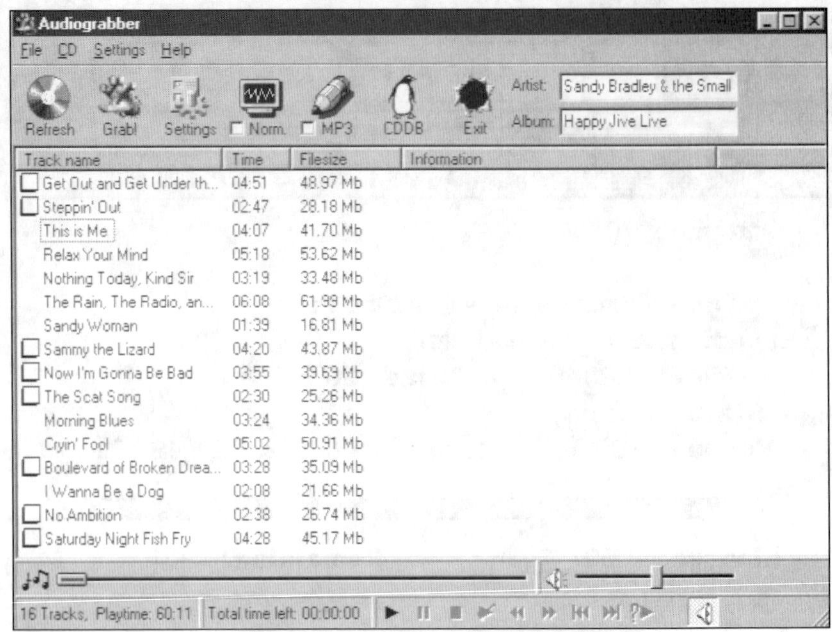

FIGURE 7.31:
The Audiograbber
main screen.

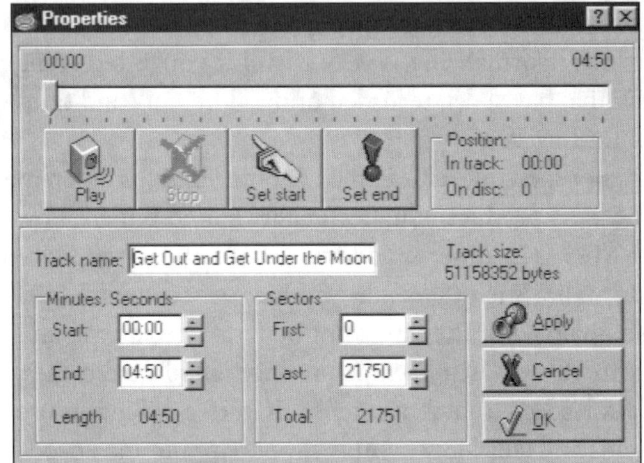

FIGURE 7.32:
The Audiograbber
Properties screen.

Audiograbber displays track information from the CD and shows you how much room each of the files will take as individual WAV files. You can play selected tracks by highlighting them and clicking the cassette buttons at the bottom of the main Audiograbber screen. If you double-click a track, Audiograbber displays a Properties screen (shown in Figure 7.32).

You can set the start and end time for the track (which is useful for creating sound bites and excerpts), retitle the track, and listen to your selection.

You can access *CDDB.com* for track information by clicking the penguin on the toolbar. (The animation of the penguins picking up data is a lot of fun, too.)

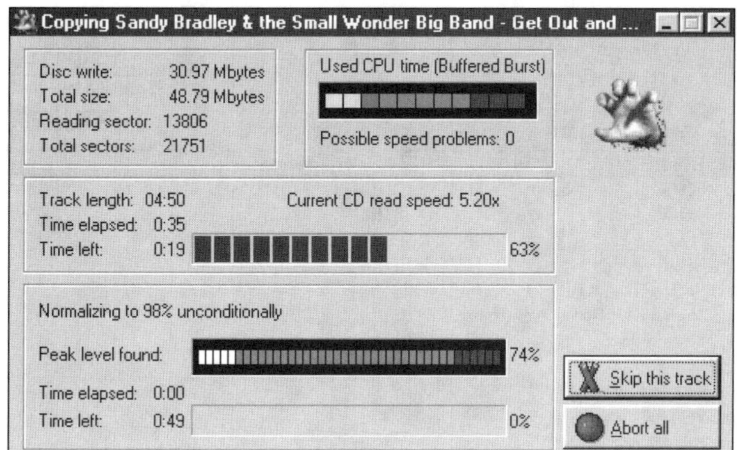

FIGURE 7.33:
The Audiograbber ripping screen.

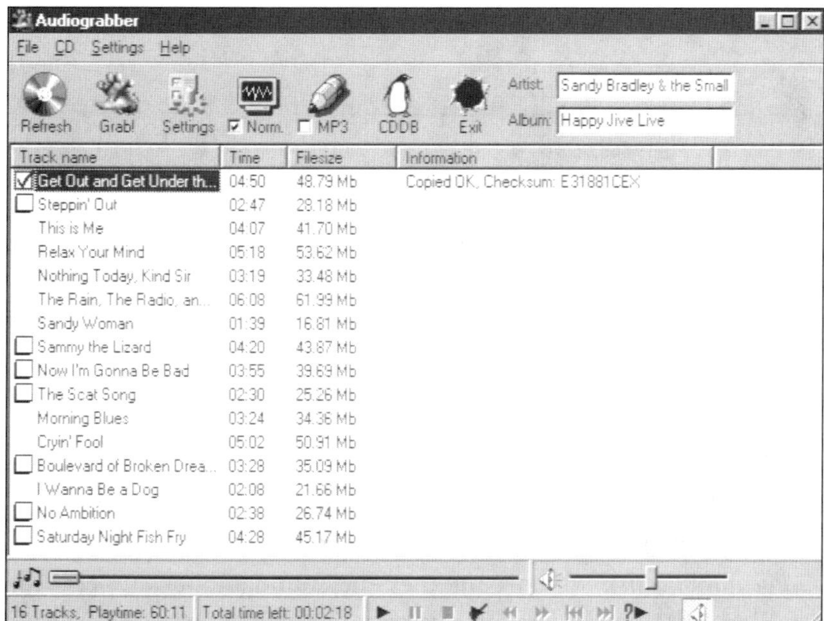

FIGURE 7.34:
The Audiograbber main screen showing a ripped file.

When you're satisfied with your entries and options, start ripping the tracks. Figure 7.33 shows a typical track being ripped.

As Audiograbber rips the file, the histograms light up to show the progress. It's worth noting that Audiograbber is capable of accessing some CD-ROM drives for digital ripping that MusicMatch Jukebox cannot. When the track has been ripped, the main screen looks something like the one appearing in Figure 7.34.

At this point, you can encode the WAV file into MP3 using an external encoder. (Audiograbber is just a ripper.)

Audiograbber has a very accessible interface, some exceptional features for ripping, and (because it copies the music digitally) it pro-

duces exact copies of the tracks you're ripping. One of the nicer things about Audiograbber is that it doesn't add files to your Windows directory, a boon for those who regularly install lots of software and have compatibility problems. All in all, Audiograbber is a bargain at $25 (which even gives you unlimited upgrades).

AUDIOCATALYST

Audiograbber is a seriously good program, but you can go one step better by using AudioCatalyst from Xing Technology (*http://www.audiocatalyst.com*), which combines the Audiograbber ripper with the Xing MP3 encoder (which is also the encoder used in Music-Match Jukebox). AudioCatalyst has a similar interface to Audiograbber, as you can see in Figure 7.35.

The big difference between Audiograbber and AudioCatalyst is that AudioCatalyst also has an encoder option. Looking at Figure 7.35, you can see an option for MP3. If you check this box and then select files, AudioCatalyst will rip the track into WAV files and then create MP3 files from the WAV files. The screen in Figure 7.36 is similar to the Audiograbber ripping screen shown in Figure 7.33, but it also shows information about the processing of the file into an MP3 file.

AudioCatalyst provides all the superior features and interface options available in Audiograbber and also lets you encode your files into MP3 files as a seamless part of the process. Registration is $29.95.

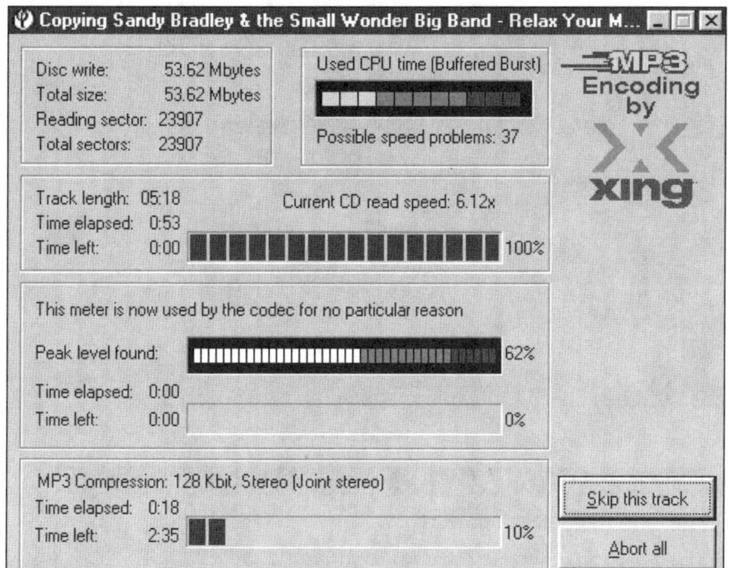

FIGURE 7.36: The AudioCatalyst ripping and encoding screen.

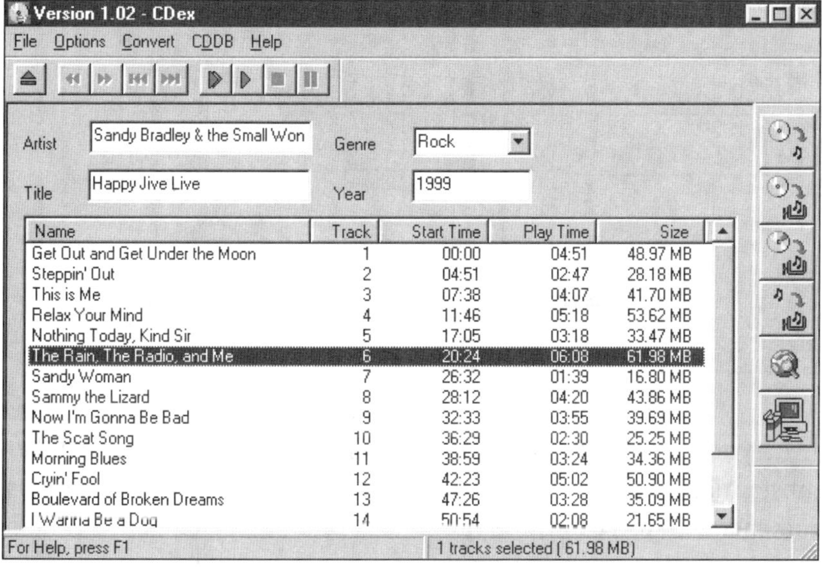

FIGURE 7.37: The CDex main screen.

CDEX

CDex is a freeware ripper and encoder from Albert Faber (*http://www.surf.to/cdex*). It's a quick, simple program. The main screen appears in Figure 7.37.

When you've highlighted the tracks you want to rip, you can click one of the buttons on the right to rip the track into a WAV file or even encode it directly into MP3. Figure 7.38 shows a track being converted to an MP3 file.

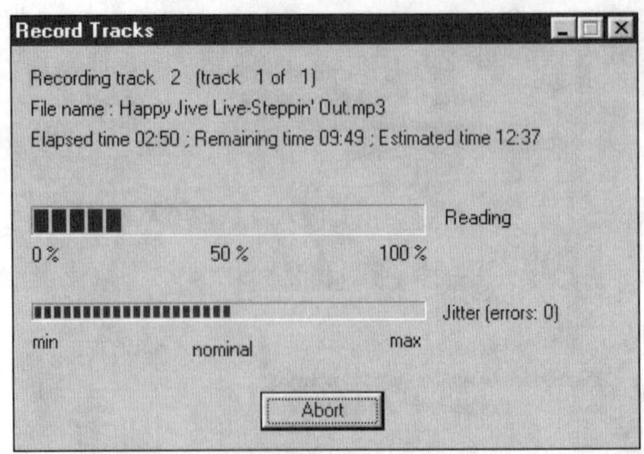

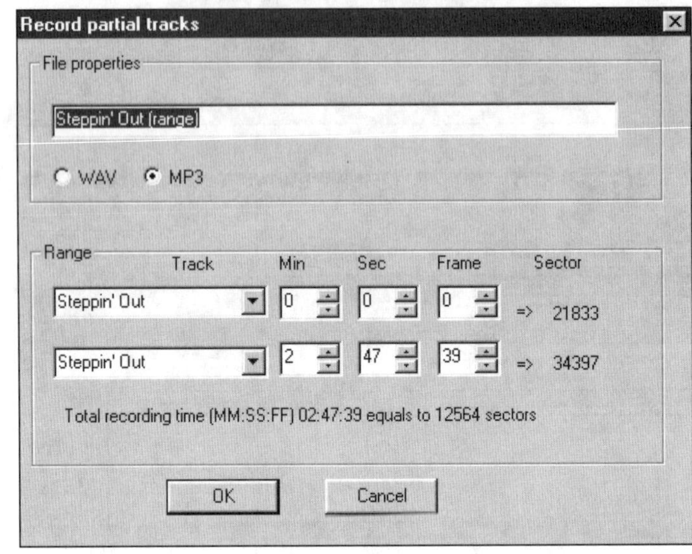

As you can see from the information in Figure 7.38, CDex takes substantially longer to rip and encode a file than the other rippers and encoders you've seen so far.

You can also record a portion of a track if you like, as shown in Figure 7.39. You can select the format to output the section of the track to by clicking the appropriate radio button on the screen.

CDex may not be the most attractive ripper and encoder out there, but it's free and it works very well. Give it a try!

EASY CD-DA EXTRACTOR

Easy CD-DA Extractor—not to be confused with Adaptec's Easy CD Creator Deluxe—is another first-rate ripper and extractor. It's from Jukka Poikolainen Software in Finland (*http://www.poikosoft.com/cdda*). Figure 7.40 shows the Easy CD-DA Extractor main screen with a sample CD displayed.

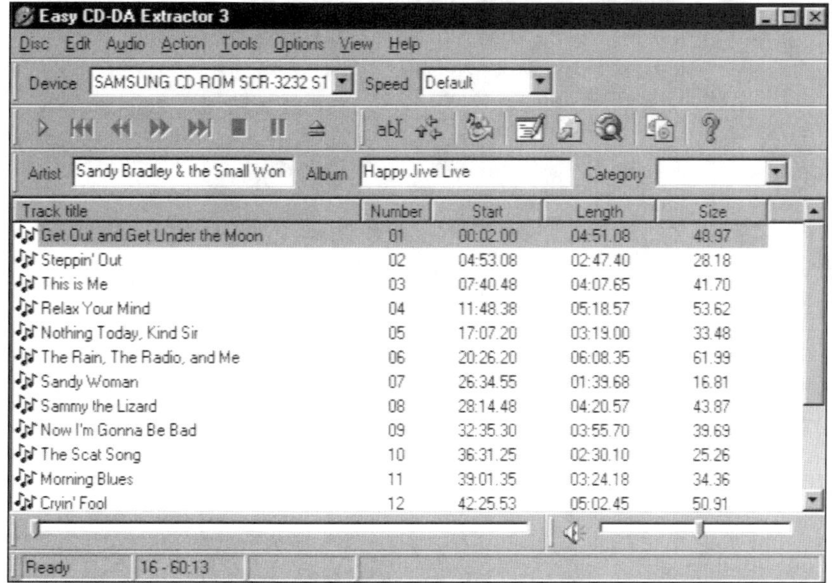

FIGURE 7.40:
The Easy CD-DA
Extractor main screen.

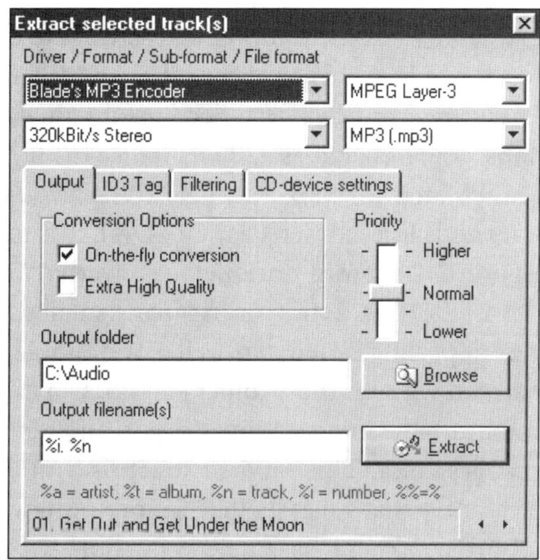

FIGURE 7.41:
The Easy CD-DA
Extractor extraction
screen.

Easy CD-DA Extractor also has features for normalizing the tracks, stripping or adding silence at the start or the end of the track, renaming and tagging tracks, and accessing *CDDB.com* for information. Double-clicking a track plays it (like many other programs, there's a built-in CD player so you can preview your selections). When you click the Extract icon, you see the screen shown in Figure 7.41. (In the demo version, you can only extract a single track at a time. Registration costs $30, after which you can extract unlimited tracks.)

Note the drop-down menus for selecting different encoders. You can select from eight different encoders and converters. Easy CD-DA

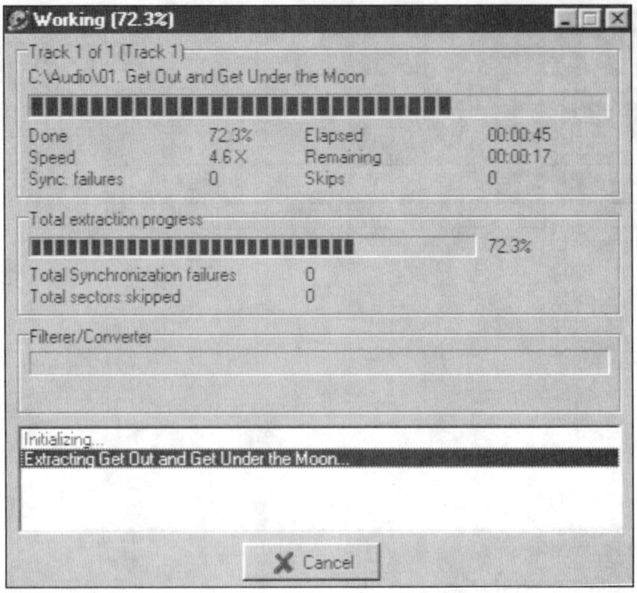

FIGURE 7.42:
The Easy CD-DA Extractor converting a track.

Extractor will use preconfigured settings to extract the track and convert it to a WAV file or encode it as an MP3 file, whichever you prefer. There are also extensive selections for the sampling rates for extractions, going as high as 320 bits (twice the high-quality settings for the MusicMatch Jukebox encoder). When you've determined your settings and click Extract, Easy CD-DA Extractor starts ripping the track. Figure 7.42 shows a track being converted to an MP3 file.

Easy CD-DA Extractor has many small user features that make it a very appealing product as well. For example, when you are looking at a screen with multiple folders on it (such as the options screens) and you move the mouse pointer over a different folder tab, the folder tab changes color. This kind of touch is a small thing, but definitely a pleasantry that suggests that the program was developed with an eye towards making it as usable as possible.

DIGITAL AUDIO COPY

Digital Audio Copy (also known as WinDAC) from Christoph Schmelnick (*http://www.windac.de*) is another good ripper. You can use it to copy tracks from a CD and strip or add silence at the start or the end of the track. Figure 7.43 shows the Digital Audio Copy main screen.

Although Digital Audio Copy is shareware, it lets you select a range of tracks for ripping. (However, in the unregistered software, after each track is ripped, there's a dialog box you need to click to continue to the next track.) Figure 7.44 shows the Digital Audio Copy processing screen.

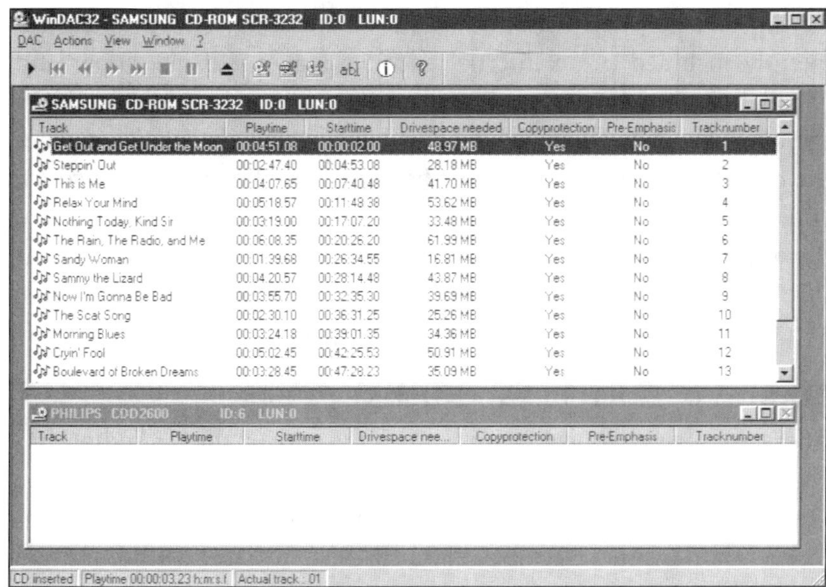

FIGURE 7.43:
The Digital Audio
Copy main screen.

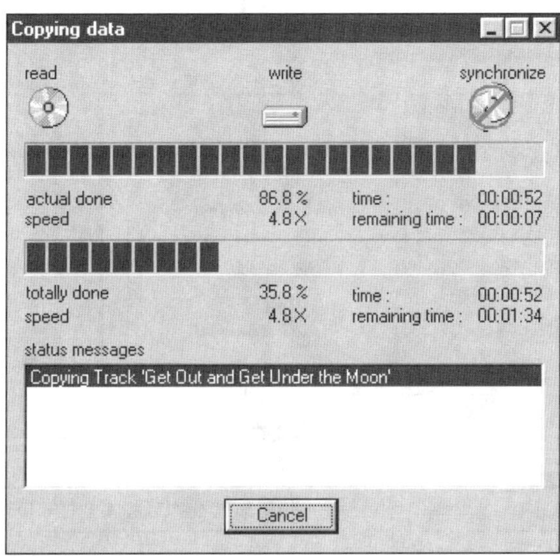

FIGURE 7.44:
The Digital Audio
Copy processing
screen.

When the tracks are ripped, you can then encode them with the encoder of your choice. Digital Audio Copy costs $31 to register. There is also a DOS version of the program if you prefer.

OTHER WINDOWS ENCODERS

There are several good encoders you can use to plug into rippers. Many of the ripper and encoder combinations ship with BladeEnc's MP3 encoder, available at (*http://www.bladeenc.cjb.net*). It's not as fast as the Xing encoder, but it's freeware, very compact, and may produce MP3 files that sound better. The Fraunhofer L3Enc encoder is very popular for high-quality MP3 files, but it's one of the slower encoders. It's frequently included as an internal encoder for an existing ripper and encoder combination, but it may be difficult to find to download. On the other hand, Plugger+ by Alberto Demichelis says that it emulates the L3Enc features, so if you can't find the Fraunhofer L3Enc encoder, you can try using that instead. Plugger+ is freeware; you can download it from (*http://members.tripod.com/~mp3nkoder*). You can also download the Xing encoder from their web site at *http://www.xingtech.com* as a stand-alone program for use with a ripper if you like.

MACINTOSH RIPPERS AND ENCODERS

There are several good Macintosh rippers and encoders. AudioCatalyst (covered earlier in this chapter) is also available in a Mac version. Figure 7.45 shows a typical screen from AudioCatalyst. The Macintosh version of AudioCatalyst costs $34.95.

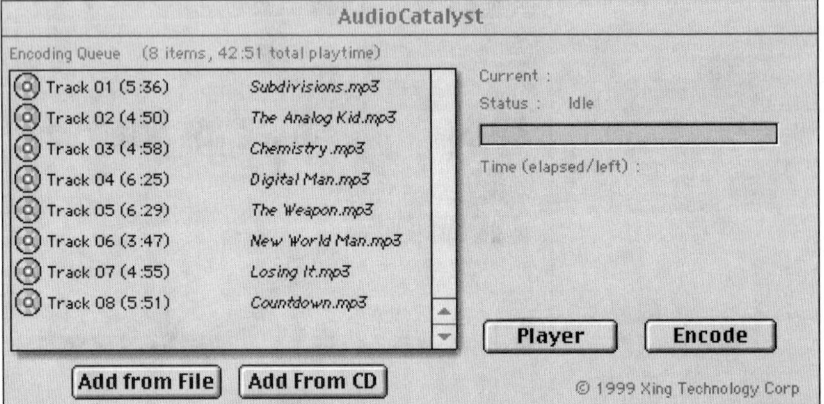

FIGURE 7.45: The Macintosh AudioCatalyst main screen.

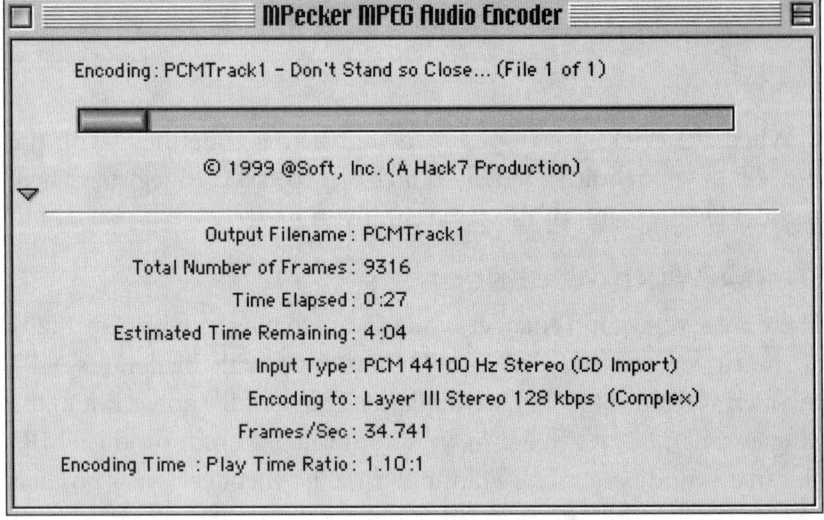

FIGURE 7.46: The Mpecker main screen.

Another popular ripper and encoder is MPecker. MPecker is a great freeware program from Rafael Luebbert (*http://www.anime.net/ ~go/mpeckers.html*), shown in Figure 7.46.

ALL-IN-ONE PROGRAMS

The last category in this chapter is all-in-one programs. All-in-one programs are programs that do everything related to MP3 files—playing, ripping, encoding, and so on. There are several other all-in-one programs besides MusicMatch Jukebox that you may be interested in.

HYCD PLAY&RECORD

HyCD Play&Record from Creative Digital Research (*http://www. hycd.com*) is a full-featured all-in-one program. It plays MP3 files, rips and encodes MP3 files, and edits WAV files. HyCD Play&Record is notable in particular for also having a built-in CD-ROM burning program. It even prints CD labels!

HyCD Play&Record is a little different from other products you've looked at in this chapter. There isn't a main screen to look at and select options from. Instead, when you install HyCD Play&Record, the features are attached to standard Windows menus in the Windows Explorer.

For example, to play an MP3 file, you display the file(s) in the Windows Explorer and then right-click to bring up the floating menu. You'll see a HyCD Play menu option at the top of the list when the file can be played by HyCD Play&Record. Select this option and HyCD Play&Record will start playing the file, as shown in Figure 7.47.

Ripping and encoding files is equally simple: you insert an audio CD in your CD-ROM drive, highlight the files in the Windows Explorer, and then right-click. Select HyCD Copy from the floating menu. Then display the destination directory in the Windows Explorer and right-click again. Select HyCD Paste from the floating menu to display the Extract Audio Option screen shown in Figure 7.48.

FIGURE 7.47:
The HyCD Player.

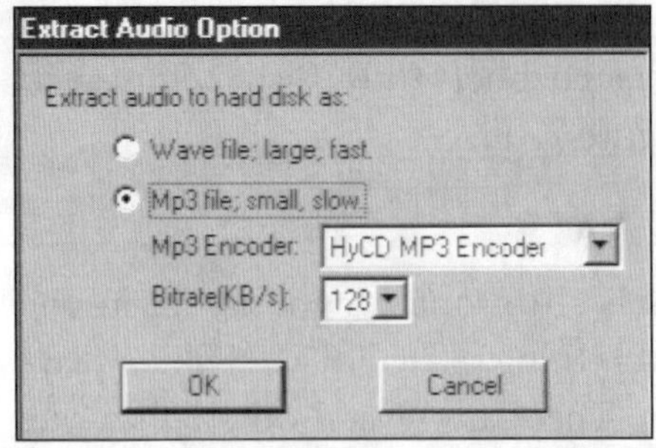

FIGURE 7.48:
The HyCD Extract Audio Option screen.

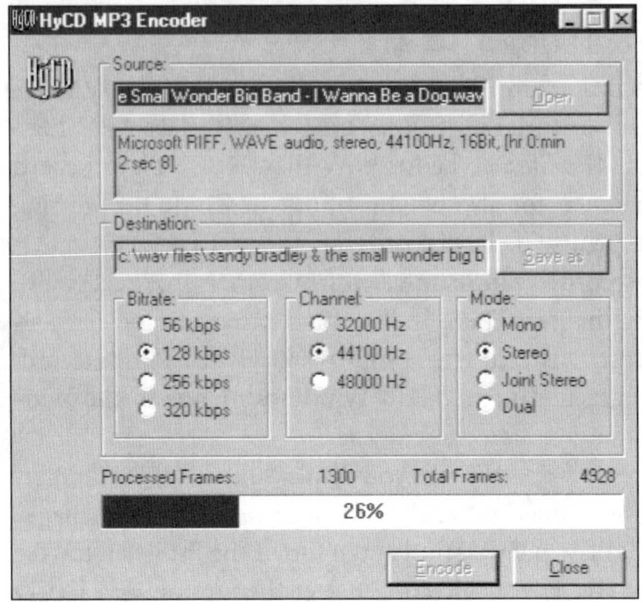

FIGURE 7.49:
The HyCD Encoder screen.

Select the options you want and click OK. HyCD Play&Record rips and encodes the file in the target directory. You can also use the HyCD Encoder (shown in Figure 7.49) to encode ripped files. Using the Encoder will give you more options than are directly available using the copy-and-paste method. You start the Encoder from the Windows Start menu rather than from a floating menu in the Windows Explorer.

If you want to edit the WAV file or add audio effects before you encode it into MP3 format, you can use the companion program, HyCD FX (shown in Figure 7.50) to clean up and filter WAV files. (HyCD FX is also accessed from the Windows Start menu.)

In addition to filtering and equalization, you can add a variety of sound effects starting with reverb and continuing with a couple dozen preprogrammed sound effects, including halls of various sizes, feedback, and cathedral sound.

FIGURE 7.50:
The HyCD FX screen.

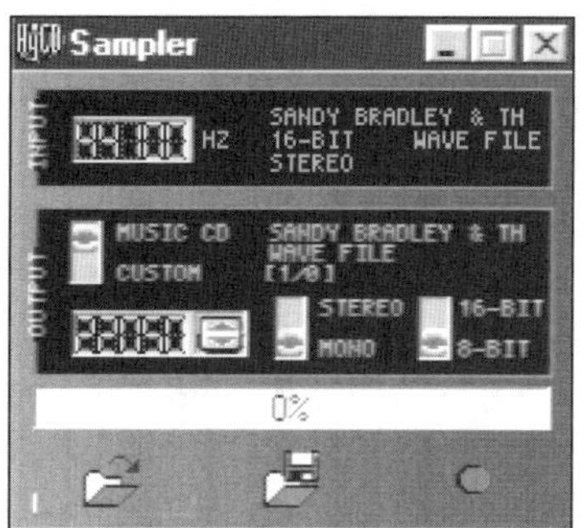

FIGURE 7.51:
The HyCD Sampler screen.

If you want to resample a file to adjust the bit rate, you can use another companion program, HyCD Sampler. The sample file shown in Figure 7.51 is about to be converted to a 22kHz sampled mono file.

Burning audio CDs is equally simple: in the Windows Explorer, you select the MP3 files you want to put on an audio CD, then right-click and HyCD Copy the files. You then right-click on the CD-ROM burner in Windows Explorer and select HyCD Paste. The Customize Play List screen appears, as shown in Figure 7.52.

As you can see, the Customize Play List screen is a standard CD mastering program that will let you copy the files to an audio CD. (If you're using a CD-RW drive, you can also do a HyCD Format that will let you reformat your CD-RW disc.)

HyCD Play&Record and its companion programs have many attractive features, but there are some disadvantages as well. For example, CD-ROM drives that are not MMC compliant are not supported. (Most CD-ROM drives are MMC compliant these days, but this may be a problem if your CD-ROM drive is more than a couple years old.) In addition, if you prefer not to use Windows Explorer in

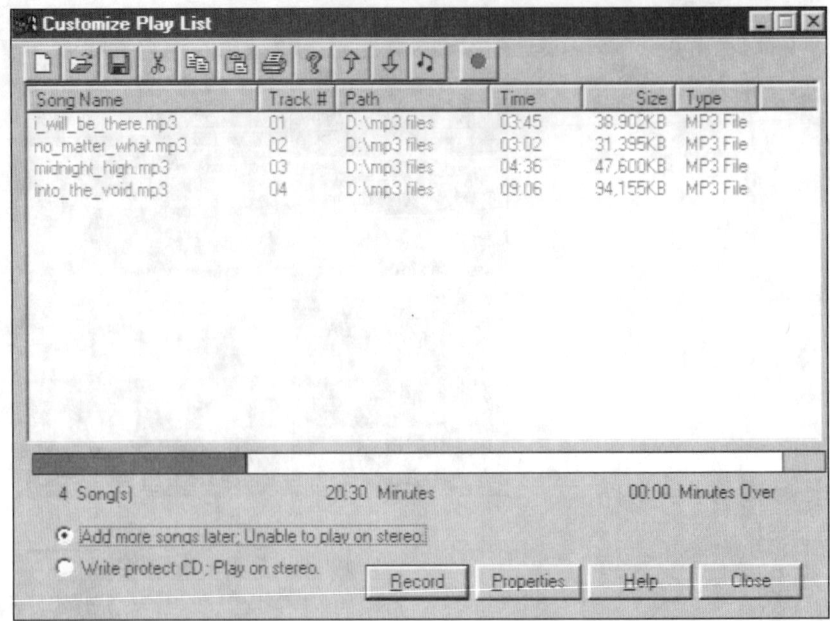

favor of another product, such as Norton File Manager, you won't see the HyCD menu options when you right-click.

HyCD Play&Record is shareware, costing $59.95. There is a professional version, which has more options for the encoder, for $79.95. For an additional $10, you can get the program on a CD with some really dazzling additional materials: a tutorial (you can download the big tutorial from the HyCD web site, but it's a 20MB AVI file, so you probably don't want to), a 1.4 million song name database, and HyCD Print, a complete CD label printing program with templates.

CDH MEDIA WIZARD

CDH Media Wizard from CDH Productions (*http://www.cdhnow.com*) is another all-in-one program worth looking at. The main CDH Media Wizard screen appears in Figure 7.53 with a sample MP3 file playing. CDH Media Wizard has a playlist editor (shown in Figure 7.54).

Unlike many other MP3 players and all-in-one programs, CDH Media Wizard also handles a wide variety of video formats.

To convert tracks to MP3 files, select Convert CD Audio to MP3 from the Conversions menu. The Convert CD Track to MP3 screen appears, as shown in Figure 7.55.

Select the tracks you want to rip and encode and click the MP3 icon in the upper left corner. CDH Media Wizard starts converting the tracks.

CDH Media Wizard isn't as rich in features as HyCD Play&Record or MusicMatch Jukebox, but it's still a product worth looking at.

FIGURE 7.53:
The CDH Media
Wizard main screen.

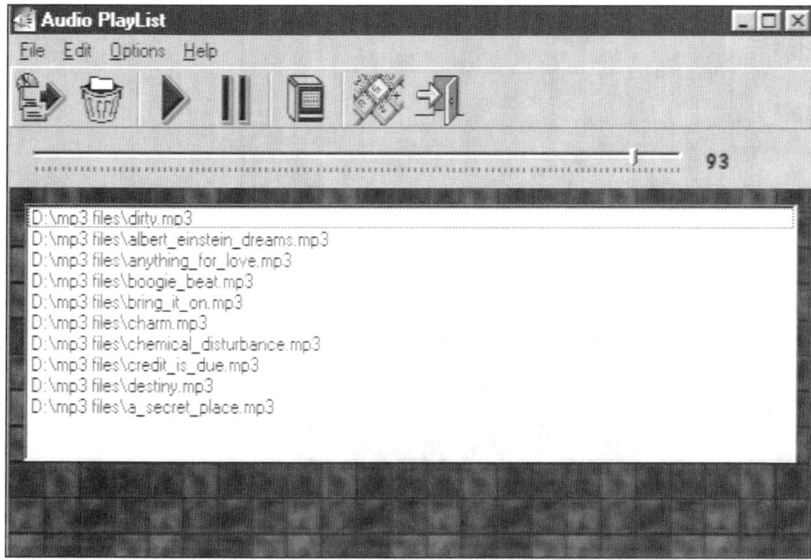

FIGURE 7.54:
The CDH Media
Wizard Audio Playlist.

CDH Media Wizard is shareware that expires after 20 days. Registration is $50.

WPLAY

One other all-in-one product to look at is WPlay from Xaudio (*http://www.xaudio.com*). WPlay is shareware that costs $10 to register after 14 days. It has a lively interface that is colorful and easy to use. Figure 7.56 shows the WPlay main screen playing a sample MP3 track. Each of the knobs on the rim of the screen are cassette buttons.

The Playlist Editor has some nice features. When you click Add, you can choose to add files using a standard Windows dialog box, by directory (which adds all the MP3 files in the selected directory), or

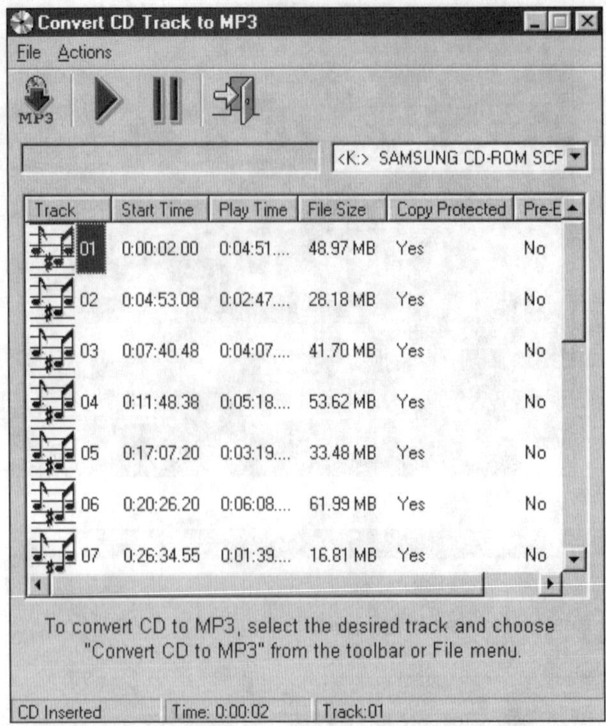

by URL, so you can get MP3 files as streaming audio. Figure 7.57 shows the Playlist screen with a sample directory added.

If you prefer a tree view of your directories (like MusicMatch Jukebox's selection screen), you can select the Use Tree View option from the Effects menu at the bottom of the Playlist screen. Figure 7.58 shows the Playlist screen with a directory ready for you to select files to add to the playlist.

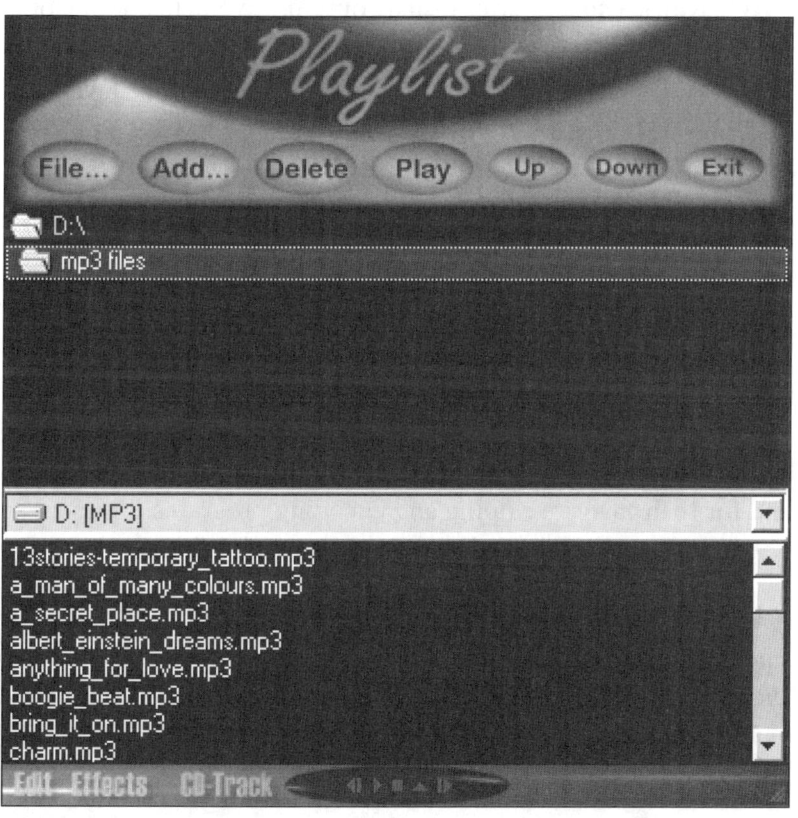

FIGURE 7.57:
The WPlay Playlist screen.

FIGURE 7.58:
The WPlay Playlist screen in tree view mode.

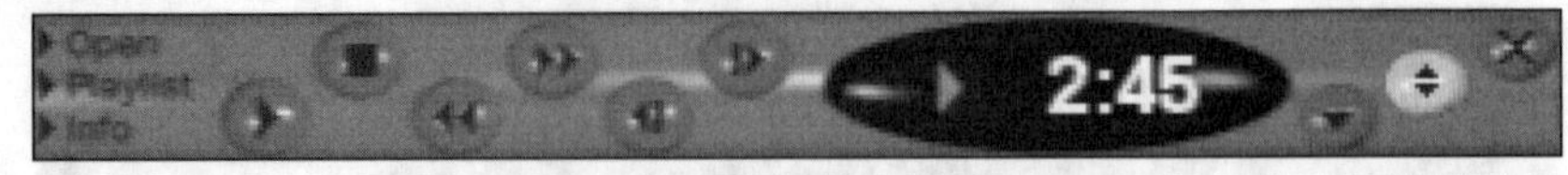

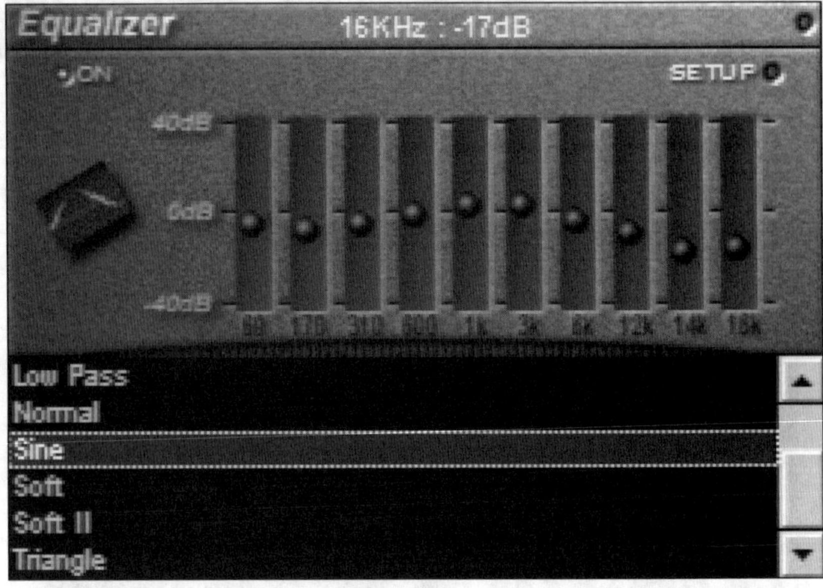

WPlay has a small player display option: if you click Mode on the main screen, the screen shrinks to a bar, as shown in Figure 7.59.

WPlay also has an equalizer (accessible by clicking Equalizer on the main screen). The equalizer, which is shown in Figure 7.60, has a number of preset equalization modes you can use.

WPlay has a built-in front end for ripping and encoding, but it doesn't supply the ripper or encoder, preferring to leave those choices up to the user. However, the program is set up to make it very easy to identify and use separate rippers and encoders. Figure 7.61 shows the conversion screen with a track selected. (You can only select the first track of each CD in the unregistered version.)

WPlay's strengths are that it is fairly attractive, easy to understand, and provides a great deal of flexibility for the people who want a front end for their favorite ripping and encoding programs. It has an analyzer and a scope trace and is able to use many Winamp skins.

VIRTUOSA GOLD

The last program in this section is AudioSoft's Virtuosa Gold (*http://www.audiosoft.com/virtuosa*). Figure 7.62 shows the Virtuosa Gold main screen.

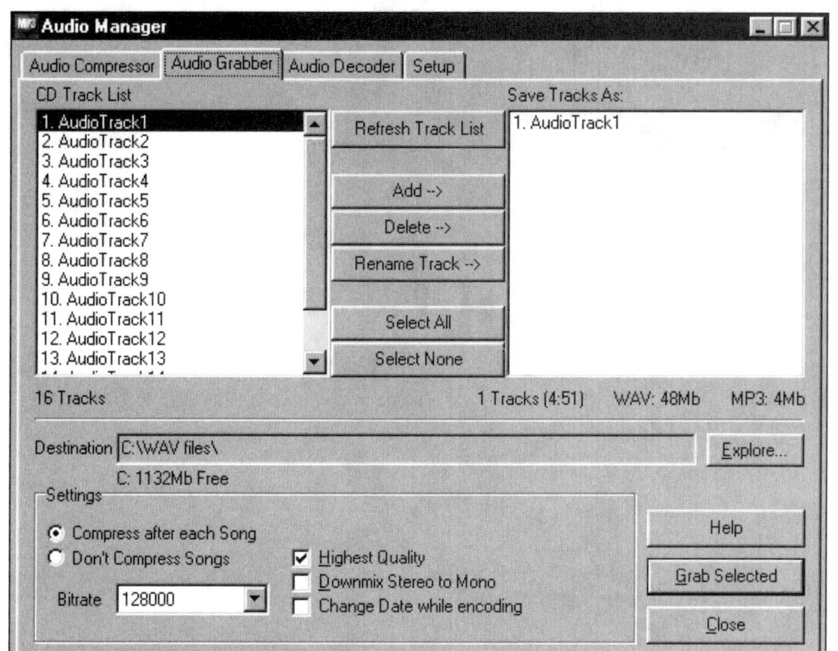

FIGURE 7.61:
The WPlay conversion screen.

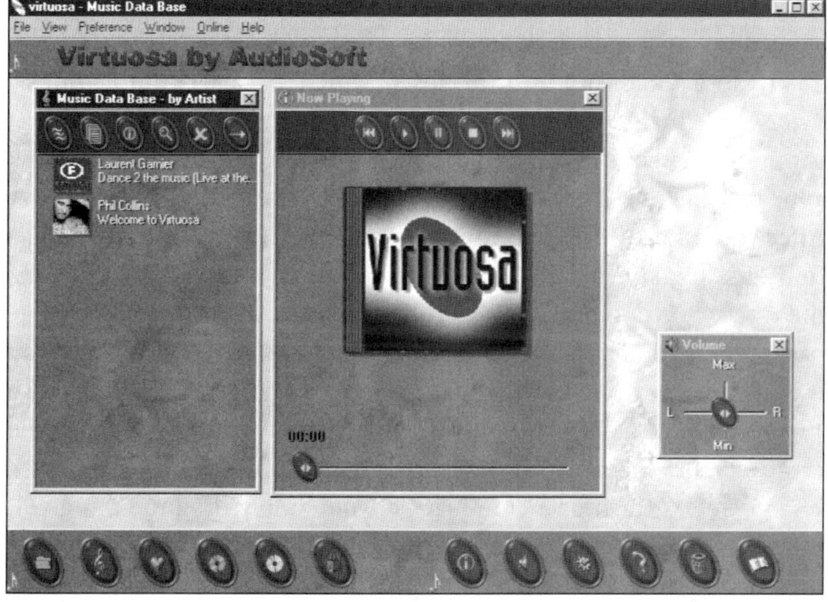

FIGURE 7.62:
The Virtuosa Gold main screen.

(By the way, Virtuosa Gold's default appearance is not the fairest of them all, but you can make a number of changes to the way the program looks by selecting Options from the Preferences menu.)

When you start a track, it appears in the Now Playing screen, shown in Figure 7.63. The volume control (shown in Figure 7.62) has a very appealing T-bar action: you can change the volume by moving

FIGURE 7.63:
The Virtuosa Gold
Now Playing screen.

it up and down; switching the balance between left and right speakers is done by moving the control horizontally.

Virtuosa Gold supports playlists, which it calls "compilations." After you click Compilations on the main screen (the little heart; some of the icons take getting used to), the Compilations window appears. Click the New Compilations tab to start a new compilation. After you name the new compilation and click OK, the new compilation window appears. As with most other playlist editors, you drag the tracks you'd like to add to the compilation from the music database. When you're satisfied with your entries, click OK. You can play the compilation by clicking the first track in it. Figure 7.64 shows the Virtuosa Gold main screen showing the various windows open while creating a new compilation called "Upbeat stuff."

To delete a track or a compilation, you simply drag the thing you want to delete to a part of the screen where there's nothing and drop it.

You can rip tracks and encode them with Virtuosa Gold. Simply drag and drop tracks from the CD Player window to the Music Database window or select the tracks and then click Record in the CD Player window. Virtuosa Gold asks you for track information in the Phonogram properties screen, shown in Figure 7.65.

When you are satisfied with your entries and have clicked the check mark, Virtuosa Gold starts ripping the file. The Digital Record Status screen is shown in Figure 7.66. (The Analog Record Screen is slightly different.)

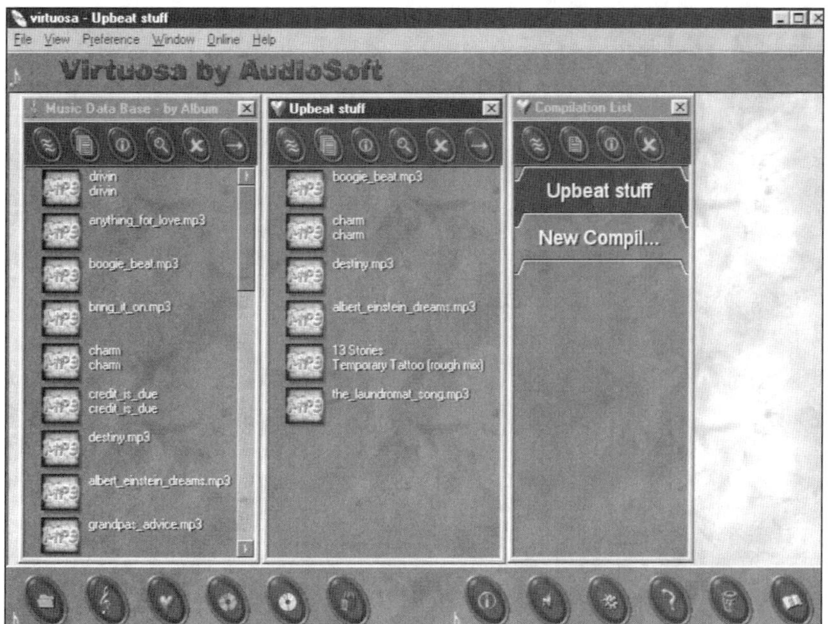

FIGURE 7.64: Creating a compilation in Virtuosa Gold.

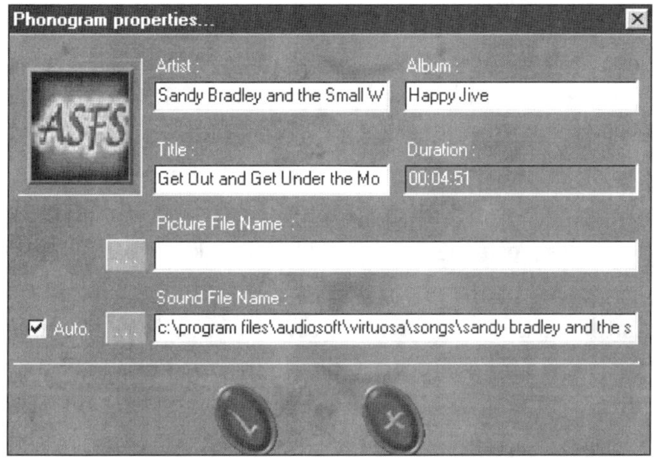

FIGURE 7.65: The Virtuosa Gold Phonogram properties screen.

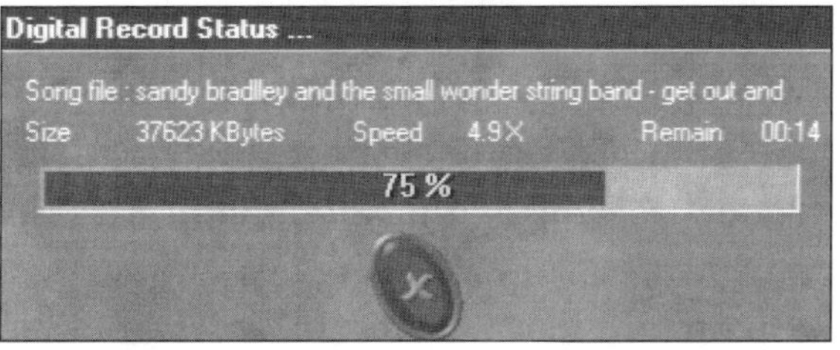

FIGURE 7.66: The Virtuosa Gold Digital Record Status screen.

After the track has been ripped to a WAV file, Virtuosa Gold converts it to MP3 and adds it to the Music Database.

Virtuosa Gold will also let you burn audio CDs directly from the program. Clicking CD Recordable brings up the CD Recordable screen, shown in Figure 7.67.

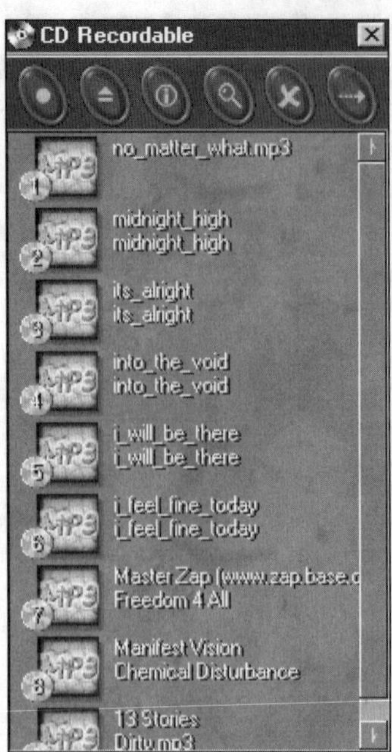

When you are satisfied with your entries, click Record. Virtuosa Gold starts burning the MP3 files to the CD.

Virtuosa Gold doesn't support skins. It also doesn't have an oscilloscope or an analyzer and the program icons may take a little getting used to. On the other hand, it's nice to have built-in CD-ROM burner support. It's also worth mentioning that Virtuosa Gold has online help files right there on your hard disk. (Most of the other programs discussed in this chapter have no help, poor help, or a help system that launches your browser and frequently requires you to be online as well.) The Virtuosa Gold help has fairly extensive step-by-step tutorials on how to do just about every task you might want to do. There are abundant screen shots, too, so you can see what the next step is. Registration for Virtuosa Gold is $29.99.

FINDING OTHER SOFTWARE

Most of the larger MP3 web sites have sections devoted exclusively to the downloading and distribution of MP3 software. *MP3.com* currently has the largest selection of software for all operating systems, including Windows, Macintosh, BeOS, Linux, Unix, OS/2, Amiga, NeXTStep, and Solaris. You can often find reviews of the various programs to guide you in your decision-making process, but the value of shareware is that you can download a program, try it out, and if you don't like it, try another one. It's also perfectly permissible to have several different programs on your computer that do basically the same thing if you like.

There are new versions of existing software being released continually. In addition, you can expect to see new freeware, shareware, and commercial products released frequently. Be sure to check on the MP3 web sites regularly for announcements of new and updated software.

In this chapter, you've been introduced to some of the other popular MP3 software options currently available for Windows and the Macintosh, including players, rippers, encoders, and all-in-one programs. In the next chapter, you'll learn about the variety of MP3 players on the market, including products like the Rio and the MPMan. You'll also be introduced to CD players that can also play MP3 files.

Playing MP3 Files Away from Your Computer

I n the previous chapter, you were introduced to a variety of popular MP3 programs, including players, rippers, encoders, and all-in-one programs. In this chapter, you'll learn about the variety of MP3 players on the market, including products like the Rio and the MPMan. You'll also read about sound cards and multimedia speakers that will improve the way your MP3 files sound when you play them. And you'll be introduced to an assortment of other types of MP3 players and gadgets for your car and home.

PORTABLE MP3 PLAYERS

Portable MP3 players are small units run by batteries. You download MP3 files into them using software that comes with the player and then play them back. Portable MP3 players have all the advantages of portable cassette or CD players, but with no moving parts, they are lightweight and durable.

Portable MP3 players have a number of things in common:

+ They're smaller than a deck of playing cards.
+ They're light (about 4–6 ounces).
+ They have a simple hardware interface to let you download MP3 files from your computer.
+ They run for about 12 hours off a small battery, usually AA.
+ They have no moving parts, meaning they don't skip when you shake the unit (perfect for when you exercise).

✦ They have an LCD display that shows the battery strength, the playing time, the volume setting, and other information about the options you've selected.

✦ They cost around $200 (although prices are dropping already).

Most portable MP3 players also let you use flash cards to augment the RAM available in the player.

Rio PMP300 Portable MP3 Player

The Rio PMP300 Portable Music Player from Diamond Multimedia (*http://www.diamondmm.com*) is the most popular MP3 player on the market. It comes with 32MB of built-in flash memory. This lets you store and play about 35 minutes of CD-quality sound or twice as much spoken information ripped at a lower radio-quality sampling rate. The Rio also has an expansion slot for a *flash memory card*, small cards of RAM you can plug into the Rio to double the number of tracks you can store and play.

The most distinctive thing about the Rio is the circular control pad on the front, as shown in Figure 8.1. The LCD display is fairly large and easy to read.

FIGURE 8.1:
The Rio PMP300
Portable Music Player.

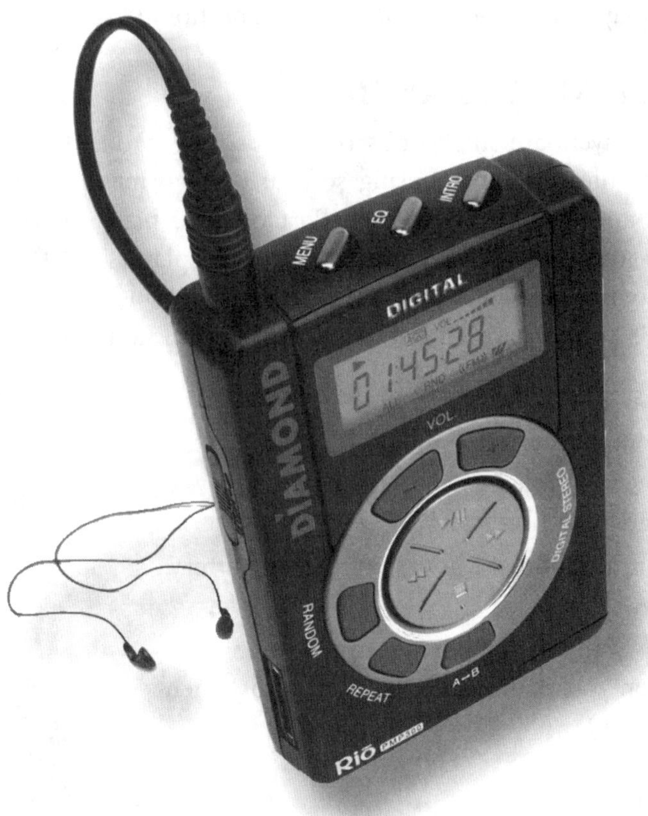

The Rio has several different equalization settings to make the music sound even better:

✦ Normal (no equalization)
✦ Classic
✦ Jazz
✦ Rock

The Rio interface software is very easy to use. When you start the Rio software, you first see the Rio player screen, shown in Figure 8.2.

The Rio player screen has the standard player controls, a volume control, and buttons to go to the other Rio screens: the Rio Playlist Manager screen, the Rio CD Player screen, and the Rio Internal/External Memory.

You use the Rio Playlist Manager screen (shown in Figure 8.3 with a sample playlist loaded) to create playlists for use in the Rio software and for downloading to the Rio itself.

Creating a playlist in the Rio Playlist Manager is similar to creating a playlist in MusicMatch Jukebox: you add files using the Add button, then save the playlist for future reference. You can also play a playlist by clicking Play. (Figure 8.4 shows the player playing a file.)

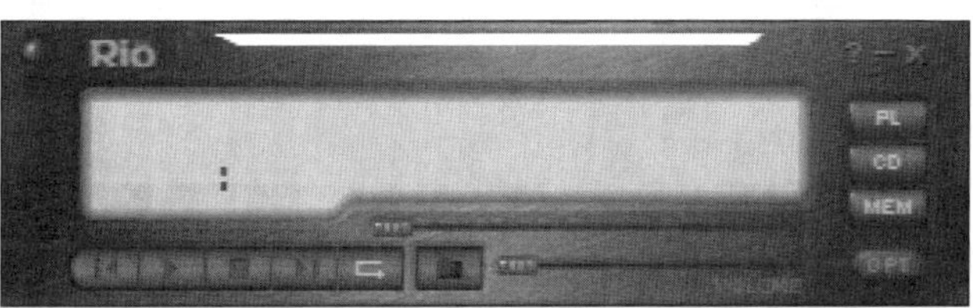

FIGURE 8.2:
The Rio player screen.

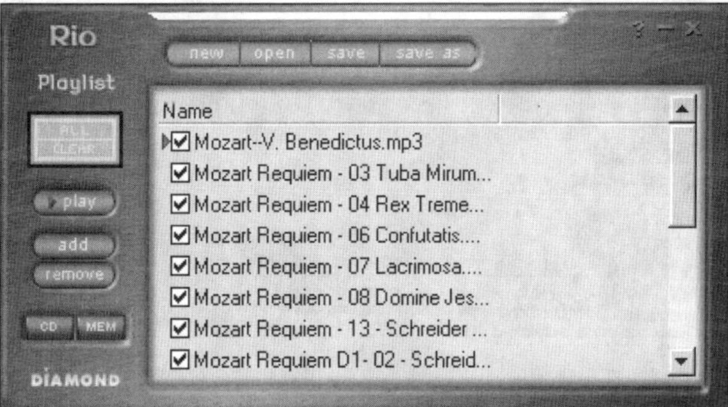

FIGURE 8.3:
The Rio Playlist Manager screen.

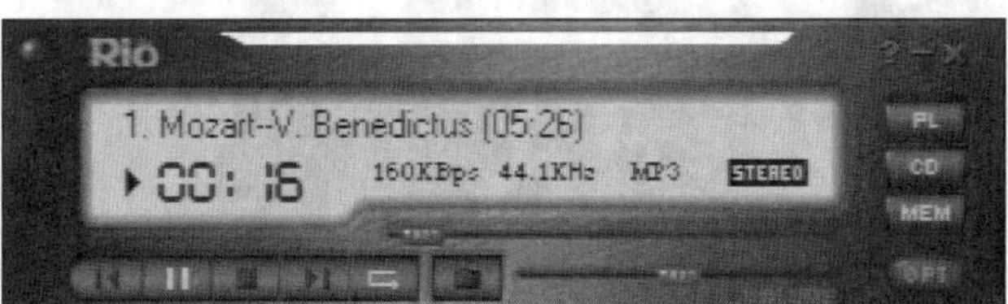

FIGURE 8.4:
The Rio player screen with a file playing.

You can also use the Rio to play CDs using the Rio CD Player screen, shown in Figure 8.5.

However, the most important reason to use the Rio software is to download files into the Rio. Figure 8.6 shows the Rio Internal/External Memory screen.

To download files, first make sure the interface cable is plugged into the Rio. Then click Open, select the files from the standard file open dialog box, then click OK. The software starts downloading files from your computer into the Rio, as shown in Figure 8.7.

When the files are completely downloaded, the Rio Internal/External Memory screen is updated with the files you've downloaded, as shown in Figure 8.8.

FIGURE 8.5:
The Rio CD Player screen with a CD playing.

FIGURE 8.6:
The Rio Internal/External Memory screen.

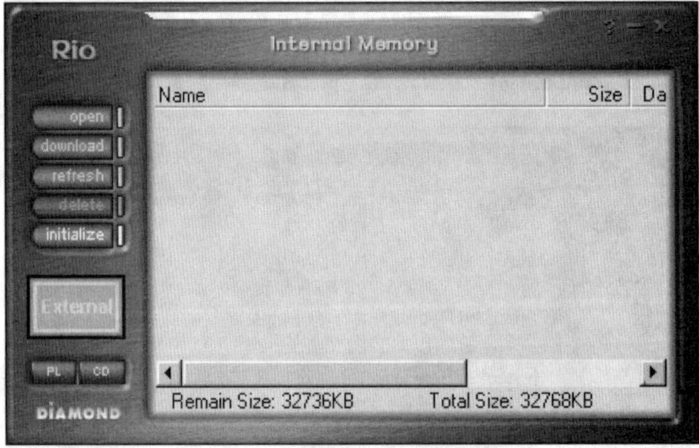

FIGURE 8.7:
Downloading files into the Rio.

When you've downloaded the selected files, the memory remaining and total memory available in the Rio appear at the bottom of the screen. As you can see in Figure 8.8, there's still room for one more track as long as it's not bigger than 3.8 MB. The Rio is now ready to play your choice of tracks. When you start playing, the tracks will be played in the order shown on the screen.

If you need more MP3 files and information on the Rio, Diamond Multimedia runs the RioPort web site (*http://www.rioport.com*), which is aimed at promoting legitimate, nonpirated music (primarily MP3) on the Internet. Figure 8.9 shows the RioPort main screen.

The Rio is a snappy little unit that is exceptionally popular. It comes with a couple of CDs of software and MP3 files, and it lists for $199.95.

The Rio PMP300 Special Edition is due to be released in the near future. It's an upscale version of the classic Rio PMP300, with 64MB

FIGURE 8.8:
Tracks downloaded into the Rio.

FIGURE 8.9:
The *RioPort.com* main screen.

of onboard RAM, which lets you store over an hour of CD-quality music. The flash memory slot lets you add an additional 16MB, for a total of 80MB of RAM. The Rio PMP300 Special Edition's case is a transparent teal plastic rather than the shiny black of the Rio PMP300. The list price on the Special Edition is $249.95.

DIAMOND MULTIMEDIA
2880 Junction Ave.
San Jose, CA 95134
800-468-5846
http://www.diamondmm.com

MPMAN

The MPMan F10 from Eiger Labs, Inc. (*http://www.eigerlabs.com*), was the first MP3 player on the market. The current model, the F20, is another snappy portable MP3 player. Figure 8.10 shows a picture of the MPMan F20.

The MPMan F20 has several advantages over the Rio. First, you can run it off an optional 3V DC adapter to save the battery. This may not necessarily be an advantage if you use the MPMan while you're working out, but it could be helpful when listening to the MPMan around the house. The MPMan also ships with very good earphones that provide good bass response. However, the LCD display is much smaller and not as easy to read. Like most competing units, you'll probably want to take a look at both and see which is best for you.

FIGURE 8.10:
The MPMan F20
portable MP3 player.

The MPMan interface program for downloading files appears in Figure 8.11.

The MPMan software makes a distinction between the flash memory and the smart media cards you insert in the player. You can load tracks into each and update them separately. The MPMan software doesn't have a player built in; instead, you can specify your favorite MP3 player as the player to use when previewing tracks.

To download MP3 files into the MPMan, click and drag the files from the file tree on the left side of the screen into the appropriate window. The software downloads the files into the MPMan. One slick trick is that you can use the MPMan as a portable file storage device. You can download files that aren't MP3 files into the MPMan, then carry them to another location and upload them there. It's not as convenient as a

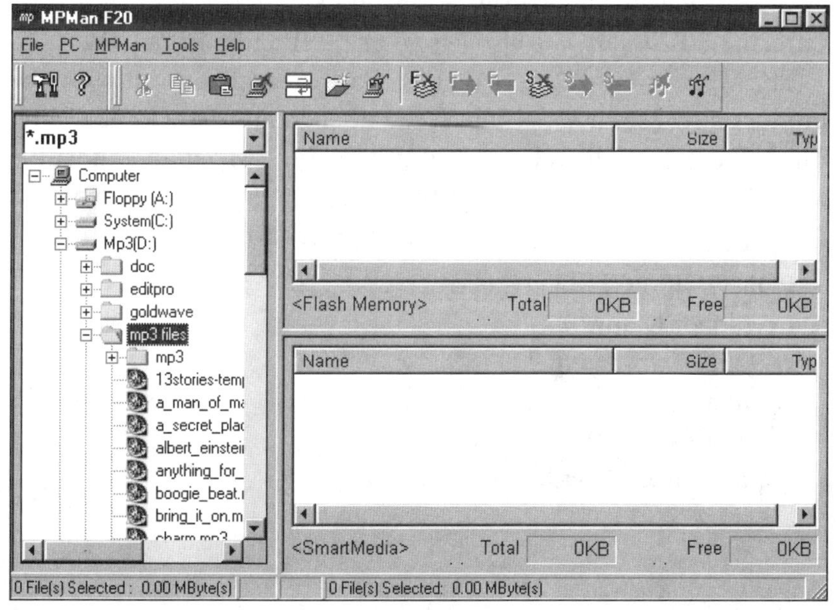

FIGURE 8.11: The MPMan interface software.

Zip drive, but you can store files of any kind up to the maximum capacity of your MPMan's RAM. This might come in handy sometime when you need to move a big file between computers.

The MPMan sells for $179. The optional 3V DC adapter costs $29.95.

EIGER LABS, INC.
37800 Central Court
City of Newark, CA 94560
510-739-5661
http://www.eigerlabs.com

MPLAYER3

The MPlayer3 from Pontis Electronic GmbH (*http://www.mplayer3. com*) is slightly different from the other MP3 players discussed in this chapter so far: it has no onboard RAM at all. Instead, the MPlayer3 uses two MultiMedia Cards for the RAM. You can record playlists on the MultiMedia Cards and then plug them into the MPlayer3. Multi-Media Cards currently have a capacity of 16MB; 32MB cards are due later in 1999. If you have several MultiMedia Cards, you can inter-change them each time to plug in a new playlist. Pontis Electronics also has a ROM version of the MultiMedia Cards called ROS (Record On Silicon), which will let distributors sell prerecorded versions of Multi-Media Cards. Figure 8.12 shows the MPlayer3 and MultiMedia Cards.

The L.E.D. software accompanying the MPlayer3 comes in both Windows and Macintosh versions. There is also support for Linux. As with other MP3 player software, it lets you create playlists and down-load MP3 files to the MPlayer3, but unlike other MP3 player soft-ware, the L.E.D. software also lets you rip MP3 files from CDs.

The MPlayer3 uses 2 AA batteries or an external power supply. The product also uses a serial interface rather than a parallel interface. The MPlayer3 is sold in Germany, Austria, and Switzerland under the name "Hexaglot MPlayer3." By any name, the MPlayer3 sells in the US for $195 with either Windows or Macintosh software.

PONTIS ELECTRONIC GMBH
Irrenloher Damm 17
D-92521 Schwarzenfeld
Germany
Fax number: +49-9435-5407-40
http://www.mplayer3.com

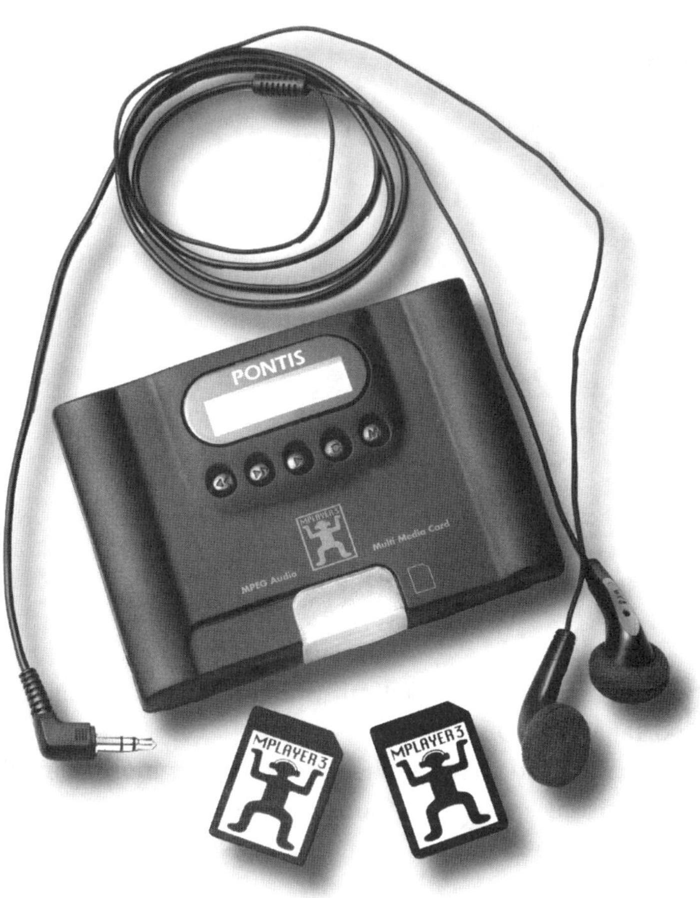

FIGURE 8.12:
The MPlayer3 and MultiMedia Cards.

NOMAD

The Nomad from Creative Labs (*http://www.soundblaster.com*) is a very small unit, about the size of a credit card. The Nomad's case is made of magnesium, giving it an attractive soft-silver look. The Nomad reads the tag off the MP3 file and displays in the LCD the name of the song being played and the name of the artist as well as the playing time. Moreover, while the song is playing, you can display the lyrics; definitely a cool feature!

In addition to the MP3 player, the Nomad has a built-in FM radio. This is a major advantage if you're using the Nomad for longer than the playlist you've recorded and want to hear something else. Another great feature of the Nomad is that it can also be used as a digital recorder: you can use it to record things like speeches and lectures.

Unlike the Rio and the MPMan, the Nomad uses two AAA batteries (rather like a typical remote control), which provides about 8 hours of play. Although this is less than the 12 hours of play for the Rio and the MPMan, the Nomad compensates by having a battery

charger in a docking station, which is very convenient if you use a portable MP3 player a lot.

The Nomad comes with CDs containing more than 100 free MP3 songs from a variety of sources and an extensive array of spoken word content. Figure 8.13 shows the Nomad plugged into the docking station.

You can also use the docking station to plug the Nomad into an external speaker or your sound system and play MP3 files that way. The basic unit (listing for $169.99) comes with 32MB of RAM in the unit. There's a deluxe unit for $249.99 that also has a 32MB flash memory upgrade card, giving you a total of 64MB.

OTHER PLAYERS

There are many other portable MP3 players under development at this time. For example, Sony is developing a digital audio Walkman using a technology called "the Memory Stick." The Memory Stick, basically a flash memory card, will hold digital audio files. Their first Memory Stick Walkman is due out sometime in 1999. For news on other developments in portable MP3 players, keep an eye on the MP3 web sites listed in Appendix A, "Resources."

SOUND CARDS

The quality of the sound you get out of your computer is largely a function of how good your sound card is. Virtually every computer sold today has some kind of sound card—in many cases, the sound card is built right into the computer's motherboard—but you may want to get a better sound card to improve the sound of the MP3 files you're playing. This section will introduce you to a couple of the leading sound cards on the market right now.

Here are a few general tips if you're looking for a sound card:

✦ Make sure that the sound card supports at least 64 simultaneous voices (a *voice* is one line of sound data, such as an instrument, lyrics, and so on; a "track" in mixing terms).

✦ You should also make sure that the card supports 3D sound. 3D sound is a relatively recent feature in sound cards.

✦ The sound card should be at least 16-bit audio, but a 32-bit sound card is better. This is most useful when recording sound from an analog source.

Also look at the software that's included with the sound card. Many leading sound cards come with customized versions of music- and WAV-editing software, including many of the programs featured earlier in this book.

SOUND BLASTER LIVE!

The name "Sound Blaster" is synonymous with sound cards. Sound Blaster cards from Creative Labs (*http://www.soundblaster.com*) have been a standard for compatibility in sound cards for more than a decade. Although there is a wide range of sound cards from Creative Labs, the Sound Blaster Live! is their most recent great sound card. (It's so cool that it has its own web site, *http://www.sblive.com.*) The Sound Blaster Live! card is shown in Figure 8.14.

FIGURE 8.14: The Sound Blaster Live! card and accompanying Digital I/O card.

The Sound Blaster Live! card can play up to 256 voices (which you can upgrade to 574 voices with software from Creative Labs). Another feature of the Sound Blaster Live! is 3D sound, also known as 3D Positional Audio. 3D sound is much like classic audiophile technology in which you have one optimal position between the speakers where the sound is just perfect. This is good for computer users, who can position their speakers so that they're automatically in the "sweet spot" for the best audio.

As if 3D sound weren't enough, the Sound Blaster Live! also has Environmental Audio. Environmental Audio lets you move beyond 3D audio effects by providing preset environmental effects such as "Hall," "Chorus," "Underwater," or "Arena." This is similar to some of the effects you saw for various WAV editors in Chapter 6, "Editing and Enhancing MP3 Files," but you don't have to edit the files themselves to do it. Furthermore, you can apply the Environmental Audio effects on the fly to any MP3 file or CD. This is also a wonderful enhancement if you play live-action games on your computer. The Sound Blaster Live! also is updatable through the Live!Ware program that lets you download new features, new sound effects, and improved software for your Sound Blaster Live! card.

Other features of the Sound Blaster Live! card are support for two or four speakers (for a real surround-sound effect). The Sound Blaster Live! also comes with a Digital I/O card that lets you break out some multimedia I/O. (You probably won't use a lot of the features unless you're doing fancy sound engineering or you want to use the digital output of your CD-ROM drive to get the very best output of your digital audio.) Upcoming features for the Sound Blaster Live! card include support for up to eight analog or digital speakers, pull-down recording software, and other improvements.

Sound Blaster Live! comes with Sound Forge XP and Mixman Studio (featured in Chapter 6, "Editing and Enhancing MP3 Files,") as well as Cakewalk Express Gold, a MIDI sequencing program, and a host of other programs, utilities, and sound files.

If you buy the Sound Blaster Live! with Digital I/O card, the price is $199, but if you buy the "value" version of the product, you get just the Sound Blaster Live! card for $99.

CREATIVE LABS, INC.
1901 McCarthy Boulevard
Milpitas, CA 95035
408-428-6600
http://www.soundblaster.com
http://www.sblive.com

DIAMOND MONSTER SOUND MX300

In addition to the Rio, Diamond Multimedia also produces a number of great sound cards. The best of the current crop is the Monster Sound MX300 (shown in Figure 8.15). The Monster Sound MX300 supports up to 320 voices and has extensive environmental 3D effects to make the sound feel real. It supports two or four speakers.

The Monster Sound MX300 has a positional 3D audio that provides extensive 3D environmental sound effects on playback. It uses a technique known as *wave tracing* to render things like sound reflecting off walls and floors. Marble, stone, glass, and water will all reflect different sounds. The Monster Sound MX300 gives you an accurate rendering of sound whether you're using headphones, two speakers, or four speakers.

For hard-core audiophiles, the Monster Sound MX300 was the first sound card to feature DVD and Dolby Digital support. You can also buy an optional add-on card for $39.95 that lets you connect your computer directly into your home theater. The Monster Sound MX300 is $99.95. The Monster Sound MX25 add-on card is $39.95.

DIAMOND MULTIMEDIA

2880 Junction Ave.
San Jose, CA 95134
800-468-5846
http://www.diamondmm.com

FIGURE 8.15:
The Monster Sound MX300 sound card.

FIGURE 8.16:
The Montego II sound card.

TURTLE BEACH MONTEGO II

One other sound card you should give serious consideration to is the Montego II from Turtle Beach (shown in Figure 8.16). The Montego II supports up to 320 voices. Like the Sound Blaster Live! and the Monster Sound MX300, the Montego II provides positional 3D audio and environmental 3D effects. You can use the Montego II with two or four speakers.

The Montego II has a built-in 10-band hardware equalizer so you can customize your sound. It also comes with Voyetra's AudioStation 32 software, a rack-component style program for equalizing and mixing your sound. AudioStation 32 has a CD player and players for MP3, WAV, MIDI, and other sound files as well as AVI and MPEG video files. The Montego II costs $99.95.

VOYETRA TURTLE BEACH

5 Odell Plaza

Yonkers NY 10701-1406

800-233-9377

http://www.tbeach.com

OTHER SOUND CARDS

There are many other sound cards on the market from manufacturers such as Yamaha (*http://www.yamaha.com*), SIIG (*http://www.siig.com*), and Hi-Val (*http://www.hival.com*). In addition, the manufacturers listed here are constantly upgrading their products and providing new features and new products at new prices. Check out the manufacturer's web sites as well as some of the more popular MP3 web sites to see what's best for your computer.

SPEAKERS

You can have the best sound card in the world, but if you have cheap, tinny speakers, you won't hear much of a difference. The PC speaker was originally a 2-1/2" speaker like you'd see in a transistor radio—most PCs still have one as a matter of fact—but these were rapidly supplanted by external speakers of increasing quality and power.

You can buy a set of speakers (frequently known as *multimedia speakers*) for about $30 from most discount houses that will provide a satisfactory level of quality in the output, but for the very best sound, you'll want to consider speakers like the ones discussed in this section. Don't worry about having to spend a paycheck for a single pair of speakers, though; you can get great sound for $50, and for no more than $300, you can get a full home-theater system for your computer that can alter time, space, and dimensions, produce nuclear-brain-damage levels of sound, and clean up the office at the same time.

SPEAKER CONCEPTS

Passive speakers have no built-in amplifier. Instead, they run off the sound card. Amplified speakers have a built-in amplifier and must be plugged into a power source to work. When people talk about a *speaker*, they are usually referring collectively to the sound-reproducing devices you're using to play the sound on each stereo channel. Each of these devices is itself a speaker, but they are usually referred to as *cones* or *drivers*. A *tweeter* is a cone that plays high-frequency (treble) sounds. A *woofer* plays low-frequency (bass) sounds. A *subwoofer* plays very low frequency (bass and subaudible) sounds. (Bass is nondirectional—you can't tell where it's coming from—so you can keep your desktop clear by putting the subwoofer on the floor behind the computer where you won't kick it.) Subwoofers are necessary for producing the best audio output.

Some amplifiers and speakers are measured in RMS watts and some aren't. RMS is an abbreviation for "root mean square," a measure of the effective wattage of the amplifier, which is about .707 times the peak wattage. If an amplifier or speaker isn't measured in RMS watts, then the equivalent RMS wattage rating is roughly seven-tenths of the total wattage.

CREATIVE LABS

For simple two-speaker sets, consider the Sound Blaster line. The SBS10, SBS20, and SBS50 are all good low-end speaker sets. The SBS10 ($19.99) is a passive speaker system. The SBS20 ($29.99) has a 5 RMS-watt amplifier and volume, bass, and treble controls. The SBS50 ($49.99) has an 11 RMS-watt amplifier and a separate woofer and tweeter to produce a wider dynamic range.

The SBS line is pretty inexpensive, but they're not the best you can do for your audio quality. The next step up from Creative Labs is the PCWorks speakers, which list for $49.99. The PCWorks speakers are an amplified three-piece system, with two small "satellite" speakers and a larger subwoofer. Figure 8.17 shows the PCWorks speakers.

For something a little better, take a look at the SoundWorks speakers ($99.99), shown in Figure 8.18. The SoundWorks speakers are larger and more powerful than the PCWorks speakers, with a 21 RMS-watt amplifier.

At the top of the line for three-speaker sets from Creative Labs are the MicroWorks speakers, selling for $249.99. The MicroWorks

FIGURE 8.17:
The PCWorks speakers.

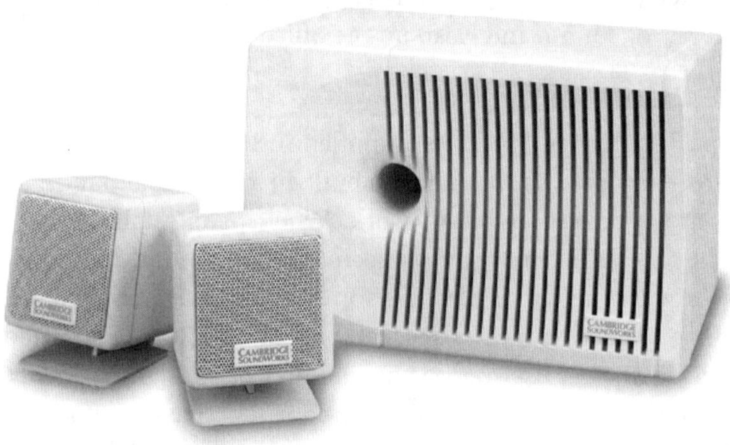

FIGURE 8.18:
The SoundWorks speakers.

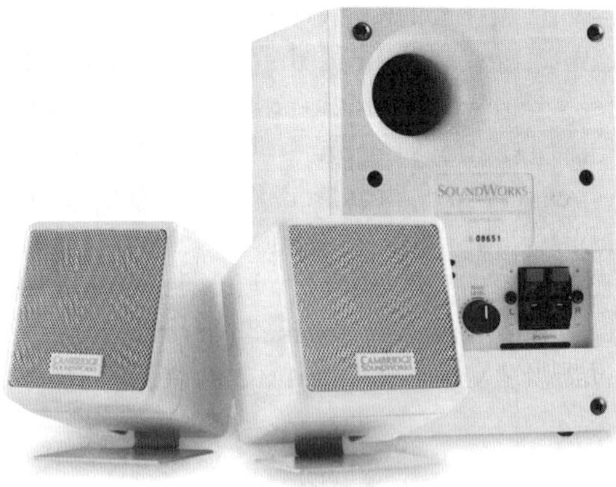

speakers (shown in Figure 8.19) have a 68 RMS-watt amplifier and provide high-end quality.

All of these speaker sets are two speakers, or two speakers and a sub-woofer. For a full sound environment, you may want to go to a set containing four speakers and a subwoofer. The first of these from Creative Labs is the FourPointSurround FPS1000, listing for $99. This set has four speakers plus a subwoofer. You set the four speakers up two in front and two behind for a complete environmental sound experience.

For $199, you can get the FourPointSurround FPS2000 Digital speakers, with a 53 RMS-watt amplifier (shown in Figure 8.20). The FPS2000 speakers handle four-channel digital output directly for crisper reproduction.

For the most in home theater sound for your PC, you'll want to look at the DeskTop Theater 5.1, appearing in Figure 8.21. This complete six-speaker system comes with a decoder-amplifier for providing the most in sound quality up to and including multichannel Dolby Digital and Dolby Surround movie sound. You can use the DeskTop Theater 5.1 with a DVD unit on your PC or with any standard DVD player. The DeskTop Theater 5.1 sells for $299.99, a fair amount of money but worth it if you want the best possible sound from your PC.

FIGURE 8.19:
The MicroWorks speakers.

CREATIVE LABS, INC.
1901 McCarthy Boulevard
Milpitas, CA 95035
408-428-6600
http://www.soundblaster.com
http://www.sblive.com

FIGURE 8.20:
The FourPointSurround FPS2000 Digital speakers.

FIGURE 8.21:
The DeskTop Theater 5.1 speakers.

ALTEC

Altec (*http://www.altecmm.com*) has had a long and distinguished reputation as a maker of great speakers, so it's no surprise that they offer a line of multimedia speakers.

For inexpensive two-piece speaker sets, the ACS90 PowerCube ($34.95) has a 15-watt amplifier. The ACS43 PowerCube 2 ($49.95) has a 20-watt amplifier. These are good speakers, but two-piece speakers won't give you the best sound, because they don't have the bass response provided by a subwoofer.

Altec's three-piece speakers start with the ACS44, listed at $79.95. It has a 33-watt amplifier. The ACS45.1 for $99.95 also has a 33-watt amplifier, but it has a wooden subwoofer, which is a pleasant change from plastic and metal speaker housings.

The ADA70 ($149.95) is a three-piece speaker system that supports digital audio. You can connect these through your computer's USB port. The ADA70 appears in Figure 8.22.

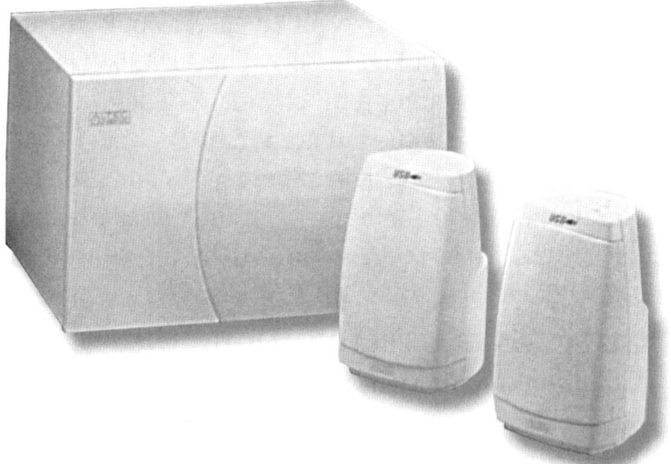

FIGURE 8.22:
The ADA70 speakers.

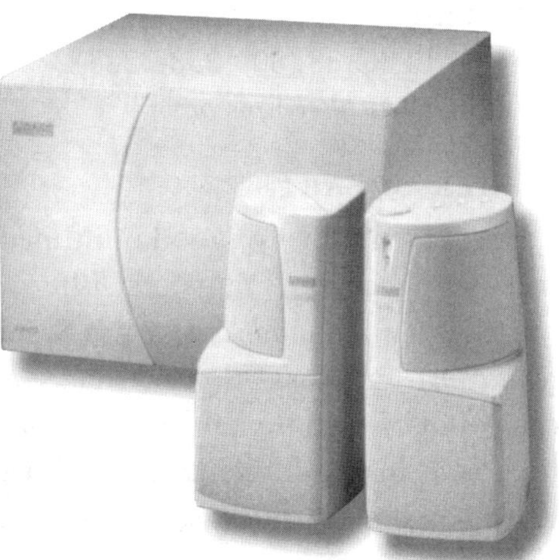

FIGURE 8.23:
The ADA305 speakers.

For something a little more powerful in a three-piece digital speaker system, you may want to take a look at the ADA305 for $199.95, appearing in Figure 8.23. The ADA305 takes an analog signal and breaks it into four channels of audio with an internal decoder. It also has a 40-watt amplifier.

The ADA880 Dolby Digital Speaker System, listing for $329.95, is the premier edition for home-computer users. It has four satellite speakers and a subwoofer powered by an 80-watt amplifier. The ADA880 (appearing in Figure 8.24) also has a remote-control unit.

ALTEC LANSING TECHNOLOGIES, INC.
Communications Manager
Altec Lansing Technologies, Inc.
Route 6 and 209
Milford, PA 18337-0277
800-ALTEC-88 (800-258-3288)
http://www.altecmm.com

OTHER SPEAKERS

There are a number of good multimedia speakers on the market. Be sure to check out Yamaha (*http://www.yamaha.com*), MidiLand (*http://www.midiland.com*), Aura Systems, Inc. (*http://www.aurasystems.com*), and Koss (*http://www.koss.com*). As with sound cards, you can count on a continual stream of new products and prices. Be sure to look at MP3 and manufacturer's web sites to see what's available when you buy your next set of speakers.

MP3 PLAYERS FOR YOUR CAR AND HOME

If you can have a CD player in your car, there's no reason why you can't have an MP3 player in your car. Although there aren't a lot of units on the market yet, there are a number in development. There are also a number of do-it-yourself units you can build if you feel like tinkering and have some spare parts.

Both the commercial units and the do-it-yourself projects all tend to have an inexpensive hard disk and a simple interface (usually a dash-mounted LCD display of some kind). The advantage of having an MP3 player in your car is that you can store a pile of tracks on the unit's hard disk. Most of these use at least a 2-gigabyte hard drive (they're really cheap these days) and they hold about 30–35 CDs' worth of music right at your fingertips!

One car unit that is about to be released is the Empeg-car from Empeg, Ltd. The Empeg-car comes with a 2.1-gigabyte hard drive in the basic model, although you can get hard drives all the way up to 28 gigabytes (about 500 CDs' worth). The Empeg-car also has a built-in FM radio and a remote-control sensor. The basic model costs $999. See the Empeg, Ltd., web site at *http://www.empeg.com* for prices and information.

Another unit due be released soon is the Impy3 from CD Systems, Inc. The Impy3 has a Pentium 200MMX computer and a keypad with a four-line, 20-character LCD display. The Impy3 can be ordered with other options as well, including Ethernet networking, a CD-ROM drive, or a bigger hard drive. (In its native configuration, the Impy3 comes with an 8-gigabyte hard drive that will hold about 130 hours of MP3 files.) Check their web site at *http://www.impy3.com* for prices and availability.

Frank Pennington's Monolith for the Automobile is a small unit that comes with a 6.4-gigabyte hard drive (which holds a little over 100 hours of music) that you can use as a car or a home MP3 unit. It has a 4-inch color LCD screen to let you select songs and create and edit playlists. You plug the Monolith for the Automobile into your computer and download new files. The Monolith for the Automobile sells for $775; the home entertainment version sells for $635. Check out the web site at *http://listen.to/digitalcar* for product information or call 888-368-DEAL or e-mail *sales@dealsdirect.com* to order.

There are a number of manufacturers of consumer electronics who are all designing CD units for your sound system that play MP3 files, but none of them are ready for the market yet.

And, although it doesn't play MP3 files itself, the Irman from Evation (*http://www.evation.com*) is a remote-control plug-in unit you can

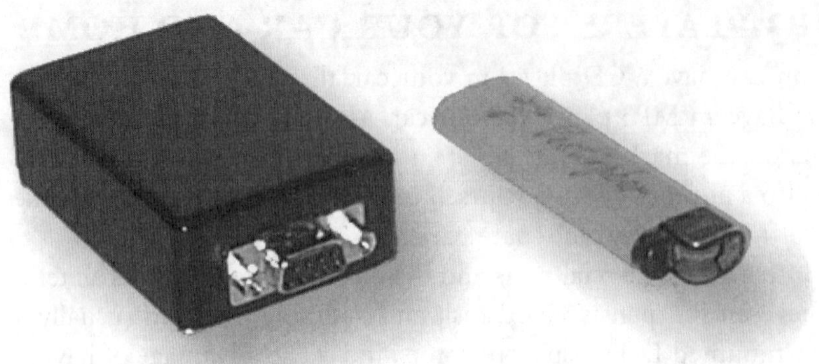

use to control your PC. It was invented by Ties Bos as a way to control Winamp using his stereo's remote control. He started selling it in the local newsgroup of Universiteit Twente in the Netherlands, where Sytse Sijbrandij saw it. Sytse struck a deal with Ties to sell the Irman in the Netherlands and abroad. Business is booming; within his first six months of operation, Sytse had to hire staff to help him ship packages.

The Irman, shown in Figure 8.25 next to a lighter for scale, is very small. You plug it into a serial port and then control it with a standard remote. Although the original software was for a Winamp plug-in, it's easy to write software for. There are now many software plug-ins and programs available on the Evation web site at *http://www.evation.com/irman* that support the Irman with Winamp, WPlay, and several general-purpose control applications. Check the Evation web site for the latest information. The Irman costs $35 plus $3 shipping and handling.

EVATION.COM
Waalstraat 219
7523 RG Enschede
The Netherlands
http://www.evation.com

In this chapter you learned about the MP3 players on the market or about to be released, such as the Rio, the MPMan, and the Nomad. You were also introduced to a few of the more popular sound cards and multimedia speakers you can use to add quality to your MP3 files. And you got a taste of the rich assortment of MP3 players and gadgets for your car and home. In the next and final chapter, you'll hear a number of experts in the field of MP3 and digital audio express their opinions on where MP3s are going and what we might have to look forward to.

What's Next?

In the previous chapter you learned about the MP3 players on the market, such as the Rio, the MPMan, and the Nomad. You also saw several of the more popular sound cards and multimedia speakers to enhance the quality of your MP3 files. You were also introduced to some of the various MP3 players and equipment for your car and home. In this final chapter, you'll hear from a number of MP3 experts, developers, and analysts, who will provide a look into the future of MP3 and digital audio.

THE FUTURE OF MP3 AND DIGITAL MUSIC

Dennis Mudd, CEO of MusicMatch, Inc., is very optimistic about MP3:

> *"MP3 truly represents a revolution in the music industry. It allows consumers for the first time to take real control over how they find and listen to music. It lets them download music from a broader range of artists than has ever been possible before. It lets people spend more time listening to music they really enjoy. MP3 truly empowers music listeners, and the industry is scrambling to figure out how to meet their new, tougher requirements."*

Paul Schatzkin (aka "The Perfesser"), President of *Songs.com*, also believes that MP3 will revolutionize the music industry:

> *"Some of my favorite recurring scenes in Star Trek are the ones where Captain Picard turns to a machine in his quarters and simply says, "Tea, Earl Grey, Hot," and*

moments later a cup of steaming brew materializes before his eyes and palate.

I think MP3 is the doorway to a future for intellectual properties quite like Picard's replicator. I rather doubt that the final format will be MP3—I know for a fact that there are already newer, better technologies being developed that offer higher fidelity (not that most people would notice) at even higher compression rates. But I believe that there will be a time—and probably sooner rather than later—when we'll be able to turn to a device in our living rooms and simply say "Beatles, 'Abbey Road,' Loud," and moments later, a crystal-clear copy of that classic LP will begin playing on our stereo (quadreo? octeo?) home-entertainment system.

When that time comes, we will no longer have our own libraries of natural-resource-consuming, digit-filled plastic wafers lining the shelves. The library will be out in cyberspace somewhere, and we will pay a modest periodic subscription fee to one or many services to obtain access to the content of our choice. We will have the option of making copies of those recordings we listen to most on our own dedicated storage device, and all the ancillary content that is bundled with music now—album cover art, lyrics, notes, etc.—will be digitally encoded and reproduced on a video display.

I'm not willing to say whether we'll ever be able to get food and other complex hard goods from a device like Picard's replicator. Who's to say even that molecules can be converted to code and digitally replicated? But I do feel that, so far as books and films and songs—intellectual property, information—are concerned, the age of the replicator is already upon us. MP3 and the Internet are just the first iterations of that potential.

"Computer: Jefferson Airplane, 'Volunteers,' VERY loud."

Another person who thinks that we're going to see music on demand is Jim Griffin, President & CEO of OneHouse LLC, a company dedicated to the digital delivery of art, with an emphasis on the transition from the analog marketplace to the digital market space. Jim sees digital music moving towards things like Nullsoft's SHOUTCast, a method of broadcasting music and audio over the net quickly and easily:

"I think that distribution isn't going to change from physical to digital distribution. SHOUTCast is the most interesting development. The future is about delivery, not distribution. Delivery is

getting the music from Point A to Point B, but it doesn't stay at Point B. The caching of digits won't be as necessary. The digits— the music—will arrive in much the same way that they arrive today: just-in-time. It's the transition from push to pull: MP3 is about push, but SHOUTCast is pull. Music will be more on-demand. One format is a very disconnected relationship; the other is highly connected. MP3 appears like the extension of a logical extension, but the paradigm will actually shift.

ATMs made access to money ubiquitous and we felt less need to have money physically in our hands as a result. Similarly, as data becomes ubiquitous, we'll be able to pull it [from the source] whenever we need it.

Push technology is designed to overcome supply inefficiency. A classic example is being in a pub. They put a lot of glasses up on the bar right before closing time (supply inefficiency) so you can get them after closing time, so around closing time, you'd need a really big glass of Guinness. But as long as you're not concerned about having a thing and there's no inefficiency, your desire to hold it will go down. Streaming and interactive streaming are the future."

Hock Leow, Vice President of the Multimedia Division at Creative Labs (who produce the Sound Blaster Live! and the Nomad MP3 player), is looking forward to supporting MP3 and digital music.

"Our goal at Creative is to continue leveraging our expertise to offer solutions for portable digital audio and to make the experience accessible to consumers worldwide. As we move forward with future products, we intend to support all popular formats for playing back Internet music and digital audio. Today that format is MP3 and there is an abundance of support from Internet audio and music enthusiasts. With the introduction of the Creative Nomad line, we are raising the bar for portable digital audio players as well as generating acceptance and understanding of a revolutionary new way to download digital music and audio from the Internet."

Frank Jin, Product Manager for the MPMan at Eiger Labs, Inc., expressed the opinion that MP3 and possibly other formats will make music more available and provide artists new creative opportunities because of the difference in the medium.

"There are many exciting things to look forward to in the future of MP3.

When the MPMan first came out as the world's very first portable MP3 player, everybody looked to it to be the Do-All, Be-All kind of a device. Now the floodgates have opened for all different kinds of configurations to satisfy every taste. It won't be long before these MP3 devices will take the place of the traditional cassette and CD players in cars, at home, and in the pocket. They'll be easier to configure and may not even require a computer.

The race is on for the standardization of a secure music distribution model. Once this is set in place, it will truly revolutionize the business of music. Consumers will be able to buy the music they want through their computer on the Internet, a vending machine at the mall, or even wireless by just placing a call and ordering what they want. It will be more convenient and will cost less money than now.

Artists will be able to concentrate on songs they are most inspired with and not waste their energy on just filling up space on the CD. There will be an avenue they can distribute their music through without the traditional record label avenue. On the Internet, the small guys would have equal footing as the big record label guys.

Eiger Labs and Saehan are working together with companies who can bring these changes to the music industry. Our near-term goal is to develop a device that can satisfy the public's desire for ease of use, flexible and expandable architecture, and much higher capacity than now.

MP3 as a compression technology may become obsolete someday, but the free and visionary spirit of MP3 will live on in the new era of digital music for the Internet generation and the business of its distribution. Ultimately, it's what people want that matters, not what some business executives think will make the most money for them."

Sytse Sijbrandij, President of *Evation.com* and the distributor of the Irman control unit, thinks that MP3 will improve the opportunities for music distribution and put more money into the musician's pockets:

"The Internet is changing the world, and it is doing that by taking down the walls that make up our normal society. Normally an artist has to give away his copyrights to get his music published. But thanks to the Internet that's changing: everybody can set up a home page and publish their MP3s. But [the RIAA's] injunction against the Rio and the modifying of protocols won't make the walls come back: intellectual freedom is here to stay.

Of course this freedom comes with some drawbacks, most notably the copying of illegal MP3s. Because of this, the RIAA started development of SDMI, a standard that would make it harder (but not impossible) to copy digital music. But this standard would also be much less flexible than MP3 (sharing it with friends, copying it to your car) and it would prevent little artists from distributing their music without a big record label. And that is what it's all about: the six big labels don't want an equal playing field because it would undermine their hold on the market.

But that's also why it shall fail. People want to be able to share their music, play it in their car, or on their Walkman. And little artists will continue to give away their music on MP3.com and other sites, not only because they want their music to be heard from an artist's point of view but also with a business sense. Yes, people, money can be made by giving your music away free. Just like Redhat makes money by giving their [Linux] software away, new record labels will make money by giving their music away. And artists will make money with advertising, concerts, T-shirts, limited edition songs, poems, fanclubs, email lists, commercials and in many other creative ways.

When the dust settles, the big six record labels will have a lot more competition from GoodNoise.com and other digital labels and from the independent labels that finally have means of distribution. People will be able to access their music anytime, anywhere, with minimal cost but great flexibility and service. Artists will retain their copyrights and will have the freedom to publish what they want. Competition and the need for selection will grow because digital distribution enables everyone to publish their songs. But as a whole, artists will earn more money while at the same time people will have to spend less. Why is that? Well, it's due to one of the oldest business tactics, to cut out the middleman: lawyers, CD shops, CD makers, distribution companies, and all other people that raise the price of a CD. 'Be afraid. Be very afraid.'"

____

Frank Pennington, Founder of DigitalCar (maker of the Monolith car and home MP3 player), also thinks that MP3 is a major tool for the independent artist and that the music industry must learn to adapt:

> *"I feel that the music industry is changing because they did not foresee how the Internet and MP3 format will drastically change their paradigm of how music can be distributed. If they do not embrace it, they will crumble to virtually nothing. Many artists I talk to are completely changing their attitudes towards record labels and contracts. They are becoming more independent now that they have this great new way of distributing their music, culture, and ideas. This trend will continue even if the laws become stiffer and the RIAA tries to fight back.*
>
> *MP3 will be remembered as the first medium that allowed any artist to express their music to a global audience. It opens up the industry in ways never before imagined! All who embrace this new change will be rewarded: not always by money, but by having an audience that they could never have reached before.*
>
> *MP3s have made the battlefield of the arts and entertainment industry fairer and more fluid for the artist. Now the audience decides which artists will be a success. I am looking forward to seeing these new types of music and artists!"*

____

Carl J. Davis, President of CD Systems, Inc. (makers of the Impy3), was not impressed with the efforts to replace MP3 with a more secure music format, and believes that MP3 will be here for a long time to come:

> *"While we sit here rockin' and rollin' and twitchin' and jerkin' to our favorite MP3 music, IBM, Microsoft, AT&T, and Sony are scrambling to come up with a copy-protectable, proprietary format to deliver CD-quality music. Like the title of one of my favorite films, I suggest that 'The Gods Must Be Crazy.' I don't think that significant improvement to music quality is even mentioned by any of the proposed new standards, so I suggest the only real motives they have are to line their own pockets and align themselves with the money-monger middlemen of the entertainment industry. Additionally, I believe that the only method at their disposal to implement such standards is by exercising the*

strangleholds that they now have on the market. Why Joe Consumer would willingly give up his MP3 format to align himself with one these behemoths for the added aggravation of 'copy protection' and proprietary format is beyond me.

Digital audio, by virtue of its undisputed quality and durability, is the method by which nearly all audio is now and will be produced for as far as I can see. The MP3 format, by virtue of its superior quality, low storage requirements, massive supply of easily available utilities, and growing acceptance by the grassroots community of computer literates will, in my opinion, extend its present popularity and become the audio distribution format of the foreseeable future."

However, not everyone thinks MP3 is going to be a permanent fixture on the digital music landscape. Mark Hardie, Senior Analyst with Forrester Research, Inc., is of the opinion that MP3 is actually on the decline in favor of other digital formats that will allow record companies and other vendors to sell digital music:

"MP3 is merely a format, and its halcyon days are probably behind it against competition from Microsoft's new audio format and other commercially viable formats from companies such as Liquid Audio and AT&T's a2b music. You're going to see that the music we all want is not going to be in MP3 format; it will be in a form that's at least as convenient for a mass-market audience.

The objective of digital distribution, if you're a record label or company making a profit, is to make music readily available and easy to consume for techies as well as nontechies. So the process can't involve multiple incompatible software packages that you have to get from different places or vendors, and you can't have concerns over whether you're using the right version. You can't have a retail environment where the content is arguably laid out in flea-market fashion. Right now, what we have are flea markets offering obscure music online. That does not make for a robust or a mass market. I don't shop at flea markets exclusively; if the world was nothing but flea markets, we'd do a lot less shopping.

There are advantages to fewer vendors and fewer brand names and having the consumers put their trust into high-quality content provided by trusted record companies. You buy a movie from Disney not because you read a critique of the movie but because it's a

Disney movie. You don't want to go to the Web and spend hours in a filtering process that radio and the record companies already do a good job of.

MP3s won't just die. But if you're going to run mission-critical systems, you need viable vendors with products that are stable and that aren't subject to multiple out-of-synch development efforts. In fact, you want to be able to take part in any changes. You don't want a vendor in, say, Amsterdam to make a new version of your product on the fly. And you don't want a vendor out of synch with your current version that your current users will find their way to and use thinking it's compatible with yours.

Van Kapeghian is a member of the band, 13 Stories, and an expert on how independent musicians can do better self-promotion. He expressed the thought that the music, not the technology, is becoming the focus again:

"My greatest fear is the MP3 community may lose its personality as MP3 becomes a mass-accepted medium. The sharing between web sites, programmers, and artists is really what made it happen. A lot of the webmasters that I bothered in chatrooms and via e-mail to post my band's songs are now great friends that I talk to about everything.

Like all big business, though, privacy becomes an issue with new technologies, and I fear that the days of living in an "open-source" type of community may be numbered. It does hearten me to see that more of the focus is shifting towards the music, and less on the technological and legal issues. I feel as less resistance is placed on this paradigm shift, the better it has become for the independent artist. Exciting as all this has been, MP3 is about music. We'll just see how MP3 incorporates itself as part of the music business."

Michael Robertson, CEO of MP3.com, believes in the value of MP3 and digital music to promote independent artists.

"MP3 is in the midst of revolutionizing music. And one of the core tenets of MP3.com is to devise a meritocracy, which shines on those musicians previously lost in obscurity."

While opinions differ about what the future of digital music may be, all these views of the future express the core belief that digital music is hear to stay.

It's not clear how long MP3 will remain the preferred digital music format. Many new digital music formats are currently being developed, each with its own unique advantages. Moreover, it's likely that there will be a strong push for a copy-protectable format that can be sold effectively that may or may not replace MP3.

Perhaps the most significant observation on the power of MP3 as a tool for musicians is this final comment from Paul Schatzkin:

> *"MP3 is the independent artist's answer to not being able to get on the radio. But even better, by using the power of the Internet and databases, the independent musicians have the ability to establish a one-to-one relationship with their fan bases, which even the people on the radio can't do."*

But, regardless of the development and acceptance of new formats, it's clear that MP3 files provide independent musicians a unique opportunity to share their music with thousands of listeners without having to go through a record company first. MP3 and digital music files will be an active part of the Internet and the independent musician for a long time to come.

Resources

This appendix contains a variety of resources for you to expand your knowledge of MP3 and digital music, download MP3 software and utilities, and find MP3 files to add to your collection. The following web sites, newsgroups, and FTP sites will help you find MP3 files, software, and products, as well as news and information about developments in MP3. In addition, these resources will give you access to a number of utilities and programs of general interest to Windows users.

WEB SITES

This section lists web sites that will be of interest to you, divided into the following categories:

- ✦ **General MP3 Resources**—Web sites, newsgroups, and other online resources for MP3 files, software, and news.

- ✦ **Technical Information**—Sources of additional information on MP3 technology, compressed audio, and other subjects.

- ✦ **Software**—Sources for MP3 software directly from the manufacturer.

- ✦ **Hardware**—Sources for MP3 hardware directly from the manufacturer.

- ✦ **Search Engines**—Search engines and other tools to help you get more information from the Web.

- ✦ **Shareware and Freeware**—Web sites to explore for shareware and freeware.

- ✦ **Other Sites of Interest**—A collection of other sites of interest to Windows users.

Bear in mind that web sites and other online resources are continu-ally changing they way they look and the features and services they offer. You may also discover that some web sites listed in this appendix may no longer be in operation at that URL. As part of your general Internet knowledge, you should learn to use one or two of the web search engines such as AltaVista, Yahoo!, and Lycos so that you can stay current with the changes in existing web sites and find out about new ones. Most MP3 web sites have links to other MP3 web sites that you should explore. You'll always be able to find another web site worth looking at.

GENERAL MP3 RESOURCES

The best place to start looking for MP3 files and information is on MP3 web sites.

MP3.com

http://www.mp3.com
MP3.com is the premier MP3 web site (shown in Figure A.1). If you can find it anywhere, you can find it here. **Recommended.**

Songs.com

http://www.songs.com
The web site of the independent music artist. Featured in Chapter 3, "Getting More MP3 Files." **Recommended.**

MP3 2000

http://www.mp3-2000.com
MP3 2000 is based in Korea. The MP3 2000 main screen appears in Figure A.2. **Recommended.**

FIGURE A.1:
The MP3.com
main screen.

MP3 Now

http://www.mp3now.com

The MP3 Now web site is a very good source of news and information about developments in the MP3 scene. **Recommended.**

MPEG.org

http://www.mpeg.org

MPEG.org bills itself as "the most complete, comprehensive and up-to-date index of MPEG resources on the Internet." It's certainly got a lot of information, that's for sure. It's run by the folks who do MPEGTV.

Dimension Music

http://www.dmusic.com

Dimension Music is another of the leading MP3 web sites. The Dimension Music main screen appears in Figure A.3. **Recommended.**

Daily MP3

http://www.dailymp3.com

The Daily MP3 web site is located in West Indonesia. It probably has the biggest collection of MP3 and related links of any MP3 web site.

CDDB

http://www.cddb.com

The *CDDB.com* web site is an essential part of creating MP3 files from CDs. It's also pretty interesting just to look around at the top 10 CD hits and other information. The main screen appears in Figure A.4.

CDnow

http://www.cdnow.com

Once you have the name for a track through CDDB, you can look up the CD and the artwork on CDnow. You can order virtually any CD through this web site as well.

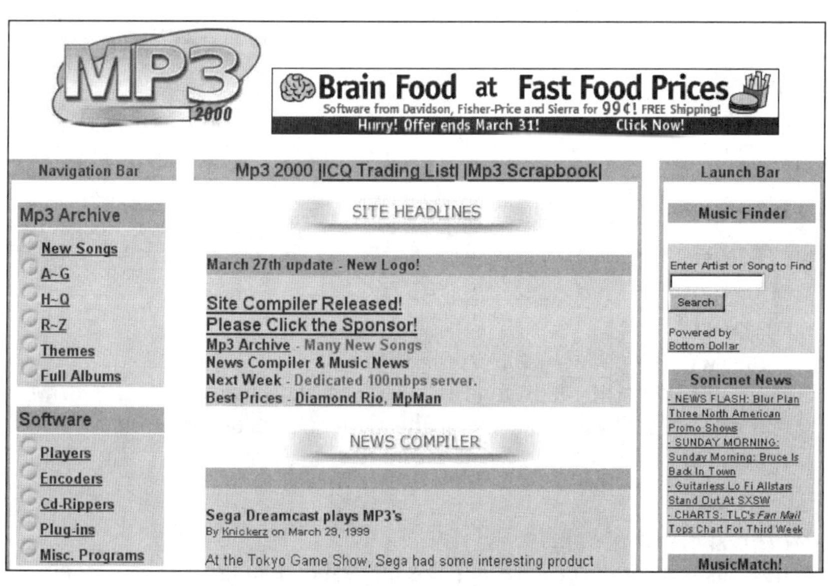

FIGURE A.2:

The MP3 2000 main screen.

MP3-World

http://www.mp3-world.net/indexe.htm
MP3s auf Deutsch! MP3-World is a German and English web site for MP3 information, software, and news. The German version of the main screen appears in Figure A.5.

MP3 Bench

http://www.mp3bench.com
How fast is your encoder, really? This interesting and approachable web site has the information. **Recommended.**

FIGURE A.5:
The MP3-World
main screen
(German version).

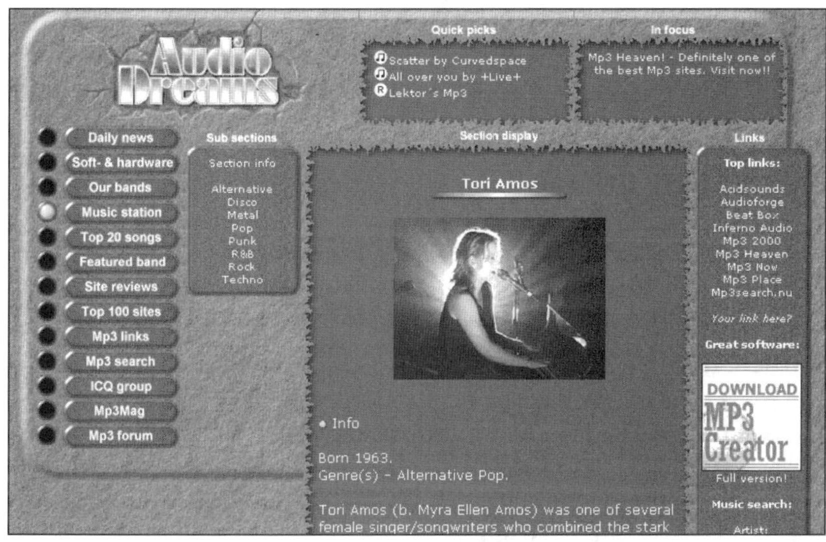

FIGURE A.6:
The Audio Dreams
web site.

Internet Audio Page

http://members.tripod.com/~s_snailham/iaf.html
A really good web site for links and information about MP3 and many other
forms of audio from Scott Snailham. He's also got a section of MP3 and WAV
files at *http://members.tripod.com/~s_snailham/Mpsongslinkwav.html* that's
worth looking at. **Recommended.**

Audio Dreams

http://www.audiodreams.com/l_amos.html
Yet another cool web site for MP3 files, news, software, and links (shown in
Figure A.6).

The Ultimate MIDI Page

http://www.ultimatemidi.com
This web site is devoted largely to MIDI files, but there is a great section of
roughly 180 MP3 links at *http://ultimatemidi.com/mp3info.html* that you
really should see if you think you've seen everything on the Web about MP3.

MusicMatch

http://www.musicmatch.com
The home page for MusicMatch Jukebox, shown in Figure A.7. Download the
latest version of MusicMatch Jukebox here. You can also download a number
of MP3 files from this site. **Recommended.**

John Vernon Hedtke's Web Page

http://www.hedtke.com
The author's web site. You can link to a variety of MP3 sites through the Links
section as well as order additional copies of this book.

Winamp

http://www.winamp.com
The home for Winamp, a first-rate player. There are also extensive skins and
plug-ins for Winamp, as well as sources for MP3 files and information. The
main screen appears in Figure A.8. **Recommended.**

100hotMusic

http://www.100hot.com/music
A fascinating web site with the Web's 100 hottest music web sites.

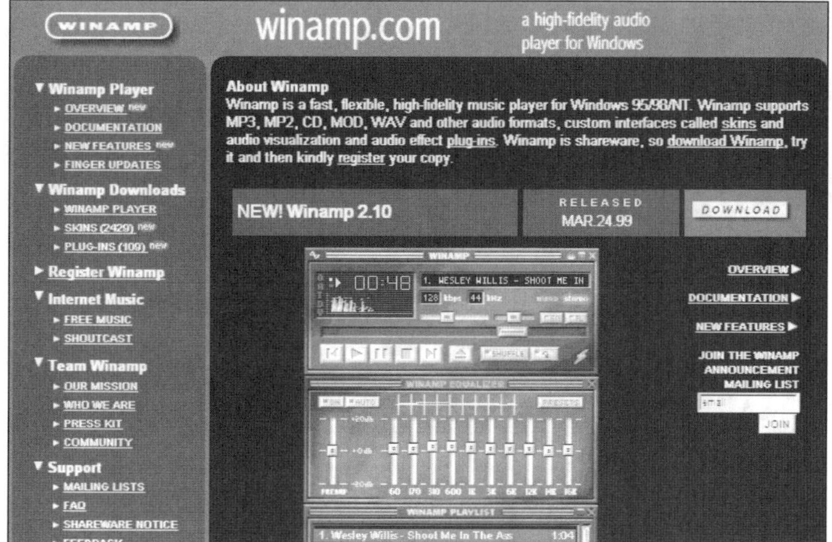

FIGURE A.8:
The Winamp
main screen.

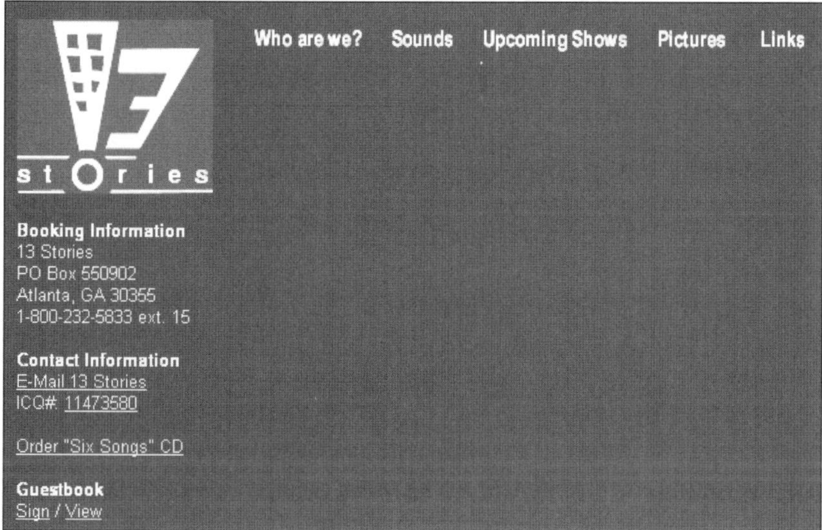

FIGURE A.9:
The 13 Stories
web site.

13 Stories

http://13stories.com

This is a great web site (shown in Figure A.9) to demonstrate how to effectively market your band through the Web and with MP3 files.

GoodNoise

http://www.goodnoise.com

Buy music online through this web site (featured in Chapter 3, "Getting More MP3 Files.")

Nordic Downloadable Music Site

http://www.nordicdms.com

Another site to buy and download music from. The main screen appears in Figure A.10.

FIGURE A.10:
The Nordic Downloadable Music Site main screen.

TECHNICAL INFORMATION

These sites will give you additional information on MP3 technology, compressed audio, and other subjects.

Compressed Audio

http://www.carte.net/wwwaudio.htm

A page of great basic information about compressed audio formats and concepts.

Best Sound Quality in Compressed Audio

http://cad-audio.fsn.net

A site with some information about compressed audio as well as recommendations by the web site author about the best programs for each class of compressed audio.

The Official FAQ for alt.binaries.sounds.mp3

http://www.top.net/taenus

This web site provides a great deal of information about the *alt.binaries.sounds.mp3* newsgroup. Most of this information applies to the other MP3 newsgroups, too. There's also some good basic MP3 information. **Recommended.**

Recording Industry Association of America

http://www.riaa.com

You can find out what the RIAA is doing and the latest word on legislation relating to MP3 and digital audio through this site (shown in Figure A.11). You should also look at *http://www.soundbyting.com*.

The Official MPEG Home Page

http://www.cselt.stet.it/mpeg

Technical information about the MPEG standards. Not for the faint of heart, but very useful information if you want to find out the details of how MPEG really works.

FIGURE A.11:
The RIAA web site.

CD-ROM Digital Audio (CD-DA) introduction

These CD-DA web pages (including all graphics thereon, with the possible exception of the background) are copyright © Stewart Addison 1997 All Rights Reserved and may not be used elsewhere without prior permission etc.
Please let me know if you intend to link this page from any commercial organisation so that I can ensure your information is accurate (And yes, a magazine counts as a commercial organisation...)
One final point: If you put a link to my CD-DA pages on your own web page, please link to this page rather than any of the others, as I can't guarantee that I'll leave all of the filenames for the other pages the same.

This is a **USER-SUPPORTED** web page. Without your help, this information cannot be kept up to date. When you download software from here, give something back to this site by sending me the results, even if it doesn't work.

CD-DA web page updates in the last month

- CD-Copy updated to version 4.507 - Now has an integrated Layer 3 encoder.
- Updated AudioGrabber, CD-Copy and CDDA Extractor to the latest versions.
- The new version of the CDDA results page is now online. Each entry in the results table now has a hyperlink to a second section of information about the drive, which includes a list of software which the drive has been used successfully/unsuccessfully, along with the number of results I've received about each drive.

FIGURE A.12:
The CD-ROM Digital Audio main screen.

RealNetworks

http://www.realnetworks.com
The home of the RealAudio player.

MPEG Audio Web Page

http://sound.media.mit.edu/mpeg4/audio
More technical information about MPEG standards.

CD-ROM Digital Audio (CD-DA) web site

http://www.tardis.ed.ac.uk/~psyche/cdda
This is a web site designed and written by Stewart Addison that provides technical information on CD-DA, CD-ROM drives, and related subjects. This is a very good site to look at if you're about to buy a CD-ROM drive and want to make sure that the drive supports digital audio extraction. Figure A.12 shows the web site's main screen. **Recommended.**

Audio Compression
http://fas.sfu.ca/cs/undergrad/CourseMaterials/CMPT365/ material/notes/Chap4/Chap4.3/Chap4.3.html
Technical information on compression.

Audio File Formats FAQ
ftp://ftp.cwi.nl/pub/audio
Guido van Rossum's FTP site containing a variety of downloadable audio file format information. Contains work by Guido van Rossum, Jack Jansen, K. Sjoerd Mullender, Carl Malamud, and Lars Hemre, among others.

Optimal Pulse Code Modulation (oPCM) and its application as an audioquality parameter
http://cips02.physik.uni-bonn.de/~scheller/audio/main.html
Very technical information about MP3.

SOFTWARE

In addition to the many links available through the general MP3 web sites in the first section, you can go to a number of manufacturers' web sites and download software directly from the source. Most of these programs were featured in detail in Chapter 6, "Editing and Enhancing MP3 Files," and Chapter 7, "Using Other Software." Listings in this section appear in alphabetic order by name of product.

Audio Forge
http://www.audioforge.net
The home page for Audio Forge, shown in Figure A.13.

Audiograbber
http://www.audiograbber.com-us.net
The home page for Audiograbber.

FIGURE A.13:
The Audio Forge web site.

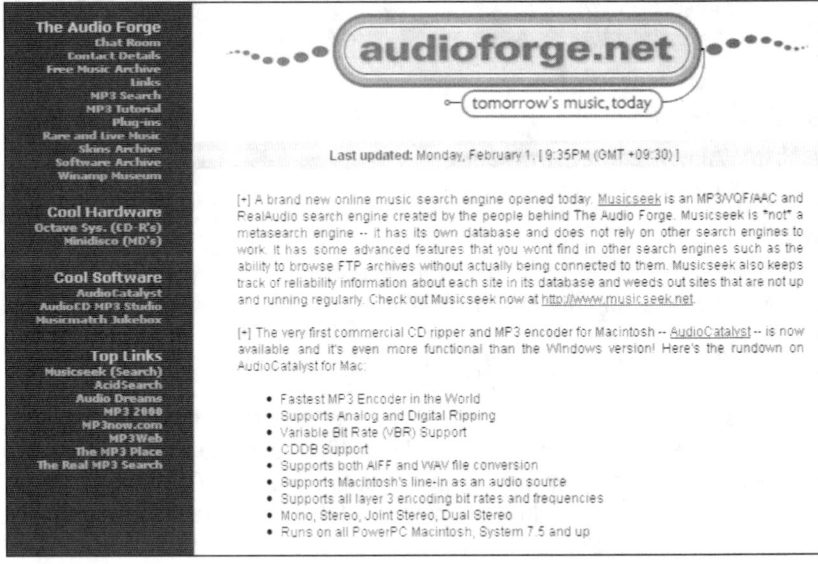

AudioCatalyst

http://www.audiocatalyst.com
The home page for AudioCatalyst from Xing Technology. The Xing encoder is available from *http://www.xingtech.com.*

BladeEnc's MP3 encoder

http://www.bladeenc.cjb.net
The home page for BladeEnc's MP3 encoder.

CDDA32

http://www.ncf.ca/~aa571/cdda32.htm
This is the web site for CDDA32 and the CDROMCHK utility. It also has some exceptional technical information for dealing with advanced recording and encoding problems. **Recommended.**

CDex

http://www.surf.to/cdex
The home page for CDex.

CDH Media Wizard

http://www.cdhnow.com
The home page for CDH Media Wizard.

CDRWIN

http://www.goldenhawk.com
The home page for CDRWIN.

Cool Edit 96

http://www.syntrillium.com
The home page for Cool Edit 96.

Digital Audio Copy

http://www.windac.de
The home page for Digital Audio Copy (also known as WinDAC).

Easy CD Creator Deluxe

http://www.adaptec.com
The home page for Adaptec products, including Easy CD Creator Deluxe and Spin Doctor.

Easy CD-DA Extractor

http://www.poikosoft.com/cdda
The home page for Easy CD-DA Extractor.

EditPro

http://www.mayah.com
The home page for EditPro.

HyCD Play&Record

http://www.hycd.com
The home page for HyCD Play&Record.

Jet Audio

http://www.cowon.com
The home page for Jet-Audio.

K-Jöfol

http://www.kjofol.org
The home page for K-Jöfol.

MacAMP

http://www.macamp.com
The home page for MacAMP.

Mixman Studio

http://www.mixman.com
The home page for Mixman Studio and Mixman Studio Pro.

MP3 to EXE

http://software.webset.de/buschjost/mp3eng.htm
The home page for MP3 to EXE.

MPecker

http://www.anime.net/~go/mpeckers.html
The home site for MPecker. This web site provides MPEG audio software for the Macintosh, including the MPecker decoding and encoding software.

MusicMatch

http://www.musicmatch.com
The home page for MusicMatch Jukebox, shown earlier in Figure A.7.

Plugger+

http://members.tripod.com/~mp3nkoder
The home page for Plugger+.

Ray Gun

http://www.arboretum.com
The home page for Arboretum Systems, makers of Ray Gun.

Sonique

http://www.sonique.com
The home page for the Sonique player.

SoundApp

http://www-cs-students.stanford.edu/~franke/SoundApp
The home page for SoundApp.

Sound Forge XP

http://www.soundforge.com
The home page for Sound Forge XP.

SuperSonic

http://www.gosupersonic.com
The home page for SuperSonic.

Uncook 95

http://www.free-music.com/uncook95.htm
The home page for Uncook 95.

Unreal Player Max

http://www.303tek.com
The home page for Unreal Player Max.

Virtuosa Gold

http://europe.audiosoft.com/virtuosa
The home page for Virtuosa Gold.

WaveLab

http://www.steinberg.net
The home page for WaveLab.

Winamp

http://www.winamp.com
The home page for Winamp, shown earlier in Figure A.8.

WinOnCD

http://www.cequadrat.com
The home page for WinOnCD.

WPlay

http://www.xaudio.com
The home page for WPlay.

HARDWARE

This section contains web sites for various kinds of MP3 hardware.
Most of these products are featured in Chapter 8, "Playing MP3 Files
Away from Your Computer."

Rio PMP300

http://www.diamondmm.com/rio
The web site for the Rio, shown in Figure A.14.

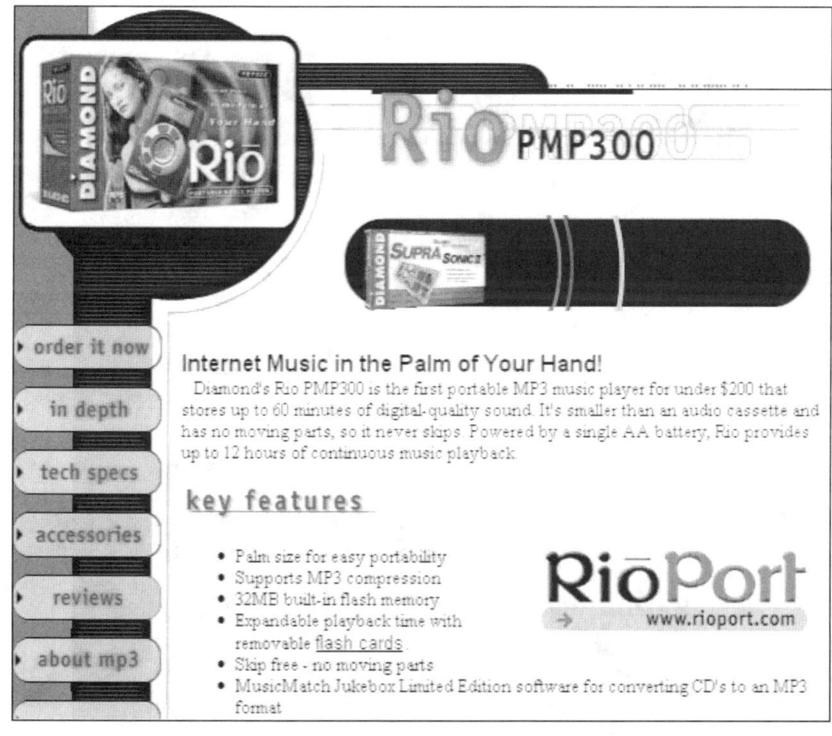

FIGURE A.14:
The Rio web site.

Neato CD Labeller

http://www.neato.com
The home page for the Neato CD Labeller, a handy device for labeling CDs.

Creative Labs

http://www.soundblaster.com
The web site for Creative Labs, makers of the Sound Blaster Live! and other great sound cards (shown in Figure A.15). This is also the site for Creative Labs' line of multimedia speakers.

MPMan

http://www.eigerlabs.com/MPMan
The web site for Eiger Labs' MPMan MP3 player.

MPlayer3

http://www.mplayer3.com/site_e/frame_e.htm
The home page for the MPlayer3 portable MP3 player.

MP3Car

http://www.mp3car.com
The home page for MP3Car, an MP3 player for your car.

Yepp

http://yepp.co.kr
The home page for Samsung's Yepp MP3 player.

Smart and Friendly

http://www.smartandfriendly.com
The web site for Smart and Friendly, maker of the CD Rocket CD-ROM burner.

FIGURE A.15:
The Creative Labs web site.

SEARCH ENGINES

This section contains information on some of the more popular search engines. Some of these (such as Lycos) have specific search facilities for MP3 files.

AltaVista

http://altavista.digital.com
AltaVista is one of the most popular search engines on the Web. Enter your search keywords and find almost anything you can think of. A typical AltaVista search for "MP3" appears in Figure A.16. (Note that AltaVista has found over 900,000 web pages dealing with MP3.) **Recommended.**

Yahoo!

http://www.yahoo.com
Yahoo! is another very popular search engine. The results of a Yahoo! search appear in Figure A.17. Yahoo! uses a different search methodology than AltaVista, which makes it frequently easier to find information using one of Yahoo!'s many predefined categories. **Recommended.**

Lycos

http://www.lycos.com
The Lycos MP3 search engine was discussed in Chapter 3, "Getting More MP3 Files." You can also use the general Lycos search engine to look for MP3 web sites and other information using the Lycos predefined categories.

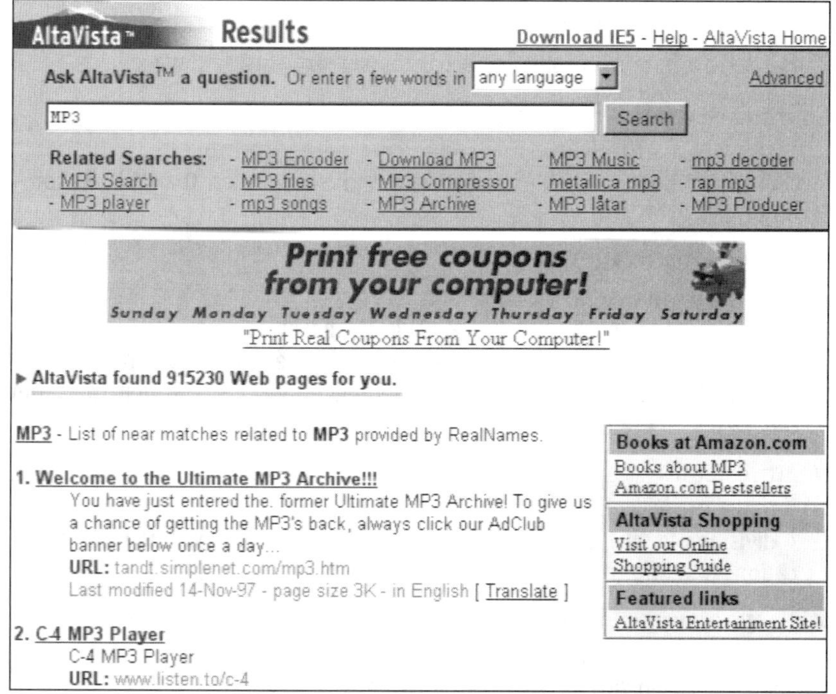

FIGURE A.16:
Sample AltaVista search.

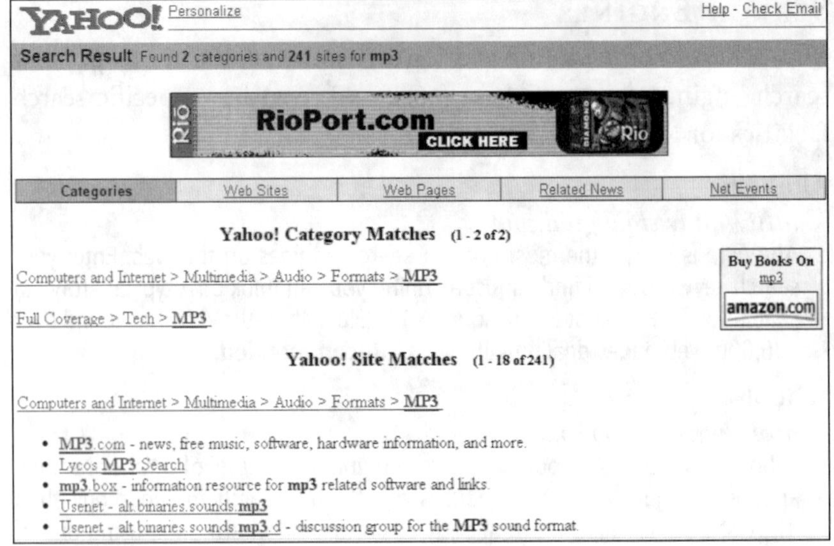

Scour.net

http://www.scour.net
Scour.net was also discussed in Chapter 3, "Getting More MP3 Files," as a way to look around the net for MP3 files.

WebCrawler

http://www.webcrawler.com
WebCrawler is a smaller search engine than the others mentioned in this section, but it has many nice features that make it worth looking at.

SHAREWARE AND FREEWARE

This section lists places to look for shareware and freeware.

Shareware.com

http://www.shareware.com
One of the best sources for shareware and freeware on the Web. **Recommended.**

Walnut Creek CDROM

http://www.cdrom.com
The home page for Walnut Creek CDROM, maker of great CD-ROM collections of shareware and freeware, shown in Figure A.18. You can download individual selections of most of the shareware available on their CDs from this web site. **Recommended.**

Winfiles.com

www.winfiles.com
A division of CNET, this is a web site for Windows 95 and Windows 98 applications and information.

ZDNet Software Library

http://www.hotfiles.com
The ZDNet web site for Windows software.

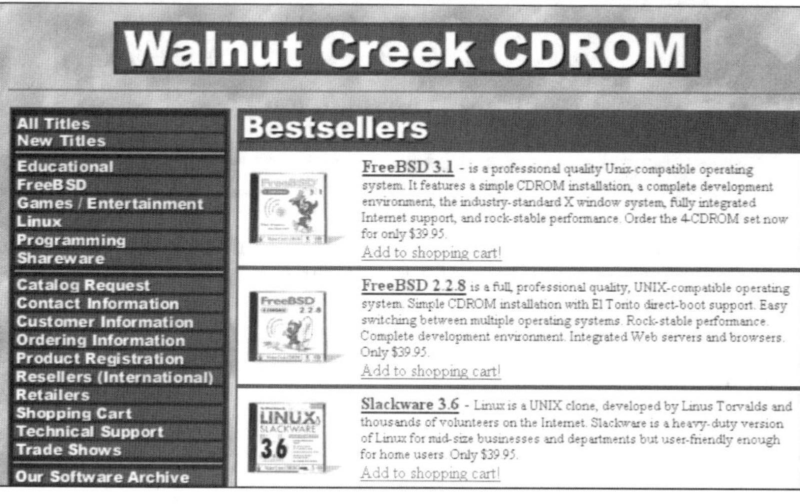

FIGURE A.18:
The Walnut Creek
CDROM web site.

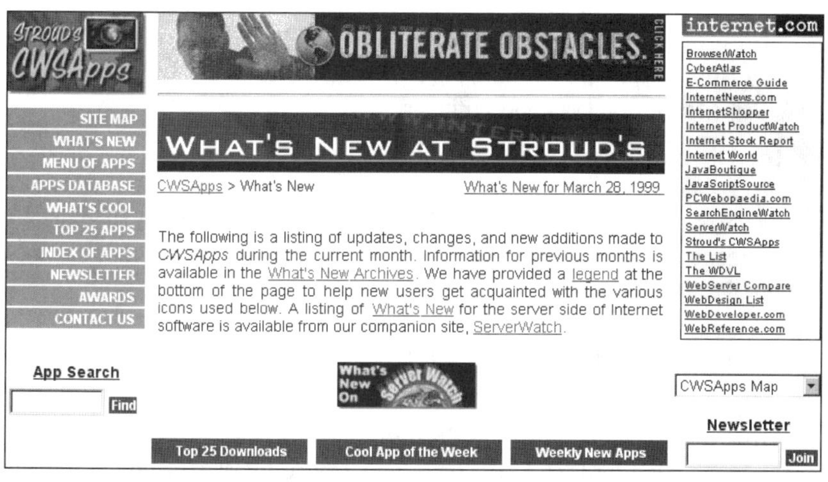

FIGURE A.19:
Stroud's CWSApps.

Stroud's CWSApps

http://www.stroud.com/new.html
A very good collection of Windows 95 and Windows 98 applications. The main screen appears in Figure A.19. **Recommended.**

TUCOWS

http://www.tucows.com
One of the most popular web sites for software, shown in Figure A.20. **Recommended.**

PCWin Resource Center

http://pcwin.com
This is a great web site run by the phenomenal Randy Burgess. The site has a variety of interesting software, hardware, and other resources. Be sure to check out the Easter Eggs section. (Easter eggs are hidden code within popular programs.)

Funduc

http://home.sprynet.com/sprynet/funduc
A web site of useful Windows utilities.

Vector Development

http://www.vecdev.com
The Vector Development web site, home of DUNCE (the Dial-up Networking Connection Enhancement), an essential tool for Windows Internet connection. **Recommended.**

OTHER SITES OF INTEREST

WinZip

http://www.winzip.com/winzip/winzip_t.htm
The home page for Nico Mak Computing, source for WinZip, one of the all-time best Windows utilities. The WinZip main screen appears in Figure A.21. **Recommended.**

Eudora

http://www.eudora.com
The home page for Eudora, one of the best e-mail programs available for Windows or the Macintosh.

Free Agent

http://www.forteinc.com
The home page for Forté and the Free Agent newsreader, the best newsreader available.

WS_FTP

http://www.ipswitch.com
The home page for WS_FTP and a variety of network monitoring products.

CuteFTP

http://www.cuteftp.com
The home page for CuteFTP, another popular FTP program.

FIGURE A.21:
The WinZip home page.

WinCode

http://www.winsite.com/info/pc/win3/util/wincode.zip
A source of the WinCode Internet decoding utility. This program is very useful for decoding files downloaded from newsgroups that were in an unusual format. (Free Agent is very good about recognizing most formats, but you'll occasionally receive a file in a nonstandard format.)

Paint Shop Pro

http://www.jasc.com
The home page for JASC and Paint Shop Pro, an excellent paint program. Use this for creating clip art for tagging tracks.

F-PROT

http://www.datafellows.com/f-prot
The home page for the F-PROT virus scanner.

McAfee

http://www.mcafee.com
The home page for McAfee VirusScan, another excellent virus scanner. The McAfee main screen appears in Figure A.22.

MTU-Speed Home Page

http://www.mjs.u-net.com/mike.htm
The home page for MTU-Speed, a very useful utility from Mike Sutherland for speeding up your Internet access. **Recommended.**

Sense Networking

http://www.oz.net
The home page for Sense Networking, the best ISP in Washington State.

CNET: The Computer Network

www.cnet.com
Home page for CNET, with news, reviews, and current information about the computer industry.

MyDesktop

http://www.mydesktop.com
Another source of current information and software, shown in Figure A.23.

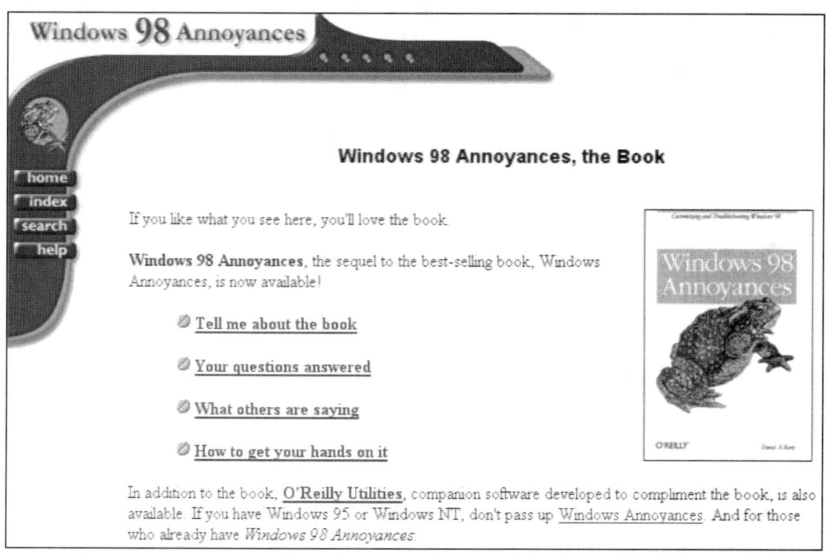

FIGURE A.24:
The Windows 98 Annoyances screen.

The Official Windows Web Site

http://www.microsoft.com/windows
The first place to go on the Web for information about Windows. Be sure to check for free downloads for Windows 95 and Windows 98. If you're running an older version of Windows 95, make sure you download the Windows 95 Service Pack, which greatly reduces all kinds of problems. There is also a kernel update for Windows 95 that fixes a memory "leak" that can cause Windows 95 to run out of memory when running Internet applications over a long period of time. You may also want to download the font-smoothing update, which rounds the fonts displayed on the screen in Windows 95, making the text more readable. Check this site regularly for updates to Windows 98 as well. **Recommended.**

Windows 95 Annoyances

http://www.creativelement.com/win95ann
Tips, tricks, and workarounds for Windows 95. **Recommended.**

Windows 98 Annoyances

http://www.annoyances.org/win98/book
Tips, tricks, and workarounds for Windows 98 (shown in Figure A.24). **Recommended.**

NEWSGROUPS

There are a large number of newsgroups for MP3 files and information, with more being created all the time. Use a newsreader such as Free Agent to read newsgroups. (See Chapter 3, "Getting More MP3 Files," for more information.)

- ✦ alt.binaries.mp3.zappa
- ✦ alt.binaries.music.mp3

- alt.binaries.remixes.mp3
- alt.binaries.sounds
- alt.binaries.sounds.1950s.mp3
- alt.binaries.sounds.1960s.mp3
- alt.binaries.sounds.1970s.mp3
- alt.binaries.sounds.1980s.mp3
- alt.binaries.sounds.1990s.mp3
- alt.binaries.sounds.78rpm-era
- alt.binaries.sounds.country.mp3
- alt.binaries.sounds.mp3
- alt.binaries.sounds.mp3.1950s
- alt.binaries.sounds.mp3.1960s
- alt.binaries.sounds.mp3.1970s
- alt.binaries.sounds.mp3.1980s
- alt.binaries.sounds.mp3.1990s
- alt.binaries.sounds.mp3.beatles
- alt.binaries.sounds.mp3.brazilian
- alt.binaries.sounds.mp3.comedy
- alt.binaries.sounds.mp3.indian.bhangra
- alt.binaries.sounds.mp3.indian.movies
- alt.binaries.sounds.mp3.indian.movies.old
- alt.binaries.sounds.mp3.indian.remixes
- alt.binaries.sounds.mp3.indian.requests
- alt.binaries.sounds.mp3.indie
- alt.binaries.sounds.mp3.requests
- alt.binaries.sounds.mp3.zappa
- alt.binaries.sounds.music.classical
- alt.music.dance.mp3.binaries
- alt.music.mp3

How to Use the CD

This appendix gives you basic information on how to load and use the software and MP3 files on the CD accompanying this book. There is a selection of MP3 software, including MusicMatch Jukebox and Winamp, but the CD primarily contains MP3 files of all kinds.

For a complete list of the programs and files on the CD accompanying this book, as well as information on how to load and use them, do the following:

1. Insert the CD into your computer's CD-ROM drive.
2. Double-click the My Computer icon. The My Computer screen (shown in Figure B.1) appears.
3. Double-click the CD-ROM icon, shown in Figure B.2. (If you've more than one CD-ROM drive, double-click the one containing the CD.) A standard contents window appears.
4. Double-click the README.TXT icon. Read the file for complete information on the programs and files that appear on the CD, as well as for instructions on how to load the software and where to find the MP3 files.

The programs on the CD have separate installation processes. Check for a README.TXT file in each of the program directories for any comments on installing the software. The main directory for MP3 files will also contain a README.TXT file cataloging the files.

FIGURE B.1:
The My Computer
screen.

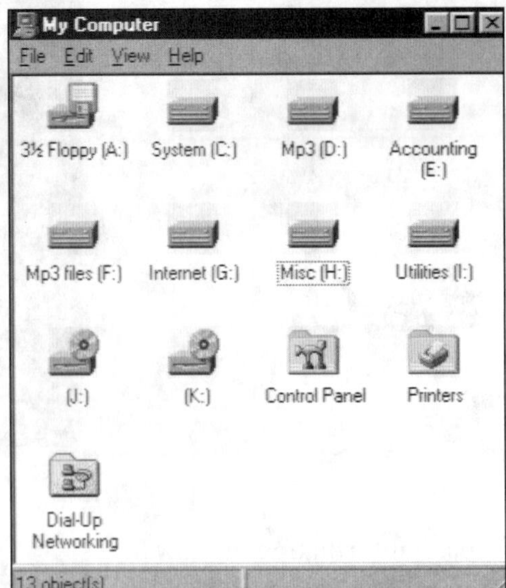

FIGURE B.2:
The CD-ROM icon.

GLOSSARY

AAC—Acronym for *Advanced Audio Compression*. AAC is a new audio format that has not yet gained wide acceptance. It's slightly more memory-efficient than MP3 files, but the source code has not yet been widely licensed from Fraunhofer (who controls the technology).

ADPCM—Acronym for *Adaptive Differential Pulse Code Modulation format*. ADPCM is a fast 16-bit file format using lossy compression.

ADSL—A high-speed connection offered by the phone companies in many areas of the country.

AIFF and AIFF-C—Acronym for *Audio Interchange File Format*. It was developed by Apple Computers for storing sounds in the data fork of a file. Macintoshes can play and create AIFF files. Common file extensions for AIFF files include .aif, .aiff, and .aifc.

analog—A wave that continuously varies in strength or quantity.

analog ripper—Takes analog signals from cassette tapes, vinyl, or radio and coverts them to WAV files. See also *ripping*.

analog-to-digital converter—Converts sound waves from their analog format (what you hear with your ear) to a digital format (what the computer can understand). See also *digital-to-analog converter*.

article—A single message posted to a newsgroup. The term "article" is being supplanted by "post" or "message."

attenuation—The total or partial reduction of the level of a signal.

attenuation threshold—Suppressing sound above a certain level.

audio CD tracks—Individual songs or cuts on an audio CD.

automatic playlists—Playlists that you create by specifying the length of the playlist you'd like and defining the types of music you want in your playlist.

AVR—A sound format created by Audio Visual Research used on Atari ST computers.

BMP—Abbreviation for *bitmap*. A type of graphic file. One of the two kinds of graphic files you can use to tag a track in Music-Match Jukebox with cover art. See also *JPEG*.

bootleg recording—The unauthorized recording of a live concert, a CD, cassette tape, record album, or a musical broadcast on radio or television. Also known as a pirate or underground recording.

BRAVADJ.CAT file—The file containing the entries for Tempo, Mood, Situation, or Preference in MusicMatch Jukebox. The categories appear at the start of each list of entries in [brackets].

burning—The process of writing information to a CD.

burn-on-demand—Creating an audio CD in response to a customer's request for specific tracks.

CD—Acronym for *Compact Disc*. Audio CDs hold about an hour of music. Digital CDs (also known as CD-ROMs) hold up to 650 MB of information.

CD-DA—Acronym for *Compact Disc Digital Audio*.

CD-DA files—Individual songs or cuts on a CD. It should be noted that there is actually only one "track" on a CD, just like there is only one groove on each side of a record album. Individual tracks are separated by start and stop information encoded as part of the digital audio on the CD. Also known as Raw WAV files.

CD-R—Acronym for *Compact Disc: Recordable*. A blank CD that you can write information to (but not erase) using a CD-R burner. Also known as a WORM (Write Once, Read Many) disc.

CD-R burner—A device that uses a CD blank that can't be reused or reburned. Once the information is on the CD, it's there forever. Also known as a CD-ROM burner.

CD-ROM—Acronym for *Compact Disc: Read Only Memory*. Generally used to identify any type of digital (as opposed to audio) CD.

CD-RW—Acronym for *Compact Disk: Read/Write* or *Compact Disc: Re-writable*. A reusable blank CD. CD-RWs are different from CD-Rs in that you can write information to them, read them, and then erase them and write new information on the CD-RW, using a CD-RW burner. CD-RWs are more expensive than CD-Rs, but the price difference is dropping significantly.

CD-RW burner—A CD-ROM writing device that uses a reusable CD. You can write data to it, use it like any other CD, and then erase it and write new information to it.

compression mode—In MusicMatch Jukebox, the process that determines the quality and format of the finished file.

copyright—The legal right to control how a song, lyric, program, book, or other piece of intellectual property is reproduced, distributed, and sold. Songs can have multiple copyrights: one for the author of the music, one for the author of the lyrics, and one for the musician or band performing the piece.

cut—An individual song or piece of music. See also *track*.

database—In MusicMatch Jukebox, a group of tracks in the Music Library.

decibel—A unit of sound.

decoder—A program that converts MP3 files back into WAV files.

digital audio—Sound or music that is stored as a series of bits rather than by a continuously varying (analog) signal.

digital modem—A special type of modem that connects your computer to a separate phone line for DSL service.

digital ripper—Extracts the tracks from the CD and converts them into WAV files on your computer's hard disk. See also *ripping*.

digital-to-analog converter—Converting digital files (such as MP3 or WAV files) into an analog format (something you can hear). See also *analog-to-digital converter*.

DSL service—Acronym for *Digital Subscriber Line*. A direct 24-hour link to the Internet at speeds of at least 144K, six times the speed of the average modem.

DVD—Acronym for *Digital Versatile Disc*. A CD format that is still new in the marketplace but which may eventually supplant CD-R and CD-RW entirely.

EIDE—Acronym for *Enhanced IDE*. A format used by disk drives, CD-ROMs, and other data storage devices for communicating. EIDE handles more data channels than the standard IDE.

encoder—A program that converts WAV files to MP3 files. As part of the conversion process, the encoder saves only the sounds that are important (that the human ear will actually hear) and throws away the rest.

equalization—The term for adjusting the relative output of frequencies in a given range to give a more balanced sound.

equalizer—A hardware or software device that lets you filter specific frequency ranges (equalize) the audio output to your speakers.

frame—The smallest "slice" of data you can play or manipulate in a track being recorded. The term comes from movie and video production and frames of films.

freeware—Software that's been developed and released to the public at no charge. See also *shareware* and *public domain*.

FTP—Acronym for *File Transfer Protocol.* The common way of transferring files online. An FTP site is a no-frills stack of files you can download.

ID3V1.CAT file—Contains the default entries for the Genre category in MusicMatch Jukebox.

IDE—Acronym for *Integrated Device Electronics.* An inexpensive and popular interface for PC hardware and devices. IDE has largely been supplanted by EIDE, which can handle more devices in a single computer. See also *EIDE* and *SCSI.*

ISP—Acronym for *Internet Service Provider.* You use an ISP to gain access to the Internet. ISPs can be local or regional (such as oz.net) or national/international such as home.net. AOL acts as an ISP for many people—you can send and receive e-mail and news articles, browse the Web, and upload and download files—although it actually does a great deal more and is technically considered an online service.

JPEG, JPG—Acronym for *Joint Photographic Experts Group.* A type of graphic file. One of the two kinds of graphic files you can use to tag a track in MusicMatch Jukebox with cover art. See also *BMP.*

leader—Blank time (silence) inserted between songs.

licensing—Contracting for the right to perform, record, distribute, and/or digitally transmit a copyrighted song or other work.

line-out jack—Bypasses any amplifier built into the sound card so you can connect the sound card to an external amplified source.

lossy compression—Compressing a file by eliminating some of the data. Lossy compression is a one-way process: converting the compressed file back to the original format will result in a file with missing information that may or may not significantly affect the quality of the reconverted file. MP3 is a lossy compression format; WAV files created from MP3 files will not sound quite as full or rich as the original WAV files used to create the MP3 files.

MIDI—Acronym for *Musical Instrument Digital Interface.* A standard for connecting musical instruments and computers using a digital interface. There are many MIDI products that let you compose and score music online and play it with the sound of a number of digitized instruments. You can also play music on MIDI instruments (most commonly keyboards, but there are MIDI wind, reed, and string instruments as well) and have the notes automatically transcribed into a MIDI format for subsequent editing and transcription.

mix—A combination of multiple tracks to create a finished song that can be heard on a CD or an album.

mixer—A device that creates several different versions of the same song depending on the volumes, tempos, and effects chosen in the mix. The individual tracks are then combined into a final mix that usually has only two tracks (stereo).

MOD, Amiga MOD—A music (rather than a sound) format that is somewhat similar to MIDI. MOD files store digitized information about the instruments and the notes played. Common MOD file extensions are .mod, .mtm, and .s3m.

morphing—Adding effects, such as reverb, that transform the way the MP3 file sounds.

MP2—One of several related standards for storing audio and video. See also *MPEG audio.*

MP3—Abbreviation for *MPEG 1, layer 3,* the portion of the MPEG standard that specifies how audio files are stored.

MP3 file—A digital audio file created using lossy compression techniques that conform to the MPEG 1, layer 3 standard. MP3 files are relatively small—about 1 MB/minute of audio—but also provide CD-quality or near CD-quality sound.

MP4—One of several related standards for storing audio and video. See also *MPEG audio.*

MPEG—Acronym for *Moving Pictures Experts Group,* pronounced "EM-peg."

MPEG audio—MPEG audio files can be created using layer 1, 2, or 3. Standard MP3 files use layer 1, the most compressed of the layers. Layers 2 and 3 provide greater quality at the cost of a larger audio file. MPEG-1, layer 3 files typically have a sampling rate of 44.1 kHz.

MTM—A type of MOD file.

multimedia speakers—A growing selection of computer speaker sets that give substantial sound quality.

music archive site—A web site or FTP site with MP3 files for downloading.

NET (No Electronic Theft) Act of 1997—The law that makes it a felony to create or distribute unauthorized digital music.

neuristic listening—Another name for *psychoacoustics.*

newsgroups (also known as **Usenet groups**)—Similar to large cork bulletin boards on a wall on which you can post messages (known in newsgroup parlance as *articles*), ask questions, and get files.

newsreader—A program that lets you read newsgroups and post articles to them.

noise—Anything that obscures the signal.

normalizing—The process of setting various frequency ranges so that the tracks sound more normal.

piracy—The unauthorized and illegal duplication or distribution of copyrighted material.

player—A type of software that plays MP3 or other audio files.

playlist—A list of the MP3 files you want to play in the order you want to play them.

playlist editor—A type of software that creates playlists.

preamp—A hardware or software device that sets the level of the music before it is amplified. Hardware preamps are often used to boost and filter the signal of a turntable or cassette deck prior to the signal being amplified. Preamps provide filtering at the source of the audio signal.

psychoacoustics—The field of study concerning what the human ear can hear.

public domain—Intellectual property of any kind that may be freely copied, performed, and distributed. Intellectual property can become public domain by having the copyright expire or by a declaration by the copyright owner(s) that the material is in the public domain.

QuickTime movies—A video format from Apple used for multimedia files. QuickTime movies usually have the extension .mov.

RealAudio—Another popular file format for sound. RealAudio files are compressed to minimize their size, but they are not as compressed as MP3 files. (There are also RealVideo formats for video files.) Both RealAudio and RealVideo formats were created by RealNetworks.

recording mode—The method used for ripping a file from a CD. Digital mode is up to five times faster than analog recording and provides a slightly cleaner MP3 file. Analog mode "listens" to the CD as it plays and records from that. Analog recording will only move as fast as the CD plays in the CD-ROM drive.

Red Book—An industry standard, defined by Philips and Sony, for CD audio and CD-ROM drives. There are several levels of standard, which are traditionally referred to by the color of the cover in which the documents were originally bound. The Red Book standard is the one most frequently used with respect to end-user CD audio and CD-ROM drives. Among other things, it specifies the standards for the recording and playback media and how audio and digital information is recorded and played back.

remix—Making different versions of a song using the same tracks.

resolution—See *sampling rate.*

RIAA—Acronym for *Recording Industry Association of America.*

ripping—The process of converting a file from a CD to a WAV file. The resulting WAV file is then encoded into an MP3 file.

S3M—See *MOD.*

sampling—Reading sound waves at regular intervals and storing the information in a digitized file.

sampling precision—The amount of information stored about a sample. Typical rates are 8-bit and 16-bit. 8-bit sampling will give up to 256 different levels, while 16-bit sampling gives up to 65,536 different levels. In general, the more frequently you sample and the greater the precision, the more closely the digital version will resemble the audio version.

sampling rate—The number of times per second that the sound card samples the sound being converted. Typical sampling rates for audio are 11 kilohertz, 22 kilohertz, and 44 kilohertz. One hertz (abbreviated Hz) is a single cycle per second, so a sampling rate of 44 kHz means that the computer is sampling the sound 44,000 times every second. The more often the computer samples the sound, the more of the sound the computer 'hears.'

SCSI—Acronym for *Small Computer System Interface,* pronounced "scuzzy." A more expensive interface than IDE that is not as common on Windows computers although it's standard on Macintosh computers.

serial number—In MusicMatch Jukebox, the unique CD identifier used by web sites to identify the CD and look up information for it. This information is automatically pulled off a CD when the MP3 files are created. The serial number frequently can be found on the CD jacket or insert.

shareware—Program that lets you try the software before you buy it. If you like it, you pay a nominal fee (usually less than $40) for the right to keep using it

signal—The song, music, or other sound recorded on a track.

skins—A way for users to alter the screen appearance of a program.

SND—A sound file format for the Macintosh, System 7 or later.

speaker-out jack—Lets you plug the sound card into a set of unamplified speakers and run them off the sound card's internal amplifier.

streaming—Playing sounds and video in real time while you download. Particularly useful for reproduction and distribution of radio broadcasts.

tagging—The process of saving additional information in an MP3 file, such as e-mail, artist bio, lyrics, and URL. There are two kinds of tagging that are in common use, MusicMatch and ID3 tagging.

track—Entire songs (whether MP3 files, WAV files, or original cuts from cassettes, vinyl, or CDs). Old industry jargon from radio DJs and the music business. When speaking of mixing and audio production, however, the term refers to a single signal or set of signals in an unmixed recording, such as the lyrics track, the drum track, or the bass track. These tracks are then mixed into the completed song.

VBR—Acronym for *Variable Bit Rate*. VBR maximizes the quality of the audio but does not limit the size of the resulting MP3 file. Not all MP3 players can handle MP3 files recorded using VBR.

VOC—A sound file format used by the Creative Labs Sound Blaster hardware. The file extension is .voc.

VQF—A sound file format similar to MP3. VQF produces files that are half again as small as MP3 files with sound qualities that are at least as good. VQF files take longer to encode and a little more CPU power to play. They are not as popular as MP3 files. For more information, as well as a number of VQF files and utilities, look at *http://www.vqf.com*.

WAV file—Pronounced "wave." Sounds that are converted directly from an analog signal into digital sound and stored as the component waveforms.

Screen, window, and field names are capitalized as they appear in the software.
Web and newsgroup entries in the index appear in *italics*.

bio, 27
Buy CD URL, 26
CD serial #, 28-29
clearing the database, 20
comment, 26
creating playlists with, 21-23
deleting tracks from, 20, 22
description, 8
duplicate tracks in, 19-20
expanding columns in, 21
filename, 28
Genre column, 26
lyrics, 27
maximizing, 20
minimizing, 20
mood, 27
notes, 27
Options menu, 20, 23, 24
playing multiple tracks,
  22-23
playing single tracks, 21-22
preference, 27
removing tracks from, 20, 22
situation, 27
Song Title column, 25
tempo, 27
Time column, 25
Music Library button, 7, 8
Music Library window, 8
music
  broadcasting over the
    Internet, 192-193
  digitizing, 53-55
  programs, 84
  reviews, 43
Musical Instrument Digital
  Interface, 55, 228musical
  instruments, connecting to
  computers, 55, 228
musicians, opportunities for,
  40, 41, 193, 194, 195, 196,
  197, 198, 199, 202
MusicMatch, 191, 206
MusicMatch Jukebox, 3, 125,
  127, 129, 155, 158
  Add Songs window, 19
  and VBR files, 68
  Auto DJ screen, 32
  Auto-Configuring screen,
    59, 60
  CDDB Connect? screen, 60,
    61
  CDDB Preferences screen,
    59, 60
  changing the player, 127
  changing your computer
    hardware, 72, 85, 93, 94,
    95, 209
  compression mode, 226
  configuring, 72, 85
  Converted Files, 78
  creating playlists for the Rio,
    171

creating your own MP3
  files, 58-63
default player, 11
determining CD-ROM
  drive settings, 59, 60
digital recording, 147
DLL files, 85
Edit menus, 16-17, 18
encoder, 148, 152
encoding, 145
error correction, 85
exploring, 9-10
features of main screen, 6-9
File Format Conversion
  screen, 77-78, 91, 92, 96, 97
File menu, 16, 17,18
filtering and editing, 144
First Auto-Configuring
  screen, 59, 60
First CDDB Preferences
  screen, 59, 60
Genre, 228
home page, 212
installing, 1, 6-9
loading from the CD,
  223-224
Macintosh compatibility, 2, 4
main screen, 6-9
Max Mismatches, 71, 72
Multipass, 71
Music Library window, 8
Music Library, 227
Options menu, 9-10
parts of, 7
Play List window, 15, 16
Player Controls, 6, 7, 11, 12,
  17
player, 7
problems installing, 5
problems when recording,
  68-69
Record Advanced Options
  screen, 69, 70-72, 82, 83, 85
Record Length, 72, 83
Record Options screen, 65,
  73, 82
Recorder screen, 61, 62, 63,
  64, 65, 68
Recording Speed, 71
recording, 69
registered version, 64
reinstalling, 85
ripping, 145
ripping tracks, 58-63
running for the first time, 6
Second CDDB Preferences
  screen, 60, 61
serial number, 231
setting CDDB options, 73
Song Selection screen, 95
starting, 6
stopping recording, 69

switching to analog
  recording, 69, 84
tagging tracks, 225, 228
Track Info window, 8
Track Information screen, 81
unregistered version, 64
using other MP3 players
  with, 11-12
using with the Rio, 171
web site, 7
welcome screen, 6, 7
Xing encoder, 148
MusicMatch tagging, 24, 232
MusicMatch-Art screen, 28
muting, 34
MyDesktop, 220

N

naming MP3 files, 60, 61, 65-66
naming tracks, 60, 61, 203
Navigation Console, 134, 135,
  138
near CD quality, 66, 72, 229
Neato CD Labeller, 103, 214
NET Act, 35, 229
Netscape Navigator, 44
neuristic listening, 57, 229
news, 43, 203, 204, 205, 206,
  207, 220
newscasts, 57
newsgroups, 4, 36, 81, 125,
  201, 208, 221-222, 230
  articles, 43, 225, 230
  downloading from, 219
  getting MP3 files from,
    43-45, 221-222
  servers, 125
newsletters, 43
newsreaders, 43-45, 125, 218,
  221-222, 230
NeXTStep software, 166
Nico Mak Computing, 218
Night 55, Inc., 134
No Electronic Theft Act, 35,
  229
no sound, 34, 82-83
noise, 80, 107, 108, 230
  in audio CDs, 94, 95
  reduction filters, 112
  reduction hardware, 109
Nomad, 177-178, 193
non-directional sound, 183
non-Windows software, 166
nonpirated MP3 files, 173
Nordic Downloadable Music
  Site, 207, 208
normal equalization setting,
  171
normalizing, 114, 144-145, 230
  tracks, 151
  WAV files, 77
Norton File Manager, 158
notes, 4, 8, 27, 81

NPR, 56
Nullsoft, 127, 132, 134, 192
number of tracks in a
  channel, 108
number of tracks written, 102

O

Official FAQ for
  alt.binaries.sound.mp3, 208
Official MPEG Home Page,
  208
Official Windows Web Site, 221
offsets, 70
old records, recording from, 80
OneHouse LLC, 192
Online Bottom 40 list, 38
online database of CDs, 60, 61
online newsletters, 43
online search engines, 47-48,
  215-216
online services, 228
Online Top 40 list, 38
open applications, 73, 84
opening databases, 21
opening playlists, 17-18
opening the playlist editor in
  Unreal Player Max, 140
opportunities for artists,
  193-199
optimal bias settings, 75
Optimal Pulse Code
  Modulation, 210
optimal recording settings, 85
optimization in encoders, 145
Options menu button, 7
Options menu in Music
  Library, 24, 20, 23
Options menu in MusicMatch
  Jukebox, 9-10
ordering books, 206
ordering CDs online, 8
OS/2, 4, 166
oscilloscope, 130, 136, 162, 166
other web sites of interest,
  218-221
output jack, 88
output levels, testing, 89
outputs, splitting, 79
outputting to cassettes, 107
outputting to CDs, 107
overdriving your amplifier, 88
Overlap, 71-72, 81-82
overwriting MP3 files when
  recording, 62
ownership, 226-227
oz.net, 228

P

paint programs, 219
Paint Shop Pro, 219
parallel interface, 176
partial attenuation, 108
passive speakers, 183, 184, 187
PC speakers, 183

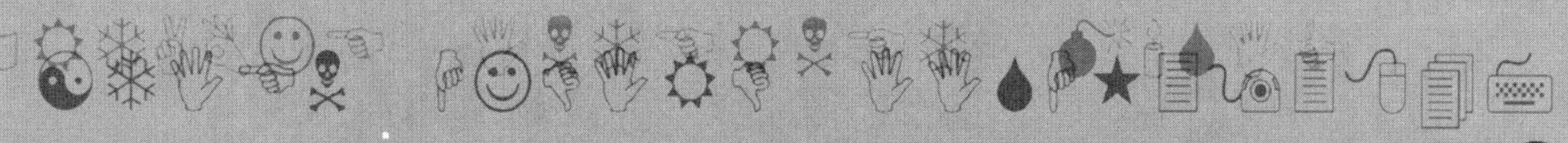

MUSIC YOU CAN'T GET ON THE RADIO.
MUSIC YOU CAN'T GET AT THE STORE.

MUSIC YOU CAN MIX THE WAY YOU WANT IT.

PORTABLE INTERNET MUSIC

RīO

ENTER TO WIN A RIO AT
RīOPort.com

DIAMOND
MULTIMEDIA